Coin Clinic 2

By Alan Herbert

1,001 MORE
FREQUENTLY
ASKED QUESTIONS

Published by

 **krause publications**

An F+W Publications Company

700 East State Street • Iola, WI 54990-0001
715-445-2214 • 888-457-2873
www.krause.com

Our toll-free number to place an order or obtain
a free catalog is (800) 258-0929.

Library of Congress Catalog Number: 95-77303

ISBN: 0-87349-875-5

Designed by Patsy Howell
Edited by Randy Thern

Printed in U.S.A.

CONTENTS

FOREWORD

Curiosity is one of the two main driving forces of coin collecting. Figuring out what something is is the first step to determining what value it might have. This book, *1,001 More Frequently Asked Questions*, is designed to satisfy reader curiosity, not to provide values. There are plenty of price guides that Krause Publications would be happy to sell to you to answer pricing questions. Instead, this book is an adventure in history, economics and numismatic lore. It is not written for professors, though they are most welcome to read it. It cannot be defined as a catalog can be defined. It cannot be organized in the same manner as a price guide, but there are similarities. This book is intended to be read from cover to cover, though any individual question is a story unto itself. In essence, this book can be read in one sitting or in 1,001 sittings, depending on reader preference.

The questions that are featured here are taken directly from the experiences of the publisher. Many of these are asked over and over again as new waves of collectors enter the field. Being more than 50 years old, Krause Publications has helped many newcomers get comfortable with numismatics. "Numismatics" is a big word that itself simply means the study of coins and related objects that range from wooden nickels to paper money. Finding out about all of these related items is fun. It is interesting. The subject also can be intimidating at first. A question-and-answer book is intended to take out the fear factor and provide information in interesting little bites and tidbits. We hope you enjoy it.

Alan Herbert, who has compiled these questions, has been active in the field of writing for hobby readers for over 35 years. There is little that he hasn't seen, or been asked, and he continues to write for *Numismatic News*, a weekly U.S. hobby newspaper, *Coins* Magazine, a monthly glossy newsstand product, *World Coin News*, a monthly for foreign coin collectors, and *Bank Note Reporter*, a monthly for collectors of paper money. With such a demanding publishing schedule, he cannot help but stay current with what coin collectors want to know about.

In our ever-changing world, as soon as something is published, the information starts to go stale. If you would like to see what other fine Krause Publications products are out there to help you in your hobby, please go to www.collect.com. The whole pantheon of numismatics will be there for you as well as publications serving other collecting hobbies. If you would happen to select one of mine, I would be honored to serve you in your quest for knowledge. First, however, I know you will enjoy this book.

Sincerely,
David C. Harper
Editor
Bank Note Reporter
Numismatic News
World Coin News

WWW.COLLECT.COM

INTRODUCTION

As I write this it has been almost nine years since I compiled the first 1,001 questions in Volume I. Re-reading those questions I found that almost all of the answers are still timely, so if you get the opportunity I would urge you to add the first volume to your reference library. It's still available from Krause Publications or your favorite bookstore or on-line bookseller.

The questions in this volume are no less important to the collector, whether beginner or expert. I would challenge you to read through the book and come away without learning something new about your hobby.

In the interim I have been answering questions from readers of *Numismatic News*, *World Coin News*, *Bank Note Reporter* and *Coins* magazine. A growing audience contacts me through the Internet. My computer database presently contains something over 16,000 questions and answers, so I had plenty to choose from—more than enough to fill these pages. The hard part was choosing between questions that have a similar demand.

Since this database dates back to 1968, when I began answering questions in *Numismatic News*, it covers virtually every topic having to do with numismatics. Don't be scared away because you aren't sure how to pronounce numismatics (NEW-Miz-MAT-iks) or how to spell it. It has always been a problem for most people, which is why "coin collector" has come to mean a collector of virtually everything having to do with money.

There is an interesting cyclical pattern to the questions that come across my desk or out of my computer. It's as if they were somehow "graduating" a new novice class of collectors every few months. Certain basic questions come in in significant numbers for a month or two. Then there's a lull for several months and suddenly the basic questions pop up again.

One of the most frequently asked questions is how I can stand answering the same questions dozens, or hundreds, of times. Perhaps I'm more tolerant than most people, but I have never had a problem with that. There are subtle differences in every letter, in every email, that make them fresh.

I depend in great measure on specialists and experts in various areas of coin collecting. The field is so vast that no one person can know everything about every specialty. In that way I am able to at least refer them to someone with the answer if I don't have it. You will find several questions where I've invited reader input, help that is often invaluable. If you have additional information, a correction or a comment on any answer, they are all welcomed.

I wish I had a dollar for every correspondent who has said something like: "I know this is a dumb question." Frankly, there are no dumb questions, no stupid questions. Once in a while there's a stupid answer, but that's my fault, not yours. My ethic is that every question needs an answer. There is no way that you are going to learn if you don't ask questions. Curiosity at any level is a plus, and it's the driving force behind any question. Simply stated, the more questions you ask, the more you can learn.

My challenge to you is to learn. Read one book on coins and you are a step ahead of more than 75 percent of the collectors out there. Read five books and you excel over 95 percent of the collectors. Read 10 books and you can start to classify yourself as an expert. You can begin with this book to broaden your general knowledge.

Send along your questions, with an unused loose first class stamp, to the Krause address:

Alan Herbert
Krause Publications FAQ
700 East State St.
Iola, WI 54990-0001

Alan Herbert
The AnswerMan
AnswerMan2@aol.com

Chapter 1

ALTERED, DAMAGED AND COUNTERFEIT COINS

Lots of things happen to coins. Many are intentional. Some are accidental. Knowing how to tell them apart is a key piece of knowledge.

Q: Is it true that all counterfeit gold coins weigh less than normal?

Many do, but many others are correct or even slightly heavier than normal. Weighing the coin is a must whenever you are checking to see if a coin is a counterfeit or not. Gold coin weights are very carefully regulated, within tolerances of one half a grain or roughly 1/31st of a gram. The U.S. Government position at one time was that if a coin was underweight or overweight by more than the official tolerances, and was found in circulation that "This is presumptive evidence that the coin is counterfeit." Today, both we and the Mint know better than that, as over the years numerous genuine coins have managed to get into circulation that were over or under weight. Weight then is an indication of possible counterfeiting, but it is not positive proof.

Q: Over the years I have seen several reports of the finding of 1915 dated Standing Liberty halves, but never an explanation of where they came from. What happened?

As is the case with most "unknown" dates of United States coins, the 1915 pieces turned up, but got turned down when experts examined them and determined that they were 1935 dated pieces which had the 3 cleverly altered into a 1. Apparently all of the reported specimens came from a single source. Trust the mint reports in most catalogs; if they don't list a date or mint, it means there were no coins officially struck for that date or mint.

Q: I have a chrome plated 1899 Morgan dollar, received from a soap company as a premium. A friend says soaking it in ammonia for a couple of months will remove the chrome. True?

At the risk of having some chemist confound me, I'd say definitely not, and even if it did it probably wouldn't do the coin any good. Once a coin is plated, it's usually worthless as a numismatic item, or will be sharply reduced in value.

Q: A friend who is a veteran collector claims that altered coins such as the 1914-D cents made from 1944-D dates were actually publicly offered for sale by people who were making them. This doesn't seem possible, or was it?

Not only possible, your friend is right as several prolific coin "manufacturers" engaged in offering these pieces to dealers and collectors, and such offers are mentioned a number of times in hobby literature for more than a decade following World War II, until the Secret Service finally put a stop to it. Typically, the makers offered the coins to dealers for $1 or $1.25 each, accompanied by a certificate stating that the date had been altered. One offer went so far as to note reduced rates for poorly executed pieces that weren't up to "standard." Thousands of 1948 and other date cents have been altered to make 1943 dates out of them. The dates altered to 1943 usually don't have the long tailed 3, another point to look for.

A Hobo nickel.

Q: Are there any American counterparts to the French coins with altered designs showing the German Kaiser?

During World War I, there was quite a stir when buffalo nickels with the Indian head turned into a spiked steel helmeted Kaiser were found in circulation. The authorities made an effort to find the "artists," but apparently without success. Later this art form would become popular - and collectible - as the "hobo" nickels. Because of their popularity with collectors, modern copies of the hobo nickels are being sold extensively. Del Romines, the author of the one available book on them, says that one enterprising engraver began making copies as soon as his first book came out several years ago.

Q: A friend has a large cent that has had the date removed, and 1809 punched in where the date should be. Why would anyone do that?

Your friend has a "filler" coin, manufactured by some early coin collector who didn't have an 1809 to put in his collection. To fill the empty space until he could afford one, he simply "made" one, which obviously wasn't genuine, but served the purpose for the time being.

Q: How serious a problem was the counterfeiting of small change during the Great Depression of the 1930s? I know a lot of lead quarters and halves got into circulation, but how about the dimes and nickels?

In today's world, where few will bother to pick up a cent they spot lying on the sidewalk, it is hard to visualize a time when nickels and dimes were counterfeited by people desperate for food. In 1934 government reports note the confiscation of $73,000 in counterfeit small change, and in January of 1935, some 49,000 fake nickels were taken up before they got into circulation. The silver dollars were faked to some extent, and fake dimes were a serious problem, especially for mass transportation. I ran across a note that the Boston Elevated Railway in 1931 was taken for a ride by a total of 117,501 dime slugs, compared to 71,000 in 1930. They were also a headache for the telephone companies. These were in the days when sophisticated slug rejectors were still a dream. Even the smaller coins got counterfeited, especially around 1900, when fake cents and nickels were turned out in New York and Philadelphia almost by the ton.

Q: Don't the metal flow lines prove that a piece is a genuine coin?

This is folklore that has long since been refuted. Flow lines, die cracks, die breaks and even hub-doubled dies can be counterfeited. When in doubt get an expert to authenticate the piece.

Q: I have several Peace dollars which have had the mintmark removed. Can I still get them graded and slabbed?

As far as the grading services are concerned these would be classed as altered coins and would be returned to you ungraded. As far as the government position is concerned they could be considered to be fraudulently altered, and might be subject to confiscation. About the only thing left to do with them is melt them down for their bullion content.

Q: *Weren't there a quantity of fake pillar dollars distributed by a Curtin and Pease?*

Curtin and Pease had a company in Ohio that sold them as "Pirate Coin replicas." They made fake 8 **reales** dated 1736 and fake pillar dollars dated 1749, along with examples cut into halves, quarters and bits. The pieces were struck around 1970 and I believe were not marked as copies. The pieces are still turning up on the Internet.

Q: *I have a silver quarter that is covered with bubbles, so that only part of the lettering can be read. How did it happen?*

I suspect that your coin has been altered, causing the bubbles, so it is not likely to have any value. They can be created artificially by the application of sudden heat, such as a welding torch. The clad coins are especially susceptible to alteration with heat. If the metal is discolored or there are traces of black soot or carbon in the design, then this is undoubtedly the cause, and the coin is worth only its bullion content. Because of the ease with which bubbles can be faked there is usually little or no extra value for genuine bubbles.

Q: *I have a coin that has a bad scar that I'd like to get repaired. Most of the dealers I've talked to say to leave the coin, which grades XF-40, alone, but I'd like to get it repaired. Any comments?*

I think you've answered your own question with your dealer survey. Any repair work is only going to make matters worse, and anyone examining the repaired coin is going to suspect more than the visible alteration. It's best to leave it alone. It's your coin, so you can do as you wish with it, but a repaired coin is an altered coin.

Q: *Is it possible to counterfeit or alter the grading service authentication certificates and slabs?*

It's possible to counterfeit anything made, but some things are more difficult to fake than others. In this case there have been several instances of counterfeit slabs. If in doubt, check with the grading service before accepting a certificate or a slab. Know your dealer.

Q: *I have a 1770 dated coin that appears to be zinc or aluminum with "CAROL III" on it. What is it?*

From the rest of the description, the coin should have been a silver coin of Mexico, so you have a counterfeit, or a copy. Aluminum wasn't even discovered until later.

Q: *Do you think dealers will "process" the copper-plated zinc cents like they did the 1943 steel cents?*

It's possible, although I think the hobby has advanced to the point where replated coins will be unacceptable to the majority of collectors. I suspect too that the technical problems involved in stripping, cleaning and replating the zinc cents will be too expensive to make it profitable. The dealers didn't process the steel cents, they bought them from companies that did the work, and then resold them.

Q: *When did PNG crack down on whizzed coins?*

The Professional Numismatics Guild adopted a resolution in August 1972, prohibiting the sale by PNG members of processed coins. It's part of their code of ethics, although "whiz" is not in the wording. A resolution forbidding whizzing was adopted at the February 1973 meeting of the ANA Board of Governors.

Q: I have a 1909-VDB cent that has what appears to be an "O" mintmark after the date. Is this some special coin, or what?

It is most probably an altered coin, or one with some coincidental damage. New Orleans shut down in 1909 after striking dimes, quarters, halves and half eagles, but never struck any U.S. cents then or at any other time.

Q: What is a "cull?"

Although there probably have been attempts in the past to use it as a grade, it is not a recognized term in any grading system I'm aware of. A cull is a coin which, while it can be identified, possibly even as to date or mint, is so badly worn or damaged as to have no real, or significant collector value. Culls are sometimes used by collectors determined to fill a gap in their series or date run of coins, but that doesn't give it any status beyond being an expedient.

Solder on a 1943 dime.

Q: Why are there so many references in ads to "solder" on coins?

This is because in the early days coins were frequently used as jewelry, or buttons, and soldered to pins or other attachments. Solder is difficult to remove, and efforts to take it off frequently result in damage to the coin, which reduces the collector value. Reputable dealers will include the solder in the description of the coin.

Q: What is meant by scoring on a coin? Is it the same thing as file marks?

File marks are a legitimate adjustment of the planchet before it was struck, to reduce it to the proper weight. Scoring is damage to the coin after being struck. This damage may well occur in the Mint, as for example damage to a coin in a counting machine is not part of the minting process.

Q: What are die marks?

Die marks are defined as wear or damage to the die that shows on the struck coin. The resulting marks on the coin usually will have rounded edges. Damage to the coin after it leaves the mint is often confused with die marks. However in nearly all cases damage will leave sharp edges, as opposed to the rounded edges of the die marks.

Q: What do notations of a "ding" mean, on a coin?

A ding is a dent or heavy abrasion damage to the piece. It traces to the German "ding" for thing. A second word, "dint" comes from the same Medieval English root, meaning to strike, or hit with a blow. There is even a special metal working tool called a dinging hammer.

Q: I recently purchased some trade dollars from a private source in Asia. What effect will the chop marks have on the value?

They will reduce the value, but a more serious problem is the probability that you may have bought counterfeit coins, as Asia is a major source of fakes, especially copies of U.S. coins, made for the tourist trade. There are reputable Asian coin dealers of course, but a man came to me recently with five silver dollars, purchased in Singapore, three Morgans and two Trade dollars. All were fakes, and didn't even contain any silver. They had been subjected to fire and other applications to give them an "aged" appearance. He told me that the dealer had "hundreds" more in his shop. I would urge that you submit all of your coins to be authenticated. Beware of bargain, or "fire sale" prices.

Q: What is a "flow" coin?

This was a nickname dreamed up for a purported minting variety back in the 1950s, with the limited knowledge of the minting process at the time. The coins exhibited a rippled surface that gave the design the appearance of double or multiple outlines. These were blamed on faulty annealing and were bought and sold as mint "errors.'" Today we know that they are nothing more than a coin that has been altered by holding it against a revolving wire brush. The point is that some of these pieces may be surfacing now in collections and might be offered for sale, so be aware that they are an alteration and that they are worthless.

Q: I have been offered an 1885 "V" nickel in VG-4 grade. The surface is pitted and there are many lines across it. Are these from the die?

Very unlikely, as any die markings would have long since disappeared on such a worn coin. The combination of wear, pits and scratches make it imperative that the seller have the coin authenticated and graded before you buy it to ensure that they aren't hiding an altered date. This is a typical problem with such big ticket items as the 1943 cents on brass planchets or 1913 "V" nickels. Damage hiding or obscuring a date or mintmark is a red flag warning to stay away from the coin. "Might be" doesn't get a ride to the pay window.

Q: What is meant by blemishes on a coin?

Blemishes can be almost any form of light damage to a coin, including such things as minor nicks, scratches bag marks, flaws or discoloration. The stronger the blemish, the more it will detract from the overall collector value of the coin.

Q: I came across several silver dollars that are missing the dates. They appear to be ground off. Any special reason?

Chances are you have uncovered some relics of the Nevada gambling casinos. When the silver dollar boom started in the 1960's, several of the casinos resorted to grinding the dates off the coins so that they wouldn't be grabbed for their collector value. As altered coins your find is worth only bullion value. The stunt got the casinos in trouble with the Feds for mutilating coins.

Q: Were the silver war nickels "reprocessed" like the 1943 steel cents?

Apparently they were, but certainly not as extensively as the steel cents that were altered by stripping them of their zinc and re-plated by the hundreds of thousands. The alteration methods used for the nickels were different, usually running to buffing or polishing the pieces to give them a better appearance.

Q: I found a large cent in a dealer's junk-box that has a square hole in the center, like a Chinese cash. Was this a pattern?

The probable cause for the hole was the practice of nailing a coin to a new building to bring good luck. In this case a square nail was used, and the coin was eventually recovered when the building was torn down, or burned. Any such hole would have to be an alteration.

Q: I have a reeded edge 1909 cent. Is this a pattern?

Sorry, but it's an alteration. No modern reeded cents or nickels were ever issued from the U.S. Mint.

Q: Is there any way to de-whiz coins?

No way. Once whizzed, always whizzed. The name applies to a coin that has been altered by some method, such as using a wire wheel, which removes metal or moves it about on the coin. It's the same as cleaning a coin, as both leave marks that are unmistakable to the trained eye.

Q: What is an "added" mint mark?

Frequently the branch mints had much lower, and thus more valuable mintages than the main mint. A popular alteration is to remove the entire mint mark from a common date branch mint coin and solder, or even glue it on a common main mint coin to increase the coin's value to collectors. Obviously the practice is illegal, and in many cases the fakes can be spotted fairly easily, but a sophisticated alteration may require an electron microscope or other exotic equipment to detect. The mint mark should always be checked carefully with a lens, and if there is the slightest doubt the coin should not be purchased until the seller has it authenticated. Old time dealers and collectors would heat a coin to see if the solder or glue would melt. I would not recommend the practice.

Q: I have a 1950-D nickel that has a very small 0 in the date. Is this a known variety?

If you will compare the 0 with the loop of the 9 on a normal 1950-D nickel, you will find that your coin has been altered, by removing the tail of the 9. This was a popular alteration back in the 1960's when the coins were selling for $5 to $15 each. Another alteration to check for is the same as the "two headed" coins - a 1950 obverse hollowed out and a "D" reverse from another date fitted into it. The joint would be along the inside edge of the rim - and could be on either side. The Standard Catalog of Counterfeit and Altered U.S. Coins describes the 1950-D nickel as the most counterfeited nickel of all time. The majority were struck in Dallas with spark erosion dies, by the same people who struck a quantity of 1939-D nickels. Both lack luster and are a dark grey. The weight is 3.9 grains light.

Chapter 2

AMERICAN NUMISMATIC ASSOCIATION

The ANA is the world's largest numismatic group, with 31,000 members. You can find lots of information at their Web site - www.money.org

Q: When did the ANA begin using a 100-point system in judging exhibits?
The 100-point system was first used at the ANA's Omaha, Nebraska, convention in 1955. Since then it has been modified several times, but in its current form it is used by most exhibit judges at coin shows all over the country.

Q: Is there any place where I can get some lessons in how to judge exhibits? Our local coin club never has enough judges and I'd like to help out.
It may surprise you to know that even the big state and regional clubs, and the American Numismatic Association (ANA) at the national level all have the same problem, as a good judge is hard to find. There is help available though, by writing to the Chief Judge, Joe Boling, in care of ANA Headquarters, 818 N. Cascade Ave., Colorado Springs, CO 80903-3279. They have some literature on the topic, including the criteria used in judging ANA exhibits, and they will be able to tell you when and where the next certification programs will be held at the ANA conventions. It's not really that difficult to become a judge, the chief specifications being knowledge of the class, an open mind and an urge to learn. While you're waiting, do some exhibiting, which will be valuable experience.

Q: When was the first American Numismatic Association Mid-Winter convention held?
Following on the heels of the long-standing tradition of the annual summer convention, the ANA decided to hold its first mid-winter show at Colorado Springs February 16 through the 18, 1978. Since then the show has been renamed the early spring show and has moved around the country in much the same fashion as the summer show.

Q: Will you recommend a source for a good lens or microscope?
Try your local coin dealer, a jeweler, an optometrist or a camera dealer. You will find both lenses and microscopes in the ANA Money Market, with a discount for ANA members. A reminder that not all microscopes are suited to coin work—some are far too powerful. Unless you are researching minute die varieties the maximum lens required is in the 20X to 50X range.

Q: Didn't the ANA at one time consider holding an eastern and a western convention each year?
Col. Robert Kriz introduced a resolution to that effect in 1973, which was defeated, but the idea later evolved into the present system of a summer and an early spring convention.

Chapter 3

SUSAN B. ANTHONY DOLLARS

Anthony dollars were the Treasury Department's trial of downsizing large coins. It didn't work, but the Treasury has yet to learn a lesson from the public's continued lack of interest.

Obverse and reverse of SBA dollar.

Q: Are Anthony dollars worth collecting?

Eventually all coins have value, the amount depending on the time that has elapsed, the number originally minted and the number that survive. The Anthony dollars - except for the varieties - probably aren't going to appreciate significantly for 25 to 50 years. After that it remains to be seen.

The question isn't, "are they 'worth' collecting?" It's whether you personally like to collect them. If you enjoy them, then by all means collect them. Don't let anyone tell you what to collect.

Q: I ran across an old ad calling the Anthony dollar an error coin. What was the error referring to?

The ad in question, which appeared in a non-numismatic publication, claimed that the Mint made a "mistake" in minting SBA dollars. It went on to suggest that the mistake justified the high price their company was charging for sets of the dollars. What the ad writer carefully forgot to mention was that at the time there were more than 500 million SBA dollars in the Treasury vaults.

Q: What was the first official act in the drive to put Susan B. Anthony on the dollar coin?

The process began with House Bill #12728, calling for Anthony's effigy on the downsized dollar. This was passed by a 6-1 vote on July 23, 1978, by the Historic Preservation & Coinage Subcommittee of the House Committee on Banking, Finance & Urban Affairs. The ceremony for the official striking of the first Anthony dollar was held December 13, 1978.

Q: I have several sets of "First Day" covers, each with three proof silver Anthony dollars from the three mints. In each set two of the three coins are gold plated. What are these sets worth?

First of all, none of the 1979 SBA dollars are silver. They are struck on a copper core with outside clad layers of an alloy of 75% percent copper and 25 percent nickel.

Secondly, only San Francisco struck proof SBA dollars, with an S mintmark, and none of these were issued outside of the regular sets of all six denomination proof coins. The Philadelphia and Denver coins cannot be proofs. Thirdly, a gold plated coin is valueless as a numismatic item. This was not done at the U.S. Mint, but is an alteration after the coin left the Mint, leaving the coin worth face value. Ironically, the $1 stamps on the envelopes are worth more than the coins. You have a privately issued item, of dubious, if any, special value.

Chapter 4

AUTHENTICATION

Authenticators sell peace of mind. To know that your coin is genuine is another key step forward in your collecting.

Q: I found a fairly valuable coin at a local flea market. The owner of the table offered it to me with a discount to cover the cost of having the coin authenticated. Should I have taken his offer?

Apparently you didn't, so consider yourself well off. Authentication is the responsibility of the seller. Even with a reputable, well-established dealer with a business address, you can avoid most potential problems by accepting delivery of the coin only after it has been authenticated by a recognized and mutually agreeable authentication service. A flea market stand is often pretty hard to trace even the next day.

Q: I have a quantity of coins (jars of cents and nickels) and rolls of silver coins, left to me by a relative. Should I send them to an authentication service to be checked?

In most cases this would be a pointless and expensive waste. From practical experience most hoards or accumulations rarely contain any coins of significant value, so your best bet would be to solicit offers from local coin dealers for the lot, remembering that the silver coins are worth about three times face value for their bullion content. Authentication services charge a minimum of several dollars for each coin, so it would rarely be worthwhile for a low value coin.

Q: What is the point of having a coin authenticated? I am sure it is valuable, and besides I wouldn't trust it out of my sight to have it checked.

While you may be certain in your own mind, as long as you fail to have any potentially valuable coin authenticated it remains worth only face value - and perhaps not even that if it is a counterfeit. Self-delusion is your choice, but your heirs will likely be a bit bitter that you left them a potential problem.

Q: I'd like to send you some coins to authenticate and grade. What is the procedure?

While I do authenticate minting varieties in a few special cases, coin grading and authentication are not a part of the free question and answer service that I provide for Krause Publication readers. Our standing instructions are to send in a drawing or rubbing of any item you have a question about (limit six at a time), but don't send the item itself until we specifically ask for it and give you the special mailing instructions needed to get it to us safely. To get your coins graded, apply to any of the several professional grading and authentication services. Don't forget the loose first class stamp required to obtain your answer.

Q: Is it worth sending my collection of silver dollars in to have it authenticated?

Probably not as the majority of coins in the average collection at best would carry only a slight premium over bullion values. However, if you are a specialist, and have key dates and top grade coins, the higher value pieces would definitely warrant authentication and grading.

Q: Will it help if I send in a picture of a coin I have a question about?

It will if the pictures are clear, sharply focused, and show both sides of the coin, at least the size of the piece, and preferably larger. Over 90 percent of the pictures that come in violate one or more of these specifications. But don't go to the expense of having a professional photo made until you have some indication that the coin is valuable enough to warrant it. A rough sketch, which shows all the lettering and numbers, will serve just as well. Actually only a very small percentage of professional photographers are equipped or experienced in taking coin photos.

Chapter 5

BARBER COINS

Charles Barber designed Barber coins. Some things in numismatics are obvious, and others are obfuscated.

A Type I and a Type II 1892 Barber quarter.

Q: Are there two varieties of the 1892 Barber quarter?

There are, but few collectors who don't specialize in the Barber coins are aware of them. The first variety struck has the eagle's wingtip covering the upright of the E in UNITED. Later in the year the die was changed and the tip covers most of the arms of the E as well, leaving just the tips showing. This latter variety is the one that is found on all the rest of the series. Despite the first variety probably being the scarcer of the two for the year, there is no distinction made in most catalogs. A third reverse and a different obverse were introduced in 1900, best identified by a shallow fork in the tip of the inner or right-hand ribbon. On the reverse, the tip of the eagle's wing is in much the same position as on the second reverse, except that the tip extends into the field between the E and the rim.

Q: Are the Barber designs of 1892 copied from a foreign coin?
The designs for Liberty, used on the 1892 dime, quarter and half dollar, are quite similar, but facing in the opposite direction from the female figure used on the silver coins of France beginning in 1848.

Q: Can you tell me anything about the coin broaches that were made from Barber coins?
You hardly ever see one of these any more. A process patented in 1903, which raised the relief of the bust, with the portrait redone, made the pieces. Before the Secret Service stepped in - it was still illegal then to mutilate a silver coin - a small number of the pieces were sold, typically 50 cents for an altered Barber quarter. There also were watch fobs made the same way from coins.

Q: Are heavily worn Barber coins worth more than just bullion?
The Barber dimes, quarters and half dollars saw extremely heavy service and it's not unusual to see them worn to the point where the design is practically level with the field. These are often referred to as "slicks," and they are discounted heavily to well below the bullion price. Many of them were melted in 1980 when the price of silver shot up.

Chapter 6

BARS AND ART BARS

No, John. Metal bars. Not drinking establishments.

Q: I have a silver bar that has an oval stamp with an eagle and the words "Mint of The United States At San Francisco." It is stamped .995 fine, has a serial number and the weight of 5.03 ounces. What can you tell me about it?

There are copies of these bars, but if the eagle is incuse you may have a genuine piece. Although they have been listed in at least one auction catalog as being from the late 1800s, bar expert John J. Ford, Jr. tells me that the genuine pieces were actually made at the San Francisco Mint but not until the 1930s. They are fairly common and sold a few years ago in the $25 to $30 range.

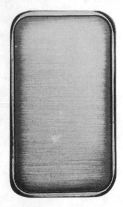

A silver art bar.

Q: Are silver art bars really numismatic items?

Mostly yes. Collecting them has had its ups and downs, peaking in the 1970s. Hundreds of private mints started making them, but when the fad ended most of them shut their doors, taking with them several big names in the minting industry.

Chapter 7

BUFFALO NICKEL

You can collect the coin, and then come to South Dakota in the fall and watch the buffalo herds get rounded up. Really bison, but who can argue with common usage.

The "End of the Trail" statue.

Q: Was the Indian on the Buffalo nickel used for any other modeling?

James Earl Fraser, well known in numismatics, is even better known in the art world for his "End of the Trail," a statue of a mounted Indian. The original was produced in 1898 more than a dozen years before Fraser designed the nickel. It's unknown who the model was. There seem to be no valid claims for any of the three models used for the Buffalo nickel for other modeling jobs.

Q: Which is which? Is the buffalo on the Buffalo nickel on the obverse or the reverse? There's more than just a nickel riding on this.

Despite the common name of Buffalo nickel, the animal is on the reverse, the side with the Indian head being the obverse. However, with plenty of Indian Head cents still in circulation in 1913 it would have been too confusing to have called it an Indian Head nickel and the buffalo gets all the honors. While a bit unusual to name a coin after its reverse design, it has happened before. Perhaps the best example is the "Chain" cents of 1793, which was rarely called a "Flowing Hair" cent.

Q: What is the status on the 1935 two-leg Buffalo nickel?

Several of these turned up in the 1970s and some may still be in collections. All of the ones I saw were low grade, and had been altered.

Q: Aren't there several other Native Americans besides the three listed models for the Buffalo nickel?

It's not too hard to find old newspaper stories from various claimants, but in all cases there is no basis in fact. Fraser named the Sioux Chief Iron Tail and Cheyenne Chief Two Moons as two of the models. In his book, *Twisted Tails*, author Robert R. Van Ryzin, who is editor of *Coins* magazine, presents convincing proof that the third was Big Tree, a Kiowa. One of the claimants was John Big Tree, a Seneca/Iroquois from the eastern U.S. He is, in fact, the one most often listed in earlier references, suggesting that he used the similarity of names to his personal benefit.

A 1937-D Buffalo with three legs.

Q: Any information on the original area where the three-legged 1937-D Buffalo nickels were found?

The late Maurice Gould is quoted as saying that he bought most of the ones he handled from the Montana area, so that apparently was where that variety got its start. A banker in Omaha, Nebraska was one of the first to spot the minting variety and accumulated three rolls, which he later sold for $2 a coin. Other reports said that the 3-legs were found in general circulation in Denver. A coin dealer who didn't give his name said Pat Eades, a Lewistown, Montana coin dealer, told him that the 3-Leg Buffalos came from the post office in Ft. Benton, Montana.

Q: If a coin is listed or described as obsolete, does that always mean that it is no longer legal tender?

Obsolete can mean that, but by no means is limited to coins that have been demonetized. It is generally used to describe coins of a series or denomination that are no longer in general circulation. For a single example, the Buffalo nickel is considered to be obsolete, yet it is still legal tender.

Type I and Type II Buffalo nickels.
Type I with the mound and Type II without the mound.

**1912 dated die trial
for the Buffalo nickel.**

Q: Somewhere I saw a picture of a 1912 Buffalo nickel. What's the story?

You probably saw the photo in one of the Krause numismatic publications, as it was one of several patterns and trial strikes loaned to us back in the 1970s to photograph. The 1911 and 1912 Buffalos were die trials of James Earl Fraser's design, which was introduced in 1913. The pieces are uniface strikes made to test the dies.

Q: Why are there two varieties of the Buffalo nickel?

This is one of those questions that frequently get ignored, on the assumption that "everyone" knows the answer. The original design shows the buffalo on a mound. This exposed the date, which wore rapidly. The mound was removed and replaced by a raised line, which helped somewhat to protect the date from wear. The first Standing Liberty quarters had the same problem, which was corrected in 1925.

Q: Wasn't the Buffalo nickel supposed to be issued in a different alloy?

Apparently the official position was that the regular 25 percent nickel-75 percent copper alloy would be used. However, the vending machine industry applied substantial pressure for a change. Several alloys, including argental, silver and aluminum were proposed, but they were dropped and the Mint went with the old alloy.

Chapter 8

BUYING AND SELLING

*One piece of sage advice - "Buy the book before you buy - or sell - the coin."
All too often collectors neglect the necessary reference material until after they
have impaired their checkbooks. The second slogan - "Know more about the
coin than the person you are buying it from." Following these two simple rules
could make you rich.*

One of the five 1913 "V" nickels.

*Q: I have a 1911 "V" nickel. After seeing the stories on the 1913 "V" nickels I want to sell
mine and retire. Where can I sell it? (Several readers.)*

The appearance of the story on the five 1913 nickels sparked a lot of interest among
collectors who have other dates in the series, but the bad news is that this is a "date
sensitive" piece. The majority of other dates in the lower grades catalog retail for only a
dollar or two. Novice collectors don't realize that values are date specific. In other
words, one date may be worth a million dollars but other dates for the same
denomination may only bring a few cents.

*Q: With the thousands of replicas and copies of early coins that are around, they must have
been pretty cheap. Do you have any idea what they cost?*

While many of the replicas were given away free—such as the Chrysler copies of
the Blake $20 gold piece and the sets that were given away by *Time* magazine with
subscriptions—a 1970 catalog offered authentic replicas of the Massachusetts pine
tree shilling for $1, the New Hampshire or Massachusetts half cent for $5, a copy of
the Confederate half for $2.75, a Sommer Island Bermuda shilling for $5, a restruck
Confederate penny token in bronze for $1, and a Confederate dime token in silver
for $1.25.

Q: Is it possible to determine when and where a bag of U.S. coins were struck?

The secret is the bag codes. However, there are several variations in the dating practice.
In general the bags carry the date they were bagged at the Mint. Older bags had the
counting machine operator's name on them, labeled at the Federal Reserve Bank.

Q: When did the roll market for coins get rolling?

In today's market it's common to see rolls and bags being sold and traded, but it wasn't that long ago that there simply weren't enough collectors around to support a roll market. According to Dave Bowers the roll market got going back in the 1940s. By the 1960s it peaked and had its first major "bust" in 1965.

Q: Where are all of the 24.2 million 1941 Walking Liberty halves?

The 1941 is considered to be a common date, so it's rarely offered in ads. Just as with cars, you'll see the later models, or the more expensive examples, in the ads. Very often you get a distorted perception of the rarity of common dates because few dealers have the capacity (or customers) to stock them.

Q: I was given several coins that are embedded in a block of plastic. Are they worth more than unprotected coins?

They probably are not. Chances are that the pieces selected for the block were common dates, so the principal value would be any silver content. The blocks make an attractive display, but are of little interest to collectors.

A group of Ancient coins.

Q: A safety deposit box, part of an estate, contained several hundred ancient coins. Local coin dealers showed no interest in them, offering only a few cents apiece. Aren't they worth more than that?

Chances are good that they are, but it's the same story, as with any other special area of the hobby, you need to contact a dealer who specializes in ancient coins. This is good advice for all collectors. Look for a dealer who specializes in the coins you are trying to sell (or buy). Numismatics is far too broad a field for any one person to be a specialist in every area. It's the same as your car. You wouldn't take a Mercedes to a Kia dealer, so use the same good judgment in picking a coin dealer. Best method - ask for a referral. Almost any dealer will know who among his or her fellow dealers is an expert on the coins you have.

Q: Aren't some of the copies of the early coins—those that were made in the 1800s—worth something?
Indeed they are, and in a few cases the copies are even worth more than the genuine pieces. However, the early copies have been copied and recopied, requiring expert authentication to determine which is a copy and which is a re-copy. A typical example of this is the famous "bar" cent, which was copied by Bolin. His copies are worth considerably more than the originals, as they are scarcer, but there are as many, or more, copies of Bolin's copy as there are copies of the original - which itself was a private issue. However, don't construe this as an indication that the thousands of copies made in the 1960s have any significant collector value. There simply are far too many of them.

Chapter 9

CANADA

Our northern neighbors have lots of interesting coins. They do things a tad differently, but in the long run they have a lot to show us.

A pitcher plant on a Newfoundland cent.

Q: I have a 1942 Newfoundland cent. What is the plant shown on the coin?

It is a pitcher plant, the provincial flower. The claim was made in some references both that the designer was unknown, and that the pitcher plant was a tropical flower, but Charleton lists the designer as Walter J. Newman, and notes that the pitcher plant is native to Newfoundland.

Q: Is it true that the French Mint prepared all the dies for the 1937 Canadian coins?

This gets to be a bit technical, but if I read the Mint reports correctly, the French Mint did make the master dies for all but the $1 obverse and the 50-cent reverse, those two master dies being prepared by the Royal Mint in England. It is likely that the Royal Mint used the French master dies to prepare hubs and from them the working dies used to strike the Canadian coins, but obviously the French Mint played a major role in getting the coins into production.

Q: Did Canada have any better luck withdrawing the tombac nickels of 1942-43 than the U.S. Mint did with the steel cents?

About 28 million of the brass-alloy coins were minted, and by 1959 the Canadian Government had withdrawn about 18 million. In the U.S., 1,093,838,670 steel cents were minted and a total of 163 million, or about 14.9 percent of the coins were recovered, leaving some 900 million still in circulation. Since the Canadians recovered 64.3 percent of their nickels they did substantially better.

Q: Were all the Canadian Confederation Centennial coins double dated?

The Canadian Mint beat the U.S. by nine years with the idea of putting both centennial dates (1867-1967) on the circulating commemoratives issued in the latter year. The 1967 $20 gold piece is the only exception.

A Canadian bank token, the forerunner of Canadian coinage.

Q: What are the Canadian bank tokens that are called Bouquet Sous?

The design is a bouquet of the heraldic flowers of England, Scotland and Ireland, along with the Canadian maple leaf and wheat ears. Some have the misspelling "un sous".

Q: Were all of the 1939 Canadian commemorative silver dollars sold?

The coin, marking the visit of the Royal Family, had a mintage of 1,363,816. Slightly more than 150,000 were unsold and melted down by the Canadian Mint between 1939 and 1945.

Q: I have a French 10 centime coin that has "Pears Soap" stamped on it. Is this a common countermark?

Here we are using countermark to mean a stamped design on one side of a coin or similar object, as opposed to a counter stamp, which puts a design on both sides. The "Pears Soap" countermark was added to some 250,000 of the French coins after they were brought into Canada in the 1850s. The French coins were selected because it was illegal to put advertising countermarks or counter stamps on British coins. They actually circulated, valued at a British penny.

Q: I have a "Northwest Territory" 1870-1970 medal. How many were struck and what was the issue price?

Mintage figures are unavailable, but the Canadian commemorative medals were issued in aluminum for 75 cents, in bronze for $1.75, silver plated for $2 and in .999 silver for $10.

Q: There have been several instances where the U.S. cent has cost almost as much to make as its face value. Has Canada had the same problem?

The Canadian cent has actually been a money-losing coin several times. The 1984 Royal Canadian Mint Report noted that despite the reduction in size and weight in 1982, the coin still cost more to produce than its face value. Despite attempts to do away with the coin, it remains a necessity to pay provincial sales taxes, the same problem that faces elimination of the U.S. cent. Other countries have done away with the problem by incorporating sales taxes directly into the price of merchandise, a much simpler method that eliminates the need for the cent.

Q: What's the difference between the "two and a half" and "one and a half" waterline versions of the "Arnprior" Canadian dollars?

The so-called Arnprior dollars of the 1950s have only partial waterlines at the right end of the canoe. Instead of the normal four, some show only two and a half lines, with this mistakenly listed by some sources as one and a half lines, because they forgot to count the upper waterline (base of the island). All of the Arnprior varieties are the result of die abrasion, and as such are valued more for the publicity they have received than their actual minting variety value, as abrasion varieties are usually too common to have any significant collector value. The name derives from a firm in Arnprior, Canada, which ordered 2,000 1955 dollars from the Royal Canadian Mint. They were found to have missing waterlines. Others were issued later but got the nickname with various numbers of lines missing.

A Canadian large cent.

Q: Please give me the weights and composition of the Canadian cents?

Beginning in 1858, the Canadian cent weighed 4.536 grams, and the alloy was 95 percent copper, 4 percent tin and 1 percent zinc. The weight was increased in 1876 to 5.670 grams. In 1919 the alloy was changed to 95.5 percent copper, 3 percent tin and 1.5 percent zinc. In 1920 the weight was reduced to 3.240 grams. In 1942 the alloy was changed to brass, 98 percent copper, 0.5 percent tin and 1.5 percent zinc. From here on we have some confusion, with one author incorrectly stating that the alloy was changed back to bronze in 1946, and two other references had conflicting figures. The official figures, quoted to us by the Canadian Mint, show in 1978 the alloy was revised to 98 percent copper, 1.75 percent zinc and 0.25 percent "other metals." J. A. Haxby tells us that over the years outside suppliers have in effect set the actual standards, which may vary from year to year. In 1980 the weight was reduced to 2.8 grams and in 1982 to 2.5 grams. In 1996 Canada struck part of the cents on bronze and some 445 million on copper-plated steel. In 1997 they switched to bronze-plated zinc. The "large" cents weighed 70.06 grains. They switched to 87.5 grains in 1876. Canada switched to a small size cent in 1920, weighing 50.0 grains. This lasted until 1980 when the Canadian cent thickness was reduced, leaving the diameter the same, dropping the weight to 43.21 grains. From 1982 to 1996 the cent was multi-sided, reverting to round in 1997.

Q: I have two Canadian proof $100 coins; one is dated 1976 and the other 1979. They are gold but different colors. Any special reason?

The 1976 coin contained copper with the .917 gold, while the 1977 and later versions were struck in an alloy containing silver instead of copper, giving the gold a more "natural" color.

Q: I know there were bans on the export or melting of silver coins but is it really true that Canada once banned the export of nickel coins?

They did, because of the Canadian nickel miner's strike in 1969. World demand for nickel, used to replace silver in many world coins, exceeded supply, and for a time Canadian five-cent pieces contained seven cents worth of nickel.

Q: Canada banned the export of silver coins as early as 1973. What was the reason?

The ban was put in effect because of wholesale export of silver as the price went above $2 an ounce. In the two months before the law went into effect in April bullion brokers and coin dealers exported more than $2 million worth of silver coins.

A 1911 cent, missing the Dei Gratia.

Q: Why is the Canadian 1911 cent listed separately from the other cents in reference catalogs?

The piece is a one-year type, as engraver Bertram MacKennal omitted Dei Gratia from the design. The change lasted for one year, and then it was restored in 1912.

Q: Is it true that the Canadian Government paid for new slug rejecters after switching away from silver coins in 1968?

The vending machine industry had enough clout to force payment for the conversion of the machines in use, and the government wound up paying the bill.

Q: Wasn't there some kind of a limit posed on the 1965 Canadian proof-like sets to inhibit speculation?

In 1965 a total of 2,904,352 proof-like sets were sold. The original limit placed by the mint was 2 million, and orders for 6 million were received. After 4 million orders had been returned, it was decided to reopen orders, but that burst the speculation bubble, and only 904,000 orders were received.

The rarest Canadian dollar - the 1911.

Q: How many Canadian 1911 dollars are known?

There are two silver and one lead specimen known. One of the silver pieces is in the British Museum, a U.S. coin dealer purchased the other in 1976 for $110,000 (later sold at auction for $325,000) and the lead pattern was found in 1977 in a vault that formerly belonged to the Finance Ministry.

Q: Most of the 1921 silver Canadian nickels were melted down in 1922. Was this the only date affected by the melt?

2,582,495 nickels dated 1921 were minted. Of this number, all but a "couple of hundred" were melted, as part of a more than three million coin melt. The remaining half million or more were mostly 1920 dated coins, but this had little effect on the rarity of that date, as 10.6 million had been minted, leaving about 10 million in circulation.

A 12-sided 1946 Canadian 5-cent coin.

Q: Why did the Canadian 5-cent switch from round to 12-sided and back to round again?

Canada switched to the 12-sided shape in 1942 to distinguish the tombac alloy from any possible confusion with the cent. In 1963 the round shape was resumed because of continuing problems with the collars cracking at the corners after the alloy reverted to nickel.

The old "ONE" and the new "1."

Q: Someone told me that there was a language change on the Canadian coins in the 1930s. Can you help, as I haven't been able to spot it?

It's rather subtle, but it's there. To satisfy both the French-speaking and English-speaking segments of the population, the new series of cents introduced in 1937 dropped the word "ONE" and instead used a numeral to make the denomination bi-lingual. It worked on the cent and five-cent coins, but the larger denomination coins already were using digits for the denomination. A case could also be made that the cent and five-cent were revised simply to bring them into line with the other denominations. Should we make the point that none of the current U.S. circulating coins carries digits identifying the denomination?

Q: I have a quantity of the gold $50, $10 and $5 coins issued by Canada. Some have the fineness as .999, while others have .9999 instead. Is there more gold in the latter?

From 1979 through 1982 the "Maple Leaf" or $50 coin carried the fineness as .999, while the 1982 fractional pieces and the 1983 $50 coins carry it as .9999. Both are considered as a minimum guarantee, and any difference in actual content would be so slight as to require very sophisticated equipment to detect. The claim is made that these are the purest gold coins in the world.

Q: Who was the designer of the Voyageur reverse for the Canadian dollar?

Emmanuel Hahn was the designer, with the canoe and two paddlers first appearing in 1935.

Q: Does the Canadian quarter come in two different sizes? It seems like some of the older ones in my collection are smaller.

Besides the change to the Queen Elizabeth II design on the Canadian quarter in 1953, the size was changed as well in that year. The coins struck early in the year have the large date reverse carried over from the George VI coins, and the obverse has no shoulder fold in the Queen's dress. These coins measure 23.62 mm (.930 inch) in diameter.

**The Voyageur reverse
for the Canadian dollar.**

With the switch to the design with the shoulder fold, a new, small date reverse was introduced, but the diameter of the coin was increased to 23.88 mm (.940 inch). If an example of each size is examined at the same time the difference in size is obvious.

Chapter 10

CENTENNIAL, BICENTENNIAL

They didn't do much for the Centennial, but they laid on a feast for collectors for the Bicentennial; lots of medals, three special coins and lots of interest from the public.

Q: I've seen several references to the 1876 U.S. Centennial, but I have an 1874 medal for the 98th anniversary. What was the purpose?

The medal was issued to mark the ground-breaking ceremonies for the buildings for the Centennial Exposition. Contrary to the 1976 bicentennial coinage, only medals were issued for the 1876 Centennial.

A medal for the U.S. Centennial.

Q: What were the issue prices for the Centennial medals of 1876?

The "Memorial" medals, as they were called at the time, came in four separate categories. The small gilt sold for $1, the large bronze for $2, in coin silver the price was $3, and a large gilt version was $5. The set came in a special case for $11. The official medals bear the words, "Act of Congress, June, 1874" or "By Authority of the Congress of the U.S." The so-called "small" pieces in the description were the size of the U.S. silver dollar. The design represents "The Genius of American Independence, rising from a recumbent position."

Q: How many privately issued Bicentennial medals are there?

Hundreds. But there is no accurate figure, as dozens of groups or individuals, including foreign sources, issued them. Many of the private firms sold the medals both before and after 1976. History tells us that a Civil War medal was issued in 1894, some 29 years after the war ended.

Q: How long before 1976 was the first Bicentennial legislation submitted?

The first bill came from Sen. Frank Church of Idaho, S-1565, filed on April 19, 1971. The bill called for the minting of 225 million sets of two or more proof, or uncirculated, 40 percent silver coins.

Q: Why is it that if the law requires that an eagle appear on our coins, that such coins as the Bicentennial quarters and some of the commemoratives and State quarters don't show one?

The law is specific, requiring an eagle on circulating coins from the quarter up, with the dime, nickel and cent exempt. However, the legislation authorizing special issues such as the Bicentennial coins and commemoratives, exempt that particular issue from the requirement.

Q: I've been told to save all the Bicentennial coins as they are becoming rare. I know I hardly ever find one in circulation.

Sorry, but you've been victimized by a rumor. A total of 1.66 billion Bicentennial quarters and over half a billion halves were minted with the 1976 date. Millions of the coins were saved in uncirculated condition, a mountain of coins, which will hang over the coin market for decades, if not centuries. With so many uncirculated coins saved, the circulated ones will not carry a premium in the next several lifetimes. Separate out any uncirculated Bicentennial coins and spend the rest. This is a prime object lesson for those who have "invested" in roll and bag quantities of the State quarters.

An ARBC medal for the Bicentennial.

Q: How many medals did the American Revolution Bicentennial Commission authorize for the Bicentennial celebration in 1976?

The ARBC, in addition to the nearly two dozen that they handled directly, authorized a total of more than 900 medals which were struck by both the U.S. Mint and a number of private mints for local, state and national Bicentennial organizing groups. A California collector, Robert Young, reportedly has the largest existing collection of these medals. Some years ago he reportedly was preparing a catalog of the medals, a task the ARBC failed to complete because of a lack of funds.

Q: Didn't another country issue the first Centennial medal for the U.S.?

That honor went to Germany. A medal was struck and issued on July 4, 1872, in Stuttgart, apparently struck at the Stuttgart Mint. It came on the heels of the March 3, 1871, Congressional authorization of the Centennial Exposition to be held in 1876.

Q: I have a silver octagonal Bicentennial piece, which is marked "One Ounce," but actually weighs closer to 1.5 ounces. Was this an official issue?

If by "official" you mean a Government Issue, the answer is no. It was struck by the Stowe Nut & Bolt Company of Stow, Ohio and sold originally for $12.50. The extra half-ounce of .999 silver is a bonus due to the die design, which required that large a planchet.

Q: How much gold was there in the $4000 gold Bicentennial medals struck by the Mint and how rare are they?

Each of the large National Medals contained 13.18 troy ounces of gold. Only 423 of them were sold. At the height of the gold boom in 1980 they were worth almost $11,000 each, so I doubt that very many survived the melting furnaces.

Q: Why don't they list prices for the Bicentennial gold medals?

The medals receive little attention as they are primarily bullion items, and are sold on the basis of the current spot bullion prices. The market was saturated with Bicentennial items, and there has been relatively little aftermarket demand for them.

There are 21 different "official" medals in various metals and cases, as well as hundreds or even thousands of other Bicentennial pieces issued by private organizations. In almost all cases the market was saturated for any particular piece, and there has been little, if any, change from the purchase price.

Chapter 11

CHECKS

*Check collecting is a little-known area of numismatics that can be a lot of fun.
And in many cases an inexpensive way to get into numismatic collecting.*

Q: Is a check written on something other than a check blank legal?

It still is, although banks are likely to refuse them. Most banks have forced customers to use personalized checks which can be read by electronic machines, so they will refuse to accept a 'counter' check, one written on a blank check form. Many odd items have been used as checks in the past, the banks going along mainly for the publicity.

Chapter 12

CHOP MARKS

Chop marks are fascinating. Even though they are alterations, some collectors are always looking for coins with chop marks. It's an area where there's plenty of room for research.

Chop marks.

Q: What is the source of the Chinese 'chop mark?'

One common answer is that it is Pidgin English, meaning to chop or cut. However, Indian Dr. P. L. Gupta says instead it traces to the Indian term chapi, or stamped. The British East India Company transferred the Indian term to apply to the Chinese practice. Dr. Gupta traces the earliest usage to a 1775 reference on BEIC trade in China. Somewhat surprisingly the practice of chop marking coins lasted until about the time the Chinese demonetized silver in 1933. The Indian term for a chop mark is schroff mark.

Chapter 13

CLAD COINS

Clad coins have been with us since 1965 and they are gradually coming into their own spot in collections. Billion plus mintages can be daunting, but there are more and more collectible coins being discovered among the "sandwich" coins, as they are often nicknamed.

A partially split off clad layer folded back.

Q: Someone told me that it's impossible for the clad layers to split off our coins. Is this true?

Examples are known for all of the clad denominations with one or both clad layers split off. At least two different methods, explosive bonding and pressure bonding, have been used. Pressure bonding is the current method. Whether there is a difference in the number of missing clad layers from the two methods is unknown.

Q: Why is it that some of the 40 percent silver 1965-1970 half dollars don't show the silver core?

Many were struck with the clad layers wrapped around the core so that it doesn't show. Plating them has altered quite a few others. Weight is the key. A 40 percent silver half weighs 177.5 grains, a copper-nickel 175.0 grains, but the 90 percent silver weighed 192.9 grains. Above all, don't try to scratch or file a coin to determine if it is plated, as it will cut the value sharply. As shown here, weight will tell you far more about the coin.

Q: All the large U.S. clad coins are the same clad material, right?

I hope this is not an argument that resulted in any kind of a substantial bet, because the answer is "No." For the clad Ike dollars and Kennedy halves, the copper-nickel clad layers are each one-sixth of the thickness of the planchet, and the core forms the other two-thirds. For the Anthony dollar, the clad layers are each one-fourth of the thickness, with the core forming the other half. The particular configuration was selected so that it would be impossible to grind down a Kennedy half and use it to replace an Anthony dollar, which would have different electrical characteristics. The electronic slug rejecters supposedly could differentiate between the two, but the point was rather moot, as few vending machine companies ever converted their machines to handle the SBA dollars.

Q: What's the difference between a clad coin and a plated coin, or are they the same?
We use "clad" to mean a planchet made by bonding three different layers of metal together. Some very early examples of clad coins exist dating back to the medieval era. Hammering the metals together created these. When the U.S. Mint switched to clad coinage in 1965 an explosive bonding process was used, but was preceded by a pressure roller system, which was much cheaper. Plating is a completely different process, even if the Mint did try to confuse the public by calling it a "coating" on the 1943 steel cents. In the modern plating process for the copper-plated zinc cents a very thin layer of metal is deposited on the planchets using an electric current to transfer the metal from an anode to the blanks.

Q: Why didn't they put arrows on the coins during the changeover from silver to clad planchets in 1965?
The Treasury Department was anxiously trying to attract as little attention as possible because of concerns that the public would refuse to accept the clad coins. At the time there were serious fears that a mass rejection—such as occurred later with the Anthony dollar—would destabilize the U.S. currency and the economy. In past instances the arrows were used to designate changes in the weight or proportions of alloy, but all of the coins were silver, both before and after the change, so switching to clad was a completely different matter.

Q: Why did the Mint switch to clad coins and not straight copper-nickel?
Extensive research was conducted at the time (just prior to 1965) to find a satisfactory substitute for the 90 percent silver coins that had been the mainstay of commerce for so many years. The researchers found that the copper-nickel cladding on a copper core was the closest match to silver coins to use in vending machines. Modern slug rejecters use electronic circuits to detect slugs and they were able to separate the clad coins from slugs as well. If the Mint had gone to the same copper-nickel alloy used in nickels, there would have been a one to three year disruption of vending.

Q: What percentage of copper and nickel are contained in our clad coins, including the copper core and clad layers?
Although the Mint published figures for the 40 percent silver clad halves and for the copper-plated zinc cents, I haven't been able to find anything official on the copper-nickel clad pieces. After searching in vain for over an hour for the figures we finally determined from the Mint Report for 1980 that all denominations of the clad coins contain 91.67 percent copper. I've got to do some more research on this, because the Anthony dollars have thicker clad layers, which should alter the percentage at least slightly. It's either another of the multitude of delightful coincidences that occur in numismatics, or a deliberate effort on the part of the Mint that the percentage of copper in our clad coins matches the centuries-old British gold sterling standard. The Sacajawea dollar contains manganese, which throws the percentages off.

Chapter 14

CLEANING COINS

Ah! A hot topic! Rule number one in coin collecting is "Don't clean your coins." The next nine rules repeat the same thing. Cleaning or polishing or even using a soft cloth can cut the collector value of your coins in half, or worse.

Q: Have you ever found a method for removing mercury from copper coins? I have several in my collection I'd like to fix.

A coin plated with mercury will have a greasy feel, which is easily recognized. As to removing the mercury, I've solicited reader help on the problem several times without success, despite having some expert chemists and metallurgists in our reading audience. One thing I can warn you about is not to use heat. This would vaporize the mercury, which is extremely, lethally toxic, so it should not be attempted under any circumstance. No coin is worth subjecting yourself to such potential harm.

Q: I've got a lot of coins that I found with a metal detector that I expect to sell to collectors. How do I go about cleaning them?

I just got off the phone with someone who had found a potentially valuable coin and promptly used a pencil eraser to clean it up to be able to read the date and inscription. My unpleasant duty was to have to tell the finder that the coin's value had automatically been cut in half. Removing accumulated dirt and grease is all right, just so long as you don't use any abrasive, abrasive cleaner or acid based cleaner.

Most non-collectors don't stop to consider that if a coin is badly corroded, covered with a thick coating of oxides, etc., that it has no special value to a collector, regardless of how much you "pretty" it up. It's still a badly pitted, corroded coin with little or no numismatic value. The most valuable coin in the world would be nearly worthless in such condition.

Q: Are silicone-impregnated tissues safe to use on coins to clean them?

Any time you wipe a coin, no matter how soft or slick the material may be you are inflicting scratches from tiny particles of grit sticking to the material or the coin. These "hairline" scratches are a dead giveaway that a coin has been cleaned, with a resulting reduction in value. And, ignore those offers on TV for coin or metal cleaners. The products being sold contain acid or abrasives, which will permanently damage your coins and sharply reduce their collector value.

Q: I've been told that using a tumbler with plastic pellets will clean up a coin and even improve the grade. Where can I get such a machine?

This method was actually published in a scholarly article on cleaning coins some years ago, but please ignore that particular piece of advice. There is no way of applying an abrasive or a burnishing material to a coin without permanently damaging the coin and reducing its value. I still remember, with horror, a collector who brought me a collection of several thousand minor coins that he had "cleaned" by dumping them in a rock polishing tumbling machine. The designs had been so severely worn down that there wasn't a single coin in the lot that was worth more than face value.

Chapter 15

COIN DEALERS

Without coin dealers a lot of us wouldn't be collecting, because we wouldn't have a source. The public has a poor perception of coin dealers, due mainly to a lack of understanding of standard business practices. Get to know your local dealers, as they are valuable sources of knowledge.

A coin dealer at work.

Q: I'm told that there are so few dealers handling Colonial coins that it is impossible to buy the coins I want, or resell them, once I have completed my collection. Comment?

The advice smacks of "sour grapes" rather than truth. Colonial coins are just one specialized area out of dozens or even hundreds in numismatics. Look for a specialist dealer and I think you will find a much different story, which is true for any specialty. You can find a large list of dealers, including those specializing in Colonial coins, at the American Numismatic Association Web site - www.money.org

Q: A "local dealer" (always unnamed) says my coin is genuine, so what is it worth, and where can I sell it?

This is a continuing problem, because readers who are not familiar with the procedures for authenticating a coin assume that any coin dealer (or experienced collector) can declare their coin good. Even if the person who made the statement were named, this tells us nothing about his or her qualifications to pass judgment on a specific piece. With all due respect to your local dealers, such a coin would have to be examined by an expert authenticator to have any credibility. Also usually missing is any indication of the grade of the coin, a vital fact in every case.

Q: Why do dealers have a large quantity of some new issue or variety when it is first offered for sale?

Dealers go out and actively seek items, plus they have to have a quantity to make the promotion work. They get them from local banks and money handling firms like anyone else. Seems you just can't convince some people that there is no big conspiracy, no private deals with the mint, no secret supplier that the dealers use to get their coins. A good part of it is sour grapes that someone else is a more astute businessman or knows more about where to buy coins. To be a successful coin dealer you have to know as much, or more, than your customers, or you don't survive. At that you are neglecting some of the major collections that are out there that have many times the coins the dealers have in stock.

Q: Who was the first coin dealer to use a computer in his business?

Sam Sloat, at a firm called Coinprice, was using a computer in 1970 to issue price lists of world coins based on auction records.

Chapter 16

COINS AND THE LAW

Laws affecting coins are sometimes specific, sometimes vague. The Coinage Acts, which have become law over the years, are a rich area for research and historical background for the coins you collect.

Q: My buddy says coins cannot be used as security for a loan. Is he right?

This is a myth that apparently got started at the time we switched to clad coins. The Coinage Act of 1965 contained the authority to impose such a regulation, but it was never authorized, so it's perfectly legal to use coins to secure a loan. Coins have a long history of use by banks as stored assets.

Q: Are one-ounce proof rounds considered bullion for tax purposes?

If they are not coins, then they are bullion for tax purposes. The simple rule here is that only a government can issue a coin, which has a denomination or stated value in commerce. If your piece does not meet that test, then it's not a coin. We are having major problems on the computer online services and the Internet with firms that are advertising bullion rounds and medals as "coins." Besides being mislabeled and misrepresented, the public is being confused as to how to handle the pieces for tax purposes, leaving them open to penalties and fines.

Q: Only one of my relatives is interested in coins, so I want him to have my collection after I die. Is there some way I can insure he will get it?

Unless you make a will specifically naming him, you may run into problems, or you can give him your collection before you die. The laws vary from state to state so consult a lawyer right away for competent advice on how best to handle the matter. Under IRS regulations, if the collection is worth less than $10,000 it meets the requirements of a gift and need not be reported. If over $10,000, the excess will reduce the estate exempted from tax when you die.

Q: I subscribe to one of the online computer services. I've noticed a number of ads offering medals for sale, but calling them coins. Is this permissible?

Calling anything a coin that isn't a coin, such as a medal or token, is either misrepresentation or false advertising. It's the same thing as a person getting on a bulletin board and offering Morgan dollars as "gold dollars." Very obviously, a novice may not know the difference between a coin and a medal, but commercial firms, who just as obviously should know better, post an uncomfortable number of ads. If some form of government didn't issue the piece to be used as money, then it can't be offered as a coin. The distinction is important for tax purposes as well, as the IRS treats coins differently than medals or tokens.

Q: Wasn't there some kind of a court battle some time ago over an Alaska Trade dollar?

In 1967 the Alaska Centennial Commission ordered 50,000 coins, which bore the illegal phrase, "good for one dollar in trade at any…" The U.S. Treasury threatened to take legal action; the Commission attempted to cancel the minting contract, but lost in court, and had to pay the contract, as well as for a substitute order of plastic coins. The Trade dollars were later sold to collectors for $2.50 each.

Q: Isn't there a law that you can't have more than 5,000 cents?
At first glance this sounds like a trick question, but it's a legitimate concern. Apparently the source was a misunderstanding of some of the regulations on legal tender. There is no law on the books that would prohibit possession of any coins (other than counterfeit), in any quantity. For a time after 1933 it was illegal to possess more than a token amount of gold coins, but that provision is long gone.

Q: Why did the Mint almost close in 1802?
The House passed a bill repealing the Coinage Act of 1792, and closing the Mint. The Senate defeated the bill, so the House tried a second time later in the year, but the measure was bottled up in committee and never came to a vote.

Q: Didn't the Coinage Act of 1970 call for a minimum of 300 million half dollars a year?
The law did not set a minimum. The announced plan of the Mint was to strike that minimum. However, in 1973 they dropped below the minimum and exceeded it only in 1976. The mintages in recent years have been far below the Mint's goal for the unwanted coins.

Q: Please send me a list of those states that do not charge sales tax on coins?
I'd like to help, but such a list would be obsolete by the time the information is gathered as the often-complicated state laws change constantly. You can learn more by reading the dealer ads, which state whether you have to pay sales tax. In some cases, purchases in another state are exempt from tax, but this is a loophole that is being plugged tighter every year. Complicating the tax picture are the hundreds of cities and counties that are charging varying added sales tax rates to the state tax.

Q: Are there any laws on the books that prohibit the melting of U.S. coins?
There is a standby law, Section 5111 (d) (1) of Title 31 U.S. Code, which gives the Secretary of the Treasury the power to prohibit the melting or export of U.S. coins at any time that it is felt there is a threat to the coinage. The power has been used in the past, but is not currently invoked. The law applies to any coin, so it could be used for whatever metal happened to go up. The Coinage Act of 1965 contained a provision, which gave the Treasury Secretary the power to invoke a ban on the melting of U.S. coins whenever it was deemed necessary. The provision was put into effect the first time on May 18, 1967, to stop the export and melting of silver coins. It was this same provision in the Coinage Act of 1965, now incorporated in Title 31, U.S. Code, which was used to ban the melting of copper-alloy cents from 1974 to 1978.

Q: Has counterfeiting always been considered a crime?
It's believed that counterfeiting began close on the heels of the striking of the first coins. Ever since then it has been considered one of the gravest crimes on the books. Up until the last several centuries it was not at all unusual for a counterfeiter to be put to death in some gruesome way as a warning to others. In ancient Egypt the counterfeiter could expect to lose both hands. In Rome making false coins meant a date in the arena with wild beasts. Constantine made counterfeiting crimes of treason and in early England counterfeiters were put to death or left to rot in jail until they died.

Q: When did U.S. coins become legal tender on the Hawaiian Islands?
Until the 1850s Mexican coins predominated on the islands. The U.S. dollar became a de facto standard as trade with the U.S. increased, but it wasn't until 1859 that a law was passed making the U.S. nickel and dime legal tender there.

Q: Is there any sort of national clearinghouse for stolen coin information?

The Federal Bureau of Investigation has a branch called the National Stolen Coin File (NSCF) just for that purpose. Access to it is limited to law enforcement agencies, so you can't contact them directly, but any loss over $2,000 can be recorded. The NSCF has equipment that can use coin photos for identification, so there's another good reason to take some clear, sharply focused photos of your more valuable coins. A scratch or nick or other marking on the coin that shows in a photo might ultimately result in the recovery of the piece if it is stolen.

Q: Didn't the Treasury Department at one time try to claim that private use of the terms "mint" and "coin" was illegal?

The Department started out on such a course back in the 1960s, but abandoned the effort when legal advisors decided that the terms were so much a part of the language that it would be difficult to enforce. However, the term "coin" has been both legally and professionally banned from use in the hobby to prevent applying it to medals, tokens and other similar items. A coin is defined as a piece that has been issued and assigned a specific value by a legal body that is entitled to issue money. Mislabeling tokens or medals as coins leaves the offender open to charges of fraud or misrepresentation.

Q: Weren't gold $2.50 quarter eagles illegal to own at one time?

It wasn't for very long, and even back then the voice of the collector was heard. In a revision of the Executive Order of 1933, which banned gold ownership except for $100 in face value in a collection, the government announced on December 28 that collectors could keep all numismatic gold except quarter eagles. The collectors protested loudly, so the order was rescinded January 12, 1934. The $2.50 gold, thus, was illegal to own for a period of 16 days. As to why the government picked the $2.50 coin, there seems to be little in the way of significant grounds.

Q: What's the law on spelling out denominations on our coins?

Actually the law has little or nothing to say on the matter. The usage is left up to the designer or the space that's available on the coin. For example, the pattern for the Buffalo nickel had the denomination as "5 CENTS." The last coin to use digits for the denomination were the Bela Pratt $2.50 gold coins of 1908 through 1929. However, the Lafayette dollar is cited as an exception, because there is a provision that the dollar denomination be fully spelled out. The Lafayette coin violated this provision by having just the word "DOLLAR," without the necessary "ONE."

Q: Isn't there some kind of a law forbidding the Mint from keeping dies and overdating them to use in a later year?

This law has been on the books since 1869, requiring that every dated coin die be destroyed on December 31 of each calendar year. If this law had been obeyed it would in theory have eliminated all overdates, but since there are a number that occurred, it obviously did not serve its purpose. The biggest loophole and the one responsible for most, if not all, of the overdates, especially those of the 20th century, is that dies for the coming year are usually made, and often actually used to strike coins in the final months of the preceding year, so that the overdates have actually been created in the two or three months before the December 31 destruction date. Some of the coins that eluded this law include the 1888/7 cent, 1869/8 two cent, 1887/6 three-cent nickel, 1883/2 Shield, 1918/1917-D Buffalo nickel, the 1918/1917-S quarter, the 1943/1942-P Jefferson nickel, 1880/79 dollars and a number of others.

The French Mint, for example, has both coin and medal dies dating back to the French and American revolutions. The Dutch Mint has dies for almost every significant variety struck in the last four centuries. One further reason for the U.S. Mint practice is the monstrous problem of storing the hundreds of thousands of dies that are used each year.

Q: I got into an argument with a lawyer friend who claims that there was at one time a federal law making it illegal for a U.S. citizen to own gold that was stored in some other country. Is he right?

He has the right dope, as an Executive Order (6260) amended and effective on January 16, 1961, required U.S. citizens and companies that had gold or securities based on gold deposited abroad to dispose of it by May 16 of that year. Violators were subject to a $10,000 fine and a ten-year jail term under an obscure 1917 law as well as civil penalties of up to twice the value of the gold under the Gold Reserve Act of 1934. The Executive Order has since been canceled and Americans may own gold anywhere.

Q: Was there any real cost to the government to redeem the Trade dollars when they were dropped from our coinage?

The Act of March 3, 1887, lobbied through Congress by speculators who had bought up all the available Trade dollars, provided for redemption of those that did not have Chinese chop marks. In the six-month life of the Act, about 7.7 million of the coins were redeemed at a loss to the Treasury of $1.8 million. At the time the coins were first struck they contained $1.04 worth of silver. When they were redeemed, silver had dropped below 80 cents an ounce.

Q: What is the official composition of the half cent?

It's quite clear in the Coinage Act of 1792, and repeated in the Acts of 1793, 1796 and 1837, all of which specify that the half cent (and the cent) be struck on 100 percent copper planchets.

Q: I'd like to see the exact wording of the Act that prohibited private ownership of gold?

There was no law passed by Congress. Instead the prohibition came in a 1933 Executive Order, signed by the President.

Q: What happened to gold coin collections in 1933?

When President Roosevelt ordered all gold coins returned to the Government there was an exemption of up to $100 face value that could be retained in a collection. However, many ignored the law despite threatened fines and jail sentences. The recall had little or no effect on the tons of gold coins in European banks.

Q: Was there any special reason why they stopped minting the $2.50 gold quarter eagle in 1930?

The Treasury Department reported to Congress that the coin was not circulating, and "is easily confused with the new one-cent piece." This is a curious piece of language since the Lincoln cent had been in circulation for two decades, and the same size cent since 1857, or about 72 years. Minting stopped in 1929, and Congress passed the Coinage Act of April 11, 1930, ending the denomination.

Q: Why did U.S. coinage laws specify Spanish "milled" dollars for exchange purposes?

The machine-made coins were less subject to clipping or other nefarious practices than the hammered coinage. In this case "milled" means machine made and not the current meaning of a reeded edge. European usage for the term is different than in the U.S.

Q: Didn't Congress authorize a new three-cent coin during World War II?

Let's say they almost did. On December 11, 1942, the Senate passed a bill authorizing the three-cent piece, but the measure died in the House. There was renewed discussion of such a coin during the 1974 coin shortage.

Q: Why did they stop minting Peace dollars in 1928 and then resume in 1934?

The total number minted up to 1928 matched the number of silver dollars melted under the provisions of the Pittman Act of 1918. The Peace dollars of 1934, 1935 and 1964 were minted under the provisions of a different act.

Hawaiian dala.

Q: Does a given coin always remain legal tender?

Not necessarily. Many coins may still be listed as legal tender issues but they were recalled, withdrawn or demonetized long ago.

Usually the law authorizing the coin specifies whether it is considered legal tender, or not. This practice may vary a bit from one country to another, but it all boils down to whether the issuing authority wants to redeem it. Legal tender status does not force acceptance, it merely establishes a legal way to pay obligations.

Q: Why isn't there an eagle on the $1 gold coins?

The law of March 3, 1849, creating the coin, specifically deleted the eagle requirement. The same legal sidestep has been used for a number of coins - especially commemoratives - since then.

Q: I had some gold coins confiscated by the Treasury. Can I recover their value?
Under a 1977 regulation, you can recover the value of the bullion content, less smelting charges, providing you meet a number of requirements, including that they were "innocently purchased and held," and voluntarily submitted to the Treasury. Write to: Department of the Treasury, 15th and Pennsylvania Ave., Washington, DC 20220 for detailed information.

Q: Didn't President Johnson say silver coins would not become scarce?
In his speech marking the signing of the Coinage Act of 1965, he said: "Some have asked whether silver coins will disappear. The answer is very definitely no. Our present coins won't disappear and they won't even become rarities. If anybody has any idea of hoarding our silver coins, let me say this: Treasury has a lot of silver on hand, and it can be and it will be used to keep the price of silver in line with its value in our present silver coins. There will be no profit in holding them out of circulation for the value of their silver content."

Q: Are the Hawaiian coins of 1883 still legal tender?
They were redeemed until January 1, 1904, and then declared to no longer be legal tender. They are one exception to the statement that all U.S. coins are still legal tender, but the 'out' of course is that at the time the coins where minted (1883) Hawaii was not part of the United States. The islands were annexed in 1898, became a territory in 1900 and a state in 1959.

Q: I'm involved in a serious argument. Can private mints issue coins?
A private mint can mint coins, but a government has to issue the coins. This is a point that many collectors overlook. Even an official mint, such as the U.S. Mint, cannot issue coins. They are a manufacturing facility and they turn the coins over to the Federal Reserve Bank, which has the authority to issue them. Thus, a coin is not legally a coin until the Mint has transferred it to the Federal Reserve Bank for issue. This raises a curious legal question as to how proof and commemorative coins struck and sold directly by the Mint become legal coins.

Q: Can you give me the Hobby Protection Act date?
President Nixon signed the law on November 29, 1973, one day before it would have gone into effect without his signature. Congress passed PL93-167, which requires marking of imitations with the word "COPY." However, they failed to plug the major loophole, which was that the law was not retroactive. Regulations to implement enforcement were not published until July 19, 1974. Final regulations were not published until March 10, 1975, in essence the effective date of the law.

Q: Why aren't the Maria Theresa thalers required to be marked as copies?
The U.S. Hobby Protection Act covers the marking of copies, but the U.S. and most other governments recognize restrikes by official government mints as legal coins that are not required to be marked. Since the Austrian Mint is restriking the thalers, they are considered to be legal coins. The Hobby Protection Act does not affect copies made before the law was enacted in 1975.

Q: What authority was there for the state monetary issues after 1776?
The state issues were covered in the Articles of Confederation of 1778. This document specifically allowed state coinage. However, the days were numbered as the Coinage Act of 1792 rescinded the right, holding it for the Federal government.

Chapter 17

COINS IN THE MAIL

The U.S. Mail is a vital part of many collectors and dealers' lives. Here too, without the mail we wouldn't have nearly as many collectors.

Q: I'm a collector, with the military in Europe. What are the laws affecting coins sent from the U.S. and what do I need to know to bring my collection of U.S. and foreign coins home with me?

You won't need to worry about any U.S. laws as far as coin collecting is concerned as long as you are getting them at an APO address. Probably even the local laws of the country you are in would not apply. To determine the procedures for returning a collection to the States I'd check with your company clerk. For future tax purposes, keep receipts for every coin you buy, U.S. or foreign, because when you sell them you will have to pay tax on the increase in value. As regulations change, I'd be interested in hearing from any returnees who have been through the process and might have some tips.

Chapter 18

COLLECTOR TOOLS

Just like any "job," coin collecting requires a variety of tools and equipment to properly implement a collection. When you start collecting don't forget to include them in your budget, right along with your reference books.

Q: Who invented the 2x2 cardboard coin holders?
My source for this answer is Chet Krause who says that Bill Eisenhart of Harrisburg, Pennsylvania invented the cardboard 2x2 with the plastic liner, and was also the first to market them.

Q: Where can I get a pen to write on plastic coin flips?
Try almost any coin dealer, an office supply store, or check the camera department in most of the big discount stores, or in a photo shop.

Q: In many of your answers you have referred to weighing coins as a safe, non-destructive method of testing a coin. Where would I find a scale that I can afford to weigh my coins with?
The least expensive source for an accurate scale that weighs in grains is your nearest gun shop, or a gun magazine, as powder scales weigh up to 500 grains with a 1/10th grain accuracy. I've used a Redding powder scale for more than three decades and have been very satisfied with it. You should still be able to find one for less than $50, and there are other similar makes on the market.

Q: Does the light that falls on a coin make any difference in what you see?
You might say that it makes ALL the difference in what you see. One of the common mistakes is to get too much light, so that glare hides much of the surface. Fluorescent lights are also likely to give you problems, frequently altering the coloration of the piece. Some dealers swear by high intensity lights, while others swear at them. A good swing-arm lamp with a 60- to 100-watt bulb is usually all you need to look at a coin. But, don't make the mistake of placing the coin flat and looking at it. You need to tilt and turn it, getting the light from several angles to see everything there is to see and, of course, to really see what's there you need magnification of some kind. When I examine a coin under my stereomicroscope I will usually turn it in a complete circle before I'm finished looking. Always try to examine coins under the same, or at least similar, lighting conditions if possible.

Q: Why is it that although the 1970-D half was only included in mint sets, the coin folders and albums include spots for it?
Underscoring the importance of at least some surveys, the manufacturers found that 84 percent of the collectors who responded wanted it in their albums and 66 percent wanted it in their folders.

Q: What does 20/20 vision mean to a collector?
It means you can read 3/8-inch high letters at a distance of 20 feet with either eye. Since few of us look at a coin from 20 feet away, it's much more important to have good close vision, and a magnifier.

Q: What are the basic tools for a collector?

At the top of the list, the first thing to buy is a good hand lens. Ultimately you will want either a combination or other lenses of different power, and eventually you may want a microscope. Next comes a scale to weigh your coins, a method that will tell you far more than any other device about your coins. Tongs or gloves are needed for upper grade or proof coins. You'll also need a set of calipers or some device to measure the diameter of a coin.

Q: What is the amount of magnification in micro and macro shots that you publish?

The coins are usually photographed at 10X to 30X, or 10 to 30 times normal size, and the photos are then blown up by varying amounts to print. Thus, there's no way, short of detailed measurements, of determining the actual printed magnification.

Chapter 19

COMMEMORATIVE COINS

Over the years commemoratives have been praised and damned by the public and collectors. Many of the coins issued in the first half of the 20th century have a fascinating tale to tell and you can find lots of background information in several books published on the topic.

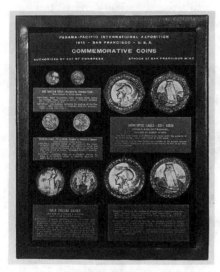

A 1915 Panama-Pacific Commemorative set.

Q: How many of the double sets of the Pan-Pacific coins were issued?
The exact number of the sets that were issued, officially described as "The most notable set of coins ever issued," is unknown, although the issue was limited to 1,500 sets. It is estimated that less than half a dozen of the double sets are still in existence.

Q: Wasn't the mintage figure for the 1893 Columbian commemorative half dollar much higher than the usually quoted 1.5 million?
Actual mintage was just over 4 million, but 2,501,700 of the coins were melted. Rather than confuse you with facts, the end result is usually quoted.

Q: I know the first strike of the 1892 Columbia Exposition commemoratives were given special treatment, but how about the 1893 date?
The Remington Typewriter Company paid $10,000 for the first 1892 commemorative, now in the Field Museum in Chicago. It got all the publicity, but the Chicago Historical Society owns the first 1893 strike. The Remington check was sold for $1,210 to Kurt Krueger at the FUN sale in 1985.

Q: How many numismatic items were issued for the 1892 Columbian Exposition?
If you want to start a collection, there's plenty to choose from. Nathan N. Eglit is quoted as listing "well over 600." Coins, medals, elongated coins, political pieces and even telephone slugs are among the items listed.

Q: Has there ever been a coin struck that was based on a quantity of energy rather than intrinsic value?
A joule is equal to about 75 percent of a foot-pound of energy, and a promoter by the name of Jim Mangan had one-joule silver coins struck for his "Nation of Celestia," which had a territory consisting of all of outer space.
The bust on the coin is that of his daughter, "Princess" Ruth. Where U.S. coins have "LIBERTY" on the hair fillet, in a play on words the Celestin has the word "MAGNANIMITY" and the 11 stars on the obverse signify both the 11 letters in the word and the 11 years of Celestia's existence.

Q: How many proofs were struck of the 1892 Columbian half dollar commemorative?

Breen said, "No reliable estimate" and reported: "About a dozen are known to exist." The standard: "There are many deceptive early business strikes" follows along, so it's not exactly a common coin. Another source estimates 100 for both dates combined. There are about two dozen of the 1893 known.

Reading the available literature on the proofs for these two years is an exercise in confusion. One source indicates that there are no (official) records for either year, but that there are a couple of dozen known examples for each year. Other quoted figures are 103 struck for 1892, including the "first" strike, purchased by the Remington Typewriter Company for $10,000, and one for 1893. The latter is also described as the "first official proof strike" of any U.S. commemorative coin. Generally agreed is that there were numerous proof-like business strikes, so before buying a Columbian half I'd strongly urge getting it authenticated by a reputable expert or grading service.

The 1932 Washington quarter circulating commemorative.

Q: Was the Washington quarter really a commemorative coin?

Yes. It was originally intended to be a one-year issue in 1932, but was popular enough to be continued. That popularity with the public is in marked contrast to many other new issues. Production was resumed in 1934, so there was none struck in 1933.

Q: Supposedly the Movie Industry sponsored a commemorative coin?

In 1923 Hollywood picked the Monroe Doctrine as the central theme of the First Annual American Historical Revue and Motion Picture Exposition, held in Los Angeles in June 1923. They sponsored the Monroe Doctrine Centennial half dollar. The coin sale was intended to pay for the Exposition, but it turned a profit, so most of the coins were sold for face value.

Q: What is a restrike of the Isabella commemorative quarter worth?

There is no record of any official restrike, so I asked for more information. It turned out that the piece in question was a silver bullion round, which is not a coin, and obviously is not a restrike. If you are buying what you think are "coins," read the fine print carefully, especially if the ad is on TV or in a non-hobby publication where there are few restrictions on claims. Several readers paid substantial sums for what they thought were original 1893 Isabella quarters, only to instead receive a silver round with a similar design.

Q: What is the significance of the palmetto and the oak branch on the 1936 Columbia, South Carolina commemorative half?
The coin marks the successful defense against the British fleet in 1776. The palmetto comes from the logs of Ft. Moultrie, which soaked up the British cannon balls with minimal damage while the oak signifies the damage the fort's cannon did to the oak ships.

Q: Didn't Susan B. Anthony have a hand in designing the Queen Isabella commemorative quarter?
Indirectly she was involved in getting the coin authorized, but apparently had nothing to do with the design. She was described as the "driving force" behind the Board of Lady Managers of the Exposition, which sponsored the coin.

Q: On the Grant commemorative half dollar, what does the 'G' stand for?
The G is for the middle name of the designer, Laura Gardin Fraser. She was the wife of James Earle Fraser, who designed the Buffalo nickel. Since that coin had been introduced in 1913, with the incuse F initial, the Mint felt that it was not practical to use an F for her as well, and as a result of the furor over the "VDB" initials of Brenner's which had barely been settled, deemed it inappropriate to "advertise" her work by putting LGF on the Grant coins. As a compromise the G from her middle name was put on the coin.

Q: On the 1990 Ike Commemorative dollar, there is what appears to be a bell in the foreground. Can you tell me if this has any special significance?
The bell was a gift from the St. Louis & San Francisco Railway, with the Presidential emblem on it. Mamie Eisenhower is quoted as saying that the grandchildren loved to ring it, "and I was always afraid the people in Gettysburg would think there was a fire."

Q: Are there any U.S. coins that recognize or take note of the Confederacy?
There are two examples. One is the 1936 Lynchburg, Virginia commemorative half dollar. It clearly shows the Confederate Monument in front of the Lynchburg City Courthouse. The Stone Mountain commemorative half shows Confederate Generals Stonewall Jackson and Robert E. Lee.

Q: Who was the first living person to appear on a U.S. coin? That is, a person who was alive at the time the coin was issued?
That distinction goes to Alabama Governor T. E. Kilby, who, with the state's first governor, W. W. Bibb, was depicted on the 1921 Alabama Centennial Commemorative half dollar.

Q: Does the figure of the kneeling miner appear on any other coins besides the California Diamond Jubilee commemorative half dollar?
The figure, which is actually panning for gold, appears on numerous tokens and game counters, but not on any other official coin.

Q: Where do I find the authorization for the two versions of the Louisiana Purchase commemorative coins?
You won't find much. One of the two, which is the original, has Thomas Jefferson on it. The other has McKinley on the obverse. The enabling act, the Act of June 28, 1902, makes no mention of there being two types. President McKinley was assassinated and died on September 14, 1901, so it's assumed that the original intent was a Jefferson gold dollar. The McKinley design was later added as a tribute to the fallen President.

Q: Does President Abraham Lincoln appear on any U.S. coin without his well-known beard?

Lincoln's visage has appeared on countless billions of U.S. cents with his beard, but the design used for the Illinois 1918 commemorative half dollar shows him clean-shaven, without his beard. By contrast, only about 100,000 of the half dollars were struck.

Q: Is the building that appears on the 1917 McKinley commemorative gold dollar the Lincoln Memorial?

The building is sometimes confused with the Lincoln Memorial in Washington, D.C. but is actually the McKinley Memorial Building in Niles, Ohio.

Q: In an old publication there's an ad for a Ft. Peck Dam commemorative half. Am I missing something here, as I can't find a listing for such a coin?

In 1937 the Ft. Peck, Montana Memorial Association asked Congress for a commemorative coin. Anticipating Congressional approval, the association went ahead and placed an ad in the March 1937 Numismatist offering the Ft. Peck commemorative half dollars for sale for $2. However, Congress, disturbed by the many excesses of the commemorative programs, showed their displeasure by killing all commemorative legislation in 1937.

Q: I have a Grant Commemorative half dollar which has the star in a slightly different position than others that I have. Is this a variety?

More probably it is a counterfeit, especially if the interior surface of the star appears different than the field surface, and the field bulges up around the star. These fakes appeared as far back as 1932.

Q: I read that the first Lafayette Commemorative dollar sold for $5,000, just like the first Columbian Exposition half dollar struck was sold for $10,000. Is this true?

The offer reportedly was made, but refused, as the first Lafayette coin went to the President of France.

Chapter 20

COPPER

Copper is a vital part of the majority of coins of the world. The U.S. has struck only one coin that didn't contain copper - the 1943 zinc-plated steel cent.

This coin may have started life as a band from a powder keg.

Q: Is it true that some early U.S. coins were made from powder kegs?

According to contemporary reports the Fugio cents were reportedly made from copper from the bands, which bound the powder kegs sent over from France. Copper was in extremely short supply and the Mint was forced to purchase copper wherever they found it.

Q: How does the price of copper compare to 1900?

Back then copper sold for 15 cents a pound. The last time I checked it was something over a dollar a pound and has been close to $1.50 a pound.

Q: Was England the only supplier of copper for early U.S. coins?

England was the main source, with interruptions such as the War of 1812. Copper from Peru was purchased beginning in 1833. Crocker Brothers & Company of Taunton, Massachusetts processed the raw metal. Later Crocker used some Wisconsin copper. The Wisconsin copper mines tried political pressure to gain more of the business but lost out. Today the Mint is buying planchets again from foreign producers.

Q: What is the "hammer test" for copper?

In the early days of metallurgy, before the ability to assay metals was common, a test for the composition of a bar of copper was to heat it red hot and hammer it on an anvil. If the metal was relatively pure, it would flatten out without splitting or cracking.

Chapter 21

DENVER MINT

The Denver Mint has a long and colorful history. It is my favorite because it was the first Mint that I visited when I was starting my career as a numismatic researcher.

Side view of the Denver Mint.

Q: What ever happened to the new mint they were building at Denver?
A new Denver Mint was planned in the early 1970s, but it never reached the building stage. Although a site was purchased, Congress failed to appropriate the money to construct it, and the building plans were canceled. Since then they have done a lot of remodeling, including construction of a die shop so that Denver could make its own dies.

Q: Wasn't there a considerable delay in putting the Denver Mint in operation?
This sounds like some of the procrastination of the British Parliament but Congress is no slouch at taking due process to the outer limits. The facts are that the Denver Mint was authorized on April 21, 1862. It struck its first coin in 1906, some 44 years later.

Chapter 22

DESIGNS, DESIGNERS, DESIGNER'S INITIALS AND ENGRAVERS

If you don't think this is an important area, then look at and listen to the controversy arising from the State quarter designs. The public takes most designs to task, but the collector has a vested interest in the designs coming out of the Mint.

Q: Didn't they get their languages mixed up on some of the Philippine coins?
Beginning in 1903 with the U.S. takeover, the Philippine coins used a mix of English and Spanish in the denominations. It's a technical point, as the denomination should have read either "one cent" or "un centavo." The mixed language has been long noted, but nothing was ever done about it. After independence, the native Tagalog language has been used on the coins.

Q: Is there any special significance to the different branches and leaves that appear on our coins?
The three principal woods that appear on our coins are the olive, the laurel and the oak. The olive signifies peace, the oak leaves are the symbol for military power and might, while the laurel leaves indicate the civic duties of our government. This is a popular question from school children.

Q: In your book you say, "the design on a hub is in relief." How does that work on a coin with incuse design elements?
"The design on a hub is in relief," is a general statement, true of most coins, which have relief designs. The hub has the design exactly as it will appear on the coin. If the design is in relief, it will be the same on the hub. Where it is incuse, it will also be incuse on the hub. Examples of incuse design include the 1984 Olympic dollars, which had incuse dates. The designer's initial "F" is incuse on the Buffalo nickels. Both would, of course, be incuse on the hub.

Q: Are historic motifs "dead" on coins?
To look at the current market, it would seem that a coin has to have a bird, fish, animal, flower or some other "collectible" object on it. Who knows what might happen if an issue of coins with historical scenes were produced. It might be a refreshing change, but a little search will find several current coins, including the State quarters, which buck this seeming trend.

Q: I have an 1855 $10 gold coin which has the 55 slanted sharply to the right. Is this a known variety?
From 1850 through 1856 the Mint used slanted 5s, but beginning in 1855 the upright "5" was introduced and both are found on the 1855 and 1856 coins. For 1857, just upright 5s were used.

Q: I've seen several examples of coins with raised center dots, but a recent find has me baffled, as it has a small indentation at the exact center of the coin where the raised dot should be. Is this legitimate?

Some of the U.S. coins, especially the $10 gold eagles and the half dollars from the mid 1800s, do have a center punch mark instead of a raised center dot. This is because the punch was applied to the master hub instead of to the master die and in the process of transfer became a raised dot on the working die and a hole on the punched coins. There are other examples of coins with punch marks, usually in the fields, assumed to be from a hardness testing machine, but probably relatively easy to fake. The center hole was used to lie out the die when it was made. A compass leg was placed in the hole and used to make the outlines and the lines for the lettering. These are fairly common on the early coins in all denominations.

Q: I made the statement that all our circulating U.S. coins have stars, but a friend questioned it. Am I right, or not?

"Some" would have gotten you by, but not "all." Stars were not used on the large cents until 1808. Neither the Indian Head nor the Lincoln cents have stars. None of the 2-cent coins have stars, nor do the 3-cent nickel pieces. The 1837-1838 half dimes and dimes are also starless. The dimes from 1860 to 1917 had no stars either. More recently the 1913 through 1938 Buffalo nickels have no stars in the design. Even the Jefferson nickel has but one star. The only Washington quarter with stars is the 1976 Bicentennial commemorative. The Franklin half has no stars, although the Kennedy half makes up for it with 63 stars, except on the 1976, which has 13 stars. The $3 gold is also without stars.

Q: Were there any other changes in the Lincoln cent besides the 1969 revamping?

The modifications in 1969 are about the only major changes, other than the change to the memorial reverse in 1959. By 1969 the master die had spread to the point that the motto was merging into the rim. Changes in several other years amounted to minor touch ups, a regular practice every few years. There were also some minor changes made during World War I that reflected new methods of making dies. A study of the series reveals that the most significant of these changes have been to Lincoln's hair.

Q: What is the source of the cap worn by Miss Liberty on the 1795 $5 gold?

Most sources describe it as a Phrygian cap tracing back to Asia Minor, but it was actually modeled after headgear that was popular in the 1790s. It is described in a letter from Samuel Moore, the Mint Director, to Thomas Jefferson.

Q: I notice that the portrait of Abraham Lincoln on the Illinois commemorative half dollar differs markedly from Brenner's Lincoln on the cent. Did Brenner do both coins?

Brenner did the cent, but not the half dollar. That was the work of Chief Engraver George T. Morgan. Morgan's portrait on the half dollar came from the head of Lincoln displayed at the state capitol in Springfield that Brenner copied from a plaque he did several years earlier.

Q: What is the story on the cross that appears on some ancient Indian coins?

The book, *New Light on the Most Ancient East*, says, "The swastika and the cross, common on stamps and plaques, were religious or magical symbols in Babylonia and Elam in the earliest prehistoric period, but preserve that character also in modern India as elsewhere."

Q: Which one of the Mint's Chief Engravers said a building should not be used on a coin?

The quote is from Charles Barber, "I am not in favor of using any building for a coin…being unsuitable for the proper display of buildings." If history had not already proved him wrong with the hundreds of buildings on coins, later and wiser heads used the Lincoln Memorial and Monticello to advantage.

Q: I've noticed some of my 1935-S Peace dollars don't match the earlier dates. They have four rays below ONE on the reverse, while the rest of my coins have just three rays.

The four-ray design is from a hub that was introduced in 1935 and used only on part of the San Francisco coins. It commands a slight premium over the three-ray variety.

Q: What's the record number of busts on a single coin?

The 1828 Convention thaler, known as the "Blessings from Heaven" thaler, was struck as a commemorative by Ludwig I, King of Bavaria (1825-48), in southern Germany. The reverse shows Queen Therese and eight children so it is often cited as one of the coins with the most portraits (10) on it. Children are Maximilian, Mathilde, Adelgunde, Hildegarde, Alexandra, Adalbert, Luitpold and Otto. A ninth child died in infancy. There is also an unusual coin, a half Reichsthaler of 1615 from Saalfeld in Saxony, which has busts of Johann Ernst and his seven brothers, four pictured on each side of the coin.

Q: I've noticed that on the Statue of Liberty coins, the obverse design has all three initials of the sculptor, but the reverse has only two. Is this a mistake?

The initials used are a matter of personal preference by the individual artists as to how they "sign" their work, so this affects whether there are two or three initials on the coin. It's not a mistake.

Two variations of John Sinnock's initials.

Q: What's the story on Joseph Stalin's initials being used on the Roosevelt dime? I'd heard it was in gratitude for Russian help during World War II.

John Sinnock shared a mutual problem with Gilroy Roberts in that both were Chief Engravers at the U.S. Mint and both had their initials derided as a "communist plot" to take over our coinage. Sinnock's J.S. initials quickly were rumored to be those of Joseph Stalin, and Gilroy Robert's monogram looked to the suspicious like a perfectly formed hammer and sickle on the truncation of Kennedy's neck on the half dollar. Whether it was Sinnock's own idea or one forced on him by pressure from mint officials, when it came time to do the Franklin half dollar Sinnock added his middle initial to make it J.R.S. He thus shares the somewhat uncommon distinction of having used two different initial combinations on different U.S. coins with Laura Gardin Fraser, who used LGF on one coin and just a G on the Grant commemoratives.

Q: While examining my Washington commemorative halves, I found two sets of initials. What do they stand for?

The E.J. stands for Elizabeth Jones on both obverse and reverse. The M.P. in the bushes at left is for Matthew Peloso, an assistant sculptor-engraver who did the plaster model for the reverse.

Q: In my coin book it notes that the VDB initials were restored to the cent in 1918. Why don't the catalog listings show this?

I suspect that you are trying to compare the 1918 listings with those for 1909. There is no special notation for the 1918 cent because the VDB was added at the beginning of the year and appears on all cents struck that year. In contrast, in 1909 the first coins were struck with the initials and then they were removed for production in the latter part of the year creating two varieties for the year, with and without the initials.

Q: I can't seem to find the VDB initials on the recent date cents I've collected. Where are they and how big are they?

The incuse VDB initials on the cent are in letters about a fourth as large as the letters in LIBERTY. They are located on the left end of the slope, or truncation, at the base of the bust, easiest to see if you turn the coin upside down. In many instances the VDB will be partly or completely missing due to abrasion of the die both by wear and by repair work on the die. Often all you can find will be the tops of the letters, or three small indentations where they should be. On most proof cents they will stand out plainly.

Q: Just exactly how much of the VDB has to be missing on these cents that are listed as having the VDB missing?

This seems to be causing some problems, because in the rush to profit from this particular minting variety, the usual standards are being ignored in some cases. When I say, "missing" I mean just that, with no trace of the VDB showing. In recent weeks I have had several coins sent to me in which have had parts, usually the tops of one or more of the letters, showing. There are some coins, which under the proper light, will show a slight indentation or break in the edge of the lower bust. I feel that these can safely be called "missing," but not if there is some part of the outline of the letter showing. The missing letters are an abrasion variety caused by the heavy use of an abrasive to repair the die surface and because of their acceptance by a number of collectors are exceptions to the general rule that abrasion varieties are too common to have any value. Most are repetitive, high mintage minting varieties.

Q: Is there any significance to the fact that Lincoln faces to the viewer's right, while all other contemporary circulation coins of the U.S. have the busts facing left?

None that I've been able to track down. V. D. Brenner set the pattern with the Lincoln cent, which was the first circulating U.S. coin to depict a real person, so the others that followed were the precedent breakers.

The 1892-93 Columbian Exposition commemorative half with a supposed bust of Columbus was the first to depict a "real" person, followed by the 1893 Queen Isabella quarter and the undated (1899) Lafayette commemorative dollar. In both cases the busts faced the viewer's left, so this question may have been based on these coins, which did circulate but were technically not part of our circulating coins. I think you may be confusing this with the tradition for the British monarchs, who changed direction with each new ruler.

Q: I'm involved in a rather heated discussion. Don't U.S. coins have to have stars in the design?

Stars play an interesting role in coin design, often as symbols, such as the 13 stars representing the original 13 states. But, they are not a required part of the design, nor are there any rules as to the number of stars, so the numbers have varied widely, down to none on a couple of coins. The Kennedy halves, at the other end of the scale, have 63 stars.

Q: I read somewhere that the Anthony dollar and the Lincoln cent have something in common but I can't find the reference. What is the answer?

The two are among the only U.S. coins to use a previously used design. The SBA dollar used the Ike reverse, and the Memorial Lincoln used the old obverse from the wheat-back cents. A third candidate is the 20-cent coin, which used the same design as the Trade dollar.

Q: I know there are a couple of coins with crosses on them, but is there any U.S. coin with a church as the design?

Apparently, adhering to the letter of the separation of church and state, the only example is the Delaware Tercentenary half dollar of 1936, which depicts the Holy Trinity Church.

Q: What was the unusual distinction of Felix Schlag's Jefferson design for the nickel?

Schlag's Thomas Jefferson and Monticello designs were the last privately executed coin design for a general circulation, or business strike, coin. There were private designs for the reverses of the three Bicentennial coins, but they are (circulating) commemoratives.

A Standing Liberty quarter displays a partially uncovered shield.

Q: Is the Standing Liberty quarter considered to be a 'War' coin?

Definitely. Take a look at the design. The partially uncovered shield, in heraldic terms, indicates that Liberty is prepared for combat.

Q: Why did they put the word "CENTS" on part of the 1883 "V" nickels?

The first coins issued for the new design reverted to the practice of not spelling out the denomination, and sharpers took advantage of the gullible by plating the coins and passing them as $5 gold pieces. The experiment failed, so the denomination was added.

Q: Why are the eagles on our coins such a poor representation of the bird?

The Bald Eagle, right from the earliest U.S. coinage, has been a required part of the design. The popular excuse for their appearance is that European engravers unfamiliar with our native birds designed the first eagles. However, they had at least one very similar bird at hand to sketch from, the European Golden Eagle, which has ironically been the subject of numerous (false) claims that it is the eagle appearing on some U.S. coins. My guess is that they attempted to get the engraving done "on the cheap," and got their money's worth.

Q: What did the public see as the main argument against the intaglio Pratt design on the $2.50 and $5 gold pieces of 1908-1929?

Since you had to be fairly well off to have a handful of them jingling in your pocket, most of the public had little contact with them. A popular myth that grew up around them was the claim that the design trapped dirt and germs. This was given new life in 1918 during the world influenza outbreak, when even the government was washing our banknotes.

Q: Why was the eagle selected as the principal symbol on our early coins?

Coin designers had a difficult time, as many people were illiterate. It was common practice to describe a coin by naming it for the prominent central design or device. The eagle went on our first gold coins to give the public a symbol that was readily identified and was distinctly different from the Spanish pillar dollar, which was the principal coin of commerce.

The law is quite vague, specifying only that an eagle be depicted, without establishing the size. The apparent intent was to give the designer as wide a latitude as possible. There is also no specification that the eagle be a bald eagle, but that has become a matter of tradition.

Q: What effect does the design have on making a die?

A coin design must be balanced in depth and placement so enough metal is there to complete the design when the die pair strikes the planchet. Actually, there has to be coordination between the obverse and reverse designs to ensure proper striking. For instance, the designer must ensure that deeper parts of the designs are not opposite each other. Most reverse designs are in deliberately low relief to accommodate the higher relief of the obverse design. The Lincoln cent is a classic example of die design problems.

Q: I have an 1859 Indian Head cent that doesn't have the shield. Is this a pattern?

Contrary to some confusing listings, it is a regular issue, and not a pattern. The design was modified and the shield was added in 1860.

Q: Has the U.S. Mint always had problems with new designs?

Almost without exception a new design guaranteed controversy. The biggest problem was rumors, often that the design would be recalled because of some flaw. The Lincoln cent had problems with Brenner's initials. The $20 gold St. Gaudens wouldn't stack, and the same complaint was made about the high relief Peace dollar. The Buffalo nickel wore rapidly, the Standing Liberty quarter wasn't dressed to go out in public, and so on. One exception was the introduction of the nickel in 1866, but that was a new coin, not a change in design. The Washington quarter seems to have been the public favorite, with demand for the coin turning a one-year commemorative into a permanent fixture.

Q: My 1957 and 1958 nickels have larger stars next to the date than the earlier and later years. Any reason?

No explanation, just the fact that the hobby is aware of the variety. For some undetermined reason the master die was changed in 1957, using a larger star. The master was used through 1958 and then discarded for the "old" design. As noted before, the Mint considers these as "minor" modifications, and doesn't make a big issue of them unless collectors make a fuss about them. This information continues to be left out of coin reference books, except in the minting variety field, so collectors rediscover them from time to time. Whenever there is a change in the master die, all the working dies will show that change, until a new master die is made.

Q: Why were so many of the "V" nickels worn nearly flat? Seems like most of them look like they had the design ground off.

Good question. The probable answer is that the design on both sides is in quite low relief, meaning it took less wear to eliminate details. The effect is similar to the rapidly wearing dates of the Buffalo nickels and Standing Liberty quarters.

Q: Were there any changes in the 1979 cent design besides the different mintmarks?

The only changes in 1979 were the new S and D mintmarks. The differences you may have noted in the rest of the design are due to wear and abrasion of the die during use, rather than a deliberate change.

Q: Why wasn't Felix Schlag's reverse design used along with the obverse on the Jefferson nickel?

As happened with the $1 banknote, President Franklin D. Roosevelt reportedly intervened and suggested the full view rather than the quartering view of Monticello.

Q: Is Brenner's bust of Lincoln on the cent an original design?

It is an original, and it is by Brenner, but it was first used for a plaque honoring Lincoln in 1907 and adapted in 1909 to fit the coin.

Q: Is it true that World War I had an influence on the design of the Standing Liberty quarter?

To avoid any show of belligerence, the eagle on the reverse was shown in peaceful flight on the reverse of the design introduced in 1916, rather than the usual perched bird clutching the arrows of war.

Q: There was a story during the first year of production of the Anthony dollar that the design was going to be changed because of the criticism of the original. Was it changed?

The design itself (Anthony bust) was not changed, but the position of the date and "LIBERTY" in relation to the rim was changed in mid 1979 on the Philadelphia strikes, and in 1980 at all three mints. These are described as having wide or narrow rims, but the width of the rim is not a valid marker as both wide and narrow rims are found on both varieties of the date position.

Q: Why are there design differences on the 1982 nickels?

The master hub for the Jefferson reverse broke in April 1982. A new master hub was made for both circulation and proof dies. The old dies showed blurred and rounded outlines of the building. The new dies had sharp and distinct outlines. On the old dies the second step from the bottom was in higher relief but has normal relief on the new dies.

Q: What is a "device" on a coin?

A device is the principal element of a design, such as a bust.

Q: Are there any foreign coins honoring the Native Americans?

At least one country has used that theme. There is a set of nine proof 10-gourdes coins, issued in 1971 by Haiti. The coins honor leaders of some of the important tribes.

Q: Was the 1793 half cent copied from a French coin?

It is copied from a French medal, the Libertas Americana medal, commemorating the American victories at Yorktown and Saratoga. Augustin Dupre was the designer. Ben Franklin supposedly suggested the design, so you could say he helped design the half cent.

Q: Why don't they identify the Lincoln Memorial on the back of the cent, like Monticello on the nickel?

The assumption was that "everybody" would recognize the Lincoln Memorial, while Monticello was not that well known. When Felix Schlag submitted his winning design for the nickel, it was not labeled; the Mint added it to the design.

Q: Seems to me we have used an enormous number of different eagle designs on our coins. Has anyone counted them?

Trust expert Walter Breen to have a figure for us. In 1964 he compiled a list of eagles and the numbers are still surprising today. Up to that time, 165 different eagle designs had been used on regular, commemorative and pattern coinage. Out of that number there were some 39 (21 regular, 5 commemorative and 13 patterns) where the eagle is holding nothing, most of the balance holding arrows or olive branches or both. Added to those numbers would be the eagle on the Kennedy half of 1964, the moon landing eagle on the Ike dollar and SBA dollar, the two eagles on the 1983 and 1984 Olympic dollars, the 1984 $10 gold, the 1986 Statue of Liberty $5 gold, the family of eagles on the gold American Eagles of 1986, and the Heraldic eagle on the silver Eagles for the same years. The additional eight designs would give us a total of 173 different eagles from 1794 to 1987. Then we add the eagles on the 1989 Congress dollars, the 1991 Rushmore, Korean War and USO dollars, the 1989 Congress $5, the 1991 Rushmore $5 and the 1992 Olympics $5. More recently there's the 1994 National Prisoner of War Museum $1, the 1994 Capitol Bicentennial $1, the 1998 Robert F. Kennedy $1, the 2001 Capitol Visitor Center $1, the 1995 Olympic Stadium $5, the 1997 Franklin Delano Roosevelt $5, the 1999 George Washington $5 and the 2000 Library of Congress $10. This makes a total of 188 eagle designs.

Q: Has anyone reported that the FG initials on the 1973 cent are larger than those on the 1972 or 1974?

Reported and forgotten. There are several other minor design changes over the years that attract little attention until new collectors rediscover them. Since all of the 1973-dated cents have the large initials there is no special value attached.

Q: With the current interest in design changes for our coins, I wonder if any of our past Presidents got involved in coin design matters?

Several of them, beginning with Washington, have become more or less involved in coin designs. Although in recent times coin design has rarely reached the attention of the resident of the Oval Office, President Teddy Roosevelt was one who got deeply involved. His view of the then current coins was described aptly in a letter to the Secretary of the Treasury, Leslie M. Shaw, in which he said, "I think our coinage is artistically of atrocious hideousness." He went on to encourage the establishing of the Saint-Gaudens designs for the gold eagle and double eagle, often considered among the most artistic of any of our coinage. Franklin D. Roosevelt is well known for his interest and the several changes he made in banknote designs.

Q: Wasn't it illegal at one time to reproduce the state emblems of the State of Vermont?

Up until 1964 it was indeed illegal to make any copies of the emblems, such as on medals or tokens. The Vermont State Legislature in 1964 finally got around to repealing this particular law. It was one of the few, if not the only specific prohibition against the reproduction of a state emblem anywhere in the country, beyond the normal requirement for permission to use the design. The Vermont statute had provided for imprisonment and fines up to $1,000.

Q: Did the 25-year minimum for coin design change established in 1890 apply to all coins?

Not too well known is the fact that the law of September 26, 1890, which required coin designs to remain in use for a minimum of 25 years, specifically exempted the V nickel. At that, the design lasted only another 22 years, for a total of 29 years of production. The Jefferson has already passed its 50th birthday by several years.

Q: Do the $5 Federal Reserve notes and the Lincoln cent have something in common?

Both have the depictions of the Lincoln Memorial; on the back of the note and on the reverse of the cent. On both it's difficult to see the statue, especially on a cent from worn dies.

Q: Did Chief Engraver John Sinnock do any Presidential medals?

He is credited with doing them for Calvin Coolidge, Herbert Hoover, Franklin D. Roosevelt and Harry S. Truman.

Q: Did the Mint ever offer an explanation as to why the engraver's initials were missing from some of the 1941 proof half dollars?

The Chief Engraver, John R. Sinnock, in a letter responding to a question about the missing initials stated that three dies were used, and went on to say that the missing initials were probably due to successive polishing of the dies after each 500 strikes. 15,412 proof sets were struck and issued in 1941, giving an average die life for the half dollar obverses of just over 5,000 coins.

Q: Which was the first U.S. coin to display the designer's initials?

Although one source lists the 1849 gold dollar as the first, bearing the same L for Longacre that eventually appeared on the Indian Head cents, it ignores an earlier coin. It was based on the premise that all of the Gobrecht dollars were patterns. In recent years some of them have been determined to be circulation strikes, which had C. Gobrecht on them.

Q: I think the 1982 half dollars with no initials are a rip-off. It looks like someone deliberately scraped them off.

While you may have seen a coin, which was altered outside the mint, on the genuine pieces the abrasions are really die scratches. Actually the die scratches help prove that the surface of the die was abraded away, removing one or both of the designer's initials in the process. Under a microscope, die scratches are in relief (raised), while abrasion of the coin itself would be incuse. The effect is the same as using a bar of soap that has incuse letters or design. After you use the soap a few times the letters disappear.

Q: Why is it there seems to be so much controversy over coin design? Seems like nobody has a good word for them.

The problem seems to be that coin designs, because of mass production, reach the attention of far more people than other works of art. Since you can't please everyone with a given design, and "complainers shout while praisers whisper," the coin designer's lot is a hard one. This has been true of the State quarters with almost every design causing some controversy. The earlier quarter is also a notable exception, as the 1932 Washington quarter was so popular that production was resumed in 1934.

Q: Designer's initials are a hot topic. Were there others besides Victor D. Brenner that were criticized for putting their initials on U.S. coins?

James Earle Fraser got flack over the incuse "F" on the Buffalo nickel. Felix Slagg bowed to the pressure and didn't want to put his initials on the Jefferson nickel until 28 years later. Critics ignored the fact that European designers had initials or full names on their coins for centuries.

Fraser's incuse "F" on the Buffalo nickel.

Q: Was the man who made the dies for our first coins an engraver?

It's all in how you define engraving. According to Robert W. Julian, Henry Voight made the dies and was described as "a skilled watchmaker and mechanic," but "not skilled in making dies."

Q: Is there any truth to the story that the eagle on our first dollars came from a piece of furniture?

It is true. The eagle was copied from the design of a Hepplewhite secretary of the late 1700s from Salem, Massachusetts.

Q: Is the eagle on the Franklin half dollar copied from the U.S. Army's Good Conduct Medal?

It could be, since the two are quite similar, and the medal preceded the medal designed by Arthur E. Dubois' coin by several years. There is no proof of the connection that I know of, but there is the fact that the eagle was rushed onto the Franklin half after Sinnock's death.

Q: Why are some coins listed as "with arrows at date," or "without arrows?"
The arrows were added, especially to the 1853 coins, to signify the reduction in weight resulting from changes in the law affecting the weight. The earlier silver coins contained silver worth more than their face value, so they left circulation rapidly. The new weights were intended to bring the silver content down to match the face value.

Q: Are the missing VDB initials on some of the cents and the missing FG initials on the 1982 half dollars from the same cause?
In both cases the missing initials are due to abrasion of the die. Die abrasion varieties are quite common because the dies are abraded several times during their life to smooth out wear and repair damage to the die face. Because they are so common, abrasion varieties usually have little or no value.

Q: Wasn't President Eisenhower supposed to replace George Washington on the quarter?
Bills were introduced in Congress to put Eisenhower on the quarter and on the $1 Federal Reserve banknote. Republicans also sponsored him as a replacement for Franklin D. Roosevelt on the dime. The first proposal to reach Congress in 1969 was for a quarter with Ike's bust, with the bills introduced in late March and April. The Treasury, however, was pushing for the dollar coin. The Department issued a press release in late April announcing a "flood" of public requests for an Ike dollar. However, this apparently contrived support evaporated as soon as the coin appeared. Although collectors were excited about the coin the public was clearly apathetic toward it.

Chapter 23

DIES, HUBS AND HUBBING

*A collector can never learn too much about the minting process, and the hubs
and dies that are used are a significant portion of the process.*

Q: I was recently offered a U.S. coin die. Can I legally buy it and keep it in my collection?

Someone at the General Services Administration had a mental lapse and sold several
hundred dies to a scrap metal dealer in 1969, and he in turn sold them to several coin
dealers, so the dies have been sold to collectors all over the country. They were an
embarrassment, as some had as much as 40 percent of the face intact and at least a
couple were used to strike fake minting varieties, but the sale was legal. There have
been subsequent sales of dies with all of the design removed and possession remains
legal. In the early days of the U.S. Mint it was relatively easy to buy worn out dies as
scrap, but by 1878 the attitude had changed. In that year a group of 22 hubs and dies,
mostly from the early 1800s, including a hub (obverse) for the 1811 half cent, were
seized by the government from the auction of coins belonging to Joseph J. Mickley.

***Q: Why is so much attention paid to the die varieties on old coins, but none to the same
varieties on modern coins?***

The key difference is the way the dies were made. The old dies were made by hand, so
each die had distinctive characteristics, which could identify the die, often on even a
well-worn coin. Modern dies are almost universally made by the hubbing process,
which means that all of them are essentially identical, especially when new. Once the
modern dies begin to wear, crack, break or get damaged, then there's collector interest
in the coins produced.

Q: How is a die canceled?

This is often misunderstood, or mislabeled. A die is usually canceled by grinding one or
more deep grooves across the face. Very often, collectors will confuse a coin, which has
had an X or other graffiti cut into the coin, with the product of a canceled die. However,
the two are completely different in appearance. A canceled die used to strike a coin,
token or medal will show a wide, heavy raised ridge of coin metal across the coin. Coin
dies are rarely, if ever, canceled in this fashion, but it is a fairly common practice with
medal and token dies.

***Q: Male and female threads are common industrial terminology. Are there such things as
male and female dies?***

While not as commonly used as in other areas of technology, there are occasional old
references to female or "maternal" dies in which the design is incuse, and male dies, or
hubs or punches, with the design in relief. A reduction punch is another name for a hub
used to make a die. The term derives from the use of a reducing lathe to produce either
a master die or master hub from a larger model. To better visualize this, take a piece of
aluminum foil and press it down on a coin. When you remove the foil, you will have an
incuse impression, which is like that of the die. The upper surface of the foil, which
shows the design in relief, is what the face of a hub would look like.

Q: Please give me all of the details on the Washington quarters struck for circulation between 1956 and 1964, and in some later years with proof dies.

The writer apparently has been looking for proof quality circulation strikes, but there's a key phrase missing. The dies were made with hubs intended for proof coins, but they were never processed or polished as proof dies and the coins were only struck once. The key markers for the proof dies are a separated E S in STATES and the leaf next to the arrow heads extends above the top arrow point, while on the circulation dies the ES is joined and the leaf just reaches the top arrow point. Herbert Hicks is credited with doing extensive research work on these two reverses and a third used only on the 1964 silver quarters.

Q: When referring to the tools used to make dies, do "punch" and "hub" mean the same thing?

A hub is a tool with the design in relief, or "positive," just as it will appear on the coin used to "sink" a die, which in turn has the design incuse or "negative." A punch usually is referred to as a tool used to sink a portion of the design, such as a letter, number or star into a die, but some mints use it to refer to the fully completed hub.

Q: Could you explain the difference between "casting" a coin using dies and "striking" a coin using dies?

This is a problem if you are not familiar with the coin making process. To see the use of 'dies' in descriptions of both casting and striking coins can certainly be confusing. The dies used in the two different processes are completely different. For casting, the dies or molds have the design cut into their faces, but then they are clamped together and the metal is poured into them. For striking, the dies also have the design cut into the faces, but then they are installed in a heavy press and the planchet is placed on one die and struck by the other die using many tons of pressure. There, of course, are variations of both processes, but striking a coin leaves a distinctive surface which is nearly impossible to obtain by casting.

Q: I ran across a statement that "only a single variety can be produced by a single pair of dies, whether coining dies, or master dies." Care to comment?

That's a new definition of variety to me and after a few moments of thought about it I would say that the premise is false. The intent is good but the author of the statement neglects that the die can change markedly during use. His statement is intended to limit the term to the narrowest possible meaning, which I think is too narrow for the modern collector. If he had limited his statement to coining dies, he might still be able to make a case, but it is readily possible to produce a number of different hubbing varieties from a single master die at one stage or another between the master and the working die. It's good for an argument, in some circles anyway.

Q: Can a worn die be repunched, rehubbed or generally reworked in some way to make it usable for striking more coins?

As a rule, the answer is no. However, there are documented instances, including a couple for U.S. coins of dies being reworked after striking a quantity of coins. In most instances attempts to soften, rework and reharden a die end in failure, as the die usually cracks or breaks apart rapidly after such treatment. There are also a few instances of world coins where a date digit was drilled out and replaced with a plug with the desired digit. Dies are routinely repaired with abrasives to smooth out rough spots or other damage to the dies. Design elements are also deepened to enable the die to continue in use.

Q: What kind of a tool is a "patrix?"

It traces from Latin literally as "father of the die." It was a tool with the design raised, or in relief, what we would call a hub, used to press the design into the surface of a die. It is, of course, closely allied with matrix, used to designate a master die from which hubs for working dies can be made, and which can be translated as "mother of the die."

Q: Isn't a "mill" also a form of hub?

If you want confusion try checking a dictionary. Mine describes a diesinker's mill as a round steel roll with the design in relief, which is used to transfer the design to another piece of metal. Curiously, it goes on to define "milling" as the striking of a coin, as well as the well known reeding on the edge of the coin! I sort of went through the mill on this question.

Q: Has the U.S. Mint ever used privately produced coin dies for an official U.S. issue coin?

The dies for the Panama-Pacific gold dollar were made privately, at the expense of the Exposition, and then sent to the Mint to strike the coins. Over the years the Mint has done many curious things in the name of coinage, including several instances where privately made dies were used to strike patterns, and in some cases to strike unauthorized "copies" of some proposed coin. One example of this was the use of the so-called "Harper" dies. These dies were for a proposed private manufacture of cents on contract to the government by one John Harper that most collectors know as the "Jefferson" cent of 1795. Harper used his dies to strike coins in a public demonstration for Mint officials, but a contract was refused. Later the dies were seized by the government and stored at the Mint. In the following years the dies were used on an "unofficial" basis to strike pieces for Mint officers and their friends. As far as actual use of privately made dies, several of the commemorative coin dies were made privately, such as those for the Arkansas Centennial and Daniel Boone made by Medallic Arts.

Q: Is the hammer die always the upper die?

In early minting practice the hammer die was always the upper and the anvil die was the lower or fixed die. Today's coin presses strike sideways and even upward so the distinction gets blurred. There are a number of different terms for the two dies so you need a numismatic dictionary to be sure you have the right die.

Q: What is a "standard" die?

The one reference I can find to the term describes it as the lower or obverse die used for striking coins with the hammer method. It apparently traces to England. The same source, dating to the 1840s, refers to the upper die as the "trussellpuncheon" die, the reference being made to two separate names for the upper, or hammer, die.

Q: When were hubs first used to make dies?

Hubs - tools with the design in relief just as it appears on the coin - were used to make dies for Roman coins and then were rediscovered in the 18th and 19th centuries. Puncheons - a form of hubs with part of the design - were used in England by 1760.

Q: What's the history of the Contamin Portrait Lathe?

It was the forerunner of the Janvier reducing lathe. The U.S. Mint purchased one of the Contamin machines in 1837. The Janvier lathe was designed as a transfer machine to reduce a design and transfer it from a Galvano to a hub or die. Le Medallier S.A. of Paris, France builds them.

Q: What does "registering" a coin or medal design, mean?

The term refers to a coin or medal, or for that matter a die being hubbed, which is struck more than once in a single strike press. For the second impression, the die and coin, (die and hub) are "mated" or registered, so that the struck design fits the design in the die (or on the hub) exactly as it was struck the previous time. It is when the die or hub is "out of register" that we get a doubling of the impression, or a hub-doubled die.

Q: Is there any record of the number of dies used to strike the 1914-D cents?

The Denver Mint records show that a total of six obverses and seven reverses were used that year to strike cents. Mintage was 1,193,000 cents, so the average obverse die life in 1914 at Denver was 198,833 strikes. Another interesting die statistic relates to the 1911-D quarter eagles, struck by two die pairs, one of which lasted for only 70 strikes.

Q: If letters and numbers are punched into the die, how is it possible to get a letter or number reversed?

You are correct in that it will not work. However, many dies were made - and some still are - by actually cutting the letters or numbers into the die with engraving tools. Since the die design is the opposite, or mirror image of the design on the struck coin, it is easy to get confused and cut a letter or number backwards, or as often happens, at the wrong end of a word.

Q: In response to questions about striking coins you've several times stated that the "final impact of the die pair" is the end of the minting process. What about proof coins that are struck twice?

I though that my statement was about as clear an answer as it was possible to give, but much to my surprise it has been misunderstood by probably more collectors and dealers than those who have recognized what I was trying to say. If I had said that it ends with the impact of the die pair, then the question about proof coins and other multiple strikes would be understandable, but the "final" placed in there covers as many strikes as could possibly occur. The minting process continues as long as the two dies keep striking the coin, regardless of whether it is in the collar or not. This includes proof coins that are struck two, three, four or more times, as well as double and multiple strikes in any combination. It also includes any combination of struck coins and planchets that get between the dies. The last contact between both dies and the coin as part of a strike is the "final impact of both dies on the coin," marking the end of the minting process. Anything that occurs up to that instant can be identified as part of the minting process and anything that happens after that final die pair impact cannot, so it's the logical place to end the minting process. Here "both dies" is crucial, because a single die bouncing or chattering on the struck coin is not striking the coin, it is damaging it.

Q: Do you have any information as to when United States coins were first struck with dies produced entirely by the hubbing process?

The earliest instance for a circulating coin was for some of the half cents of 1794, the so-called "heavy wreath" variety. Walter Breen listed the following dates, as full hubs were introduced at different times for different denominations: The half dollar in 1836, cents, half dimes and dimes in 1837, quarters and $10 eagles in 1838, half eagles in 1839, half cents, quarter eagles and silver dollars in 1840. The obverses did not include the dates, and the dates were not hubbed into the dies until 1907 for the larger gold, 1908 for quarters and half eagles, 1909 for cents, 1913 for nickels and 1916 for the silver coins with the exception of the dollar, which wasn't done until 1921.

Q: Flip and non-flip - do these two terms have anything to do with plastic flips for coins?
The plastic flips as they are called have nothing to do with these two terms. It has to do with the die axis of the obverse and reverse of a coin or medal, the "non-flip" position being the one with both obverse and reverse upright so that when the medal or coin is turned over from top to bottom (flipped) the reverse would be upside down. It follows that the flip position has the reverse die pointed down so that when flipped the reverse is upright. Two more terms to add to the lengthy list of those used to describe die positioning or rotation. Arrows are often used to designate the relationship. If the arrows are pointing in the same direction this signifies medal alignment and if pointing in opposite directions means coin alignment.
Coin:= Flip, anti-book wise, coin rotation, coin alignment.
Medal:= Non-flip, book wise, medal rotation, medal alignment.

Q: In discussing early dies, was it true that the lower die was more often the obverse, different from modern practice?
Early hammer dies reportedly wore out from two to four times faster than the anvil or lower die. For this reason the complicated designs were reserved for the lower die, and since these were often the main, or obverse design, the lower die was more often the obverse. This seems to be the cause for the confusion in definitions mentioned in answering earlier questions.

Q: Please explain what 'raising' and 'sinking' in connection with a coin die mean.
Almost all modern coin dies are made by using a hub to impress the design into the face of the die. The hub, hob, matrix or 'father die,' as it has been variously called, is a tool that has the coin design in relief, exactly as it appears on the coin. It is used to 'sink' the design into the face of the master die. Dies in turn are used to strike coins by 'raising' the design on the planchet. Heavy use can cause portions of the die face to sink below the normal level, resulting in a raised area on the struck coin, which is somewhat confusingly classed as a sunken die.

The early strikes of the 1982-No-P dime had a flat date.
Later strikes were better adjusted.

Q: Are first strikes from a new pair of dies always the best examples from the die pair?
Usually they are, but not always. If the dies are not adjusted properly, or the coin press is out of adjustment, the first strikes may exhibit problems. A good example is the 1982 no-mintmark dimes. The early stage has a flat date. The dies apparently were readjusted and later strikes show a normal date. Stages of the die life can be determined by wear on the die, which shows up on the coin.

Q: What is understood in the term "complete reduction" of a coin design?
It simply means that the engravers started with a model, transferred it to a galvano, and ultimately to a new master die or hub.

A major die break,
a victim of brittle die steel.

Q: Die wear seems to be a constant problem. Why don't they just make them out of some really hard steel?
Any steel that is hard enough to resist wear would be too brittle. Die steel must be hard but it must also be elastic because it has to withstand the repeated hammering under many tons of pressure caused by striking the coins. If it weren't elastic, it would shatter on the first strike. To make a die steel that will resist wear and yet will be capable of withstanding hundreds of thousands of blows requires compromises in the makeup of the steel. The steel also has to be able to be softened to take the impression of the hub and then hardened to strike the coins. There are some spectacular major die breaks from the 1970s caused by the use of new die steel that was too brittle.

Q: Does a pair of dies remain together while in use?
A pair of dies is the set of two dies, one obverse and one reverse. Most collectors assume that a pair of dies is installed and used until they are both worn out. This is not always the case because the obverse dies wear out faster than the reverse dies. This is because the obverse, or hammer die, is affected more by the impact of striking thousands of coins. In the old days of hammered coins the hammer die lasted half or less of the life of the fixed or anvil die.

Often a single die will be removed for repair work to clean up wear. Rather than shut down the press, a different die is installed so that it can keep running. Even on modern coins it's possible to trace die marriages through a number of complicated pairings, replacements and re-pairings.

Chapter 24

EDGES AND EDGE DIES

Edge dies are another important part of the minting process. They've been with us since the 1500s, so they have a long history.

Q: Do all the half cents have a plain edge?

All of the 1794 and part of the 1795 and 1797 half cents have a lettered edge, "200 FOR A DOLLAR."

Q: Are all of the early half dollars made with lettered edges? I've seen information that some aren't.

All of the regular reference works list the half dollars as having lettered edges from 1794 through 1835, so I'm not sure which source you are referring to. The possible confusion may arise because at least one catalog lists the edge lettering for the first dates, then for later varieties merely says "specifications as before."

Q: Are there more than two early U.S. coins with lettered edges?

There are four—the dollar, half dollar, cent and half cent.

Q: Years ago you were listing die slippage as the cause of the overlapping letters on the lettered-edge half dollars until someone questioned that as a cause. Then you switched to slippage in the drive mechanism as the cause. Isn't that wrong too?

Andrew Wells raised the point and sent me several drawings to back up the conclusions reached by Michael Hodder. Back at the beginning I was repeating what I'd learned from another expert on the minting process. I thought at the time that the die drive slippage had gotten lost in translation. When Wells' letter came in I was still not convinced that slippage - even a belt slipping on the drive to the moving die - would not duplicate the irregular or overlapping spacing on the coin. But when I started to visualize it in order to describe it I realized that slippage is not the answer. If the drive slips, the moving die stops, and so does the planchet. So, it's got to be the moving die being out of position at the start of the rotation. Obviously the planchet cannot slip against either die without tearing the relief letters off the die or seriously gouging the edge of the planchet. The basic process involved here is the lettering of the planchet (or coin) by rotating it between two bar dies, each of which has half the lettering. One die is fixed, the other moves, turning the planchet. While die position is not a new theory, it now would seem to be the single key to overlapping letters. As always, reader input is welcomed.

Q: One of the rare 1907 ultra-high-relief proof double eagles is described as having the edge lettering inverted. How was the edge inscription put on the coin?

Breen said that the segmented lettered edge die was first used (in the U.S.) for the 1907 eagles and double eagles. This would mean that either the description was incorrect, or the segments were inverted, suggesting that these first segmented edge dies were different from later versions, which would have been impossible to invert because of their design. It's an interesting problem needing more research. One possible answer is that they struck the proofs with a method different from that used for the circulation strikes.

Q: Wouldn't striking a coin obliterate any buckling of the planchet caused earlier by the edge dies applying pressure to the planchet?

Robert Julian, one of our favorite sources for early minting knowledge, indicates that this is true (I agree), but that most of our early coins received their edge lettering after being struck, the opposite of most present day practice, so the edge dies could in fact buckle a struck coin.

Q: Is it possible to strike a lettered edge coin in a fixed collar?

It's physically impossible to strike a lettered edge coin in a fixed or closed collar. To demonstrate, lace your fingers together and then try to move one hand sideways without moving the other. The only way it would work would be to shear one set of fingers off. In the same way, the relief letters on an edge die stick into the incuse letters formed on the coin, so they would have to be sheared off before the coin would come out of the collar. Back in the 1600s coins were struck with an engraved strip of steel between the planchet and the open collar. Otherwise, the only way is with a segmented collar that closes around the coin, by rolling the planchet through an edge die or by rolling it between two edge dies before it is struck by the coining dies.

Q: Are there any half cents with blundered edge inscriptions such as those on the early half dollars?

Breen lists a single report, lot 591 in the Kagin sale of September 11, 1972, cataloged as "HUNDRED FOR A DOLLAR," and mentions a second. I apparently at one time had a report of several others, but it seems to have been misplaced. If others are known, I'd appreciate a listing.

Q: The 1907 $20 gold coin is listed in the catalogs as having either "large" or "small" letters. How do you tell the difference?

The large lettered edge proof for the 1907 $20 gold is unique - one known - so the question is moot, but unfortunately a mistake in language used to describe the coins has been locked in, making it difficult for the collector. The "small" letters are really the normal size letters, which appear on every one of the other 361,667 1907 $20 coins, so all you need is a second 1907 to compare your coin with. To be correct, the descriptions need to say "large" and "normal" letters, as this would eliminate most of the confusion.

Chapter 25

EISENHOWER COINS

"Ike" was a beloved General, thanks to his work in World War II. That popularity took him to the White House and onto a couple of coins.

A non-silver circulating Ike dollar.

Q: Why were there so many ads back in the 1970s offering "silver" Ike circulation strike dollars?

The two principal causes were ignorance or an attempt to play on public gullibility. The ads pretty much stopped when the silver price reached the point where the public was aware of the difference. However, with an entire new generation growing up in the meantime, there are plenty of people today who think the Ikes were 90 percent silver like the Morgans and Peace dollars. The proof and special uncirculated Ikes, those with an S mintmark, are 40 percent silver, but the rest are copper-nickel clad on a copper core.

Q: Wasn't there a scandal a number of years ago in connection with the U.S. Mint profiteering on Ike proofs and special uncirculated strikes?

It wasn't so much a scandal as it was a black eye for the Mint. In testimony before Congress, the Secretary of the Treasury said that the Mint was making a profit of $3.89 a coin. He admitted under questioning that the charges for the Ike proofs were "unconscionable."

Chapter 26

EXONUMIA

You asked, "What is exonumia?" Very simply it's anything on the fringes of numismatics. Stocks and bonds are just two of the many collectibles that fall under this heading.

A stock certificate.

Q: *Are old stocks and bonds worth anything?*

Almost any old stock certificate should be checked. Frequently companies merged, changed to a new name or successfully emerged from bankruptcy. Even if the stock is worthless, it is often worth money to collectors. Stockbrokers usually charge a fee for checking a stock, but if you have an account, or get lucky, you can avoid the expense.

Chapter 27

FORT KNOX

Fort Knox is probably the country's best-known storage facility because that's where much of our gold is stored. You have to take their word for the fact that the gold is still there as there is an extremely strict "No Visitors" rule. All that gold is the subject of many a dream.

The United States Bullion Depository
Fort Knox, Kentucky

A view of Fort Knox.

Q: My brother claims that at least some of the gold that is buried at Ft. Knox was struck into coins there. Is this true?

Brother loses this argument. Ft. Knox has been our principal gold bullion depository since it was built in 1936, but there never have been any coins struck there. Gold has been withdrawn from Ft. Knox and used for gold coins, but they were struck somewhere else.

Q: Is there any practical use for all that gold in Ft. Knox?

Not exactly practical, but there's enough gold stored there to pave a 16-foot-wide highway from New York to Chicago, one fourth of an inch thick. The U.S. Gold Bullion Depository at Ft. Knox was built in 1936. In the first six months of 1937 445,501 gold bars weighing 157,820,192 troy ounces were brought by train from the New York Assay Office and the Philadelphia Mint. The gold was then valued at 5.52 billion dollars.

Chapter 28

GOBRECHT DOLLARS

The Gobrecht designs for the dollar have always been controversial and only through diligent research have we learned enough about them to make some positive statements.

An 1836 Gobrecht dollar.

Q: What evidence is there that the 1,000 Gobrecht dollars of 1836 were coins and not patterns?

Bob Julian cites a copy of the Mint's bullion journal for December 31, 1836, showing that the coins were delivered to the Mint and to the Bank of the United States. The coins matched the legal silver content (established in 1792), two points that prove that the coins were intended for circulation.

Q: Are there official specifications for the Gobrecht dollars?

According to ANACS research, there were no official standards. Unofficial measurements indicate a diameter of 38.1 mm, struck in 90 percent silver and weighing 26.73 grams, the standards adopted in 1840.

Q: Are there any of the Gobrecht dollars of 1838 which were struck over other coins?

In a 1956 auction Lewis Werner discovered a restrike of the 1838 dollar in proof, which had been struck over an 1859 silver dollar. The 1859 date from the original coin shows just to the right of the 1838 date. This is restrike evidence similar to that of the 1804 dollar struck on a cut down 1857 Swiss (Bern) shooting thaler, which also shows the underdate.

Chapter 29

GOLD, SILVER AND PLATINUM

Three of the precious metals and the three we are most familiar with. While you may never have seen a platinum coin, they are coming into the marketplace in increasing numbers.

One of the last of the circulating 90 percent silver coins.

Q: Why did silver coins disappear so rapidly after 1965?

There were several reasons that triggered the demise of the silver coinage. The silver price was climbing. Despite President Johnson's flat statement that the silver coins would continue to circulate alongside the new clad coins, the Treasury was secretly intercepting all the silver that went to banks. The last of the recovered coins were melted in 1969 at the New York Assay Office and the Denver Mint. Of course much of the public saw through the government's protestations and hoarded every silver coin they could lay hands on.

Q: A friend claims that silver and gold are no longer used as coinage metals. Is that true?

Very much not true at all. Both metals are still being issued, mostly for commemoratives or bullion coins, but there are even a few circulating silver pieces, such as the Mexican 10, 20 and 50-peso coins.

Q: Did the U.S. Mint keep all the silver coins they recovered?

For some time after they stopped making 90 percent silver coins they did, but when the returns got down to less than 3 percent silver quarters per bag they quit sorting them.

Q: It's been said that U.S. silver coins didn't circulate until the Civil War era. What was the problem?

It was the same problem that arose in 1965. The early silver coins contained bullion that was worth more than the face value of the coin, so most were melted down. Many of the half dollars and dollars went straight to bank vaults to be used as backing for privately issued bank notes. The 1853 reduction in the bullion content helped to turn things around.

Q: What is the size ranking for the silver dollar, double eagle and the "quint" eagle ($50 gold)?

The gold double eagle ($20) is the smallest of the three with a diameter of 34.0 mm. The dollar is next at 38.1 mm, and as would be expected, the round $50 gold piece is the largest at 46.0 mm in diameter. The dollar weighs 26.730 grams, the $20 weighs 33.436 grams, and the $50 gold is the heaviest at 83.592 grams.

Q: Did the Federal Reserve Banks not release some 1964 silver coins for circulation?

Eyewitness reports indicate some shipments of the coins arrived after the announcement that silver coins were to be retired, and late shipments were to be returned immediately for melting. The Feds only kept totals, without specifics. The Federal Reserve actually released some silver coins into circulation after 1965. Their bags were checked by weight and if they were within 3 percent of the proper clad weight they were released, although, some 90 percent silver coins still got into circulation. The silver coins were heavier than the copper-nickel clad.

Q: Wasn't there a big run on silver dollars in 1964, before the switch to clad coins?

Rising silver prices at least in part were responsible for a heavy amount of buying. The Treasury Department's over-the-counter sales from January 1 to March 23, 1964, totaled 25 million coins.

Q: Why did the Treasury Department allow silver prices to increase? Wasn't the Treasury controlling prices?

The basic reason was that the Treasury didn't have enough silver to be able to hold the line on price. They removed price controls on silver in May 1967 and then ended redemption of Silver Certificates on June 24, 1968. While the Treasury was not responsible for the steep rise in 1980, the removal of the price controls actually laid the groundwork for the price increase.

Q: Has the price of silver always been at $1.29 up until the 1960s?

One rather remarkable statistic about the U.S. price of silver is that the $1.29 figure was set in 1792. The price was maintained at that figure until 1963. However, as a point of reference, this was the monetary value of the metal, not the market value. The official monetary value of gold is currently $42.22 an ounce, but the market value for gold is around $375.

Q: What would the market price of silver have to be to match the face value of 90 percent coins?

If silver were $1.39 an ounce it would make the 90 percent silver coins equal to face value. Of course, silver has been well above that figure for several decades.

Q: What are the known amounts of gold, silver and platinum that have been recovered over the centuries?

As might be expected there are few, if any, records of much of the early gold and silver recovery. I've seen several figures, one that estimates that approximately 3 billion ounces of gold and 25 billion ounces of silver have already been mined. It's interesting to point out that if the figures are correct, then silver should be valued at about 1/8th the price of gold. As any reference chart will show you the current price ratio is far above 8-1. One source indicates that only 2,000 tons of platinum has been mined throughout history.

Q: Does fool's gold have any value?

Fool's gold is a nickname for iron pyrite. This mineral is found in large quantities and has a brassy golden color which is easily mistaken for gold, hence the nickname. Under the right conditions it forms some fairly spectacular crystals and these specimens do have a small value, but nothing like real gold. The first supposed gold discovered in the U.S. in 1576 turned out to be fool's gold after two cargoes of it were carried back to England.

Q: What's the reasoning behind the desire for high-grade coins?

Besides the obvious desire to have something that is "perfect," there is a more mundane reason having to do with money. The original desire to have high-grade coins traces to the common practice of hoarding gold. It's a simple matter of economics, the higher the grade of a coin the more gold it contains. There's a bit of a miser in all of us.

Q: The Bible records what sounds like some staggering amounts of gold and silver in use. Are they as tremendous as they sound?

Description of the Tabernacle records the use of 46,058 ounces of gold and 158,432 ounces of silver to build it, but the totals were dwarfed by a gift from the Queen of Sheba to King Solomon - 188,700 troy ounces of gold and the yearly tribute to Solomon was 666 talents, which converts to more than a million ounces.

Q: My grandfather, who served in the Pacific during World War II, told me once that they used gold ore to pave a road in New Guinea. Is that a barracks tale or did it actually happen?

That is a true story. It was known as the Golden Road. Military engineers needed a large quantity of fill to build a road on the island. A local mine had a large heap of gold ore that the engineers used as the surfacing material for a two-mile stretch of jungle road. The ore was estimated to contain 45,000 ounces of gold. At $20 an ounce this would have been over $900,000.

Q: Where would I find a gold coin with a Florentine finish?

I don't know of any country in the world that has used this finish on a legal coin. It's possible that tokens or medals have been given a Florentine finish, but no coins. The finish is described as a textured surface produced with engraved crosshatch lines. It is a popular finish on jewelry.

Q: Which U.S. branch mint was the first to strike coins?

On March 28, 1838, a $5 half eagle gold coin was struck at Charlotte, North Carolina, giving that mint the honor. Charlotte struck only gold, and the coins bore a C mintmark.

Q: Why was it that only gold coins were struck at Charlotte and Dahlonega?

For one very simple reason; When the two mints opened in 1838, gold was the only coin metal available locally. Actually, some of the California gold found its way to the southern mints in the years before the Civil War.

Q: Why did the ancient Egyptians hold gold in such high esteem?

The underlying cause seems to be religious. The Egyptians considered gold to be the earthly embodiment of the sun god Horus. The Pharaohs considered gold to be as immortal as the god and in order to ensure their own immortality they surrounded themselves with gold both while they were alive and after death, giving rise to the vast stores of gold objects found in the many tombs in Egypt.

Q: Did the Philippines issue a gold peso after the U.S. takeover in 1903?
Congress established the gold peso, weighing 12.9 grams, of .900 fine gold, but none were ever issued. It probably would be considered to be only a money of account, used for figuring the rate of exchange with other countries.
Designating a gold peso also would have helped to stabilize the currency.

Q: What was the grand total of gold coinage struck by the U.S. Mint?
Between 1795 and 1933 the Mint struck $4,526,218,477.50 in U.S. gold coins. The Mint also struck gold coins for other countries, and has struck additional gold coins in recent years.

Q: How many 1933 $20 gold coins are in private hands?
Other than the single celebrated specimen that was sold recently, the number that reached - and is still in private hands - is unknown.

Q: What was the first gold coin struck in the U.S. after the gold ownership ban was lifted in 1974?
Panamanian 100 balboas were struck at midnight on December 30, 1974, marking the end of the 41-year ban.

Q: What was the official name for the octagonal $50 gold pieces issued in 1851?
In Mint literature they were called "ingots." But the public generally ignored the Mint term; so they were also called "slugs," "quintuple eagles," or "five eagles."

Q: How many of the 1927-D $20 gold pieces are still in existence?
The last count we saw was six or seven, with three of those in the Smithsonian Institution. Bowers and Ruddy auctioned one in MS-65 in 1982 for $160,000, up from the $32,000 that it brought in 1969. We currently list the coin in *Coin Prices* magazine at $750,000 in MS-65.

Q: Which was smaller, the gold dollar or the silver three cent piece?
Hedge your bets on this one. The Type I gold dollar (1849-1854) measured 13 mm. The Type II and III (1854-1889) measured 15 mm, while the silver three cent piece measured 14 mm.

Q: Is dental gold .900 fine like coin gold?
Dental gold is considered to be .750 fine, and is alloyed with metals other than copper.

Q: Didn't the Federal Reserve resist the restoration of the right to private ownership of gold in 1975?
To use an old saying, Chairman Arthur Burns "fought tooth and nail" to get the ban extended for at least six months. After Congress passed the bill rescinding the ban as of January 1, 1975, a bill was introduced by Sen. Adlai Stevenson III to repeal the new law, but despite widespread official support for the repeal attempt, it failed. The rest is history.

Q: Wasn't there a $25 California Gold coin made by Templeton Reid?
The only known specimen was once in the U.S. Mint collection, but was stolen in 1858 from the Philadelphia Mint and never recovered. The piece was one of the few to bear a dollar sign ($) rather than spelling out the denomination. A sketch of the piece appears in the book, *New Varieties of Gold And Silver Coins* printed in 1851.

Q: Did the world price of gold match the $20.67 figure set by the U.S. prior to World War II?

The world price was above the U.S. price from 1907 to 1930, ranging from $21.90 to $30 an ounce.

Q: When did the Mint stop refining private gold?

The end came on December 31, 1969. Earlier the Mint had refined private gold for a fee, and even earlier than that, had struck the gold into coins for the gold's owner.

Q: What happened to the silver borrowed by the Atomic Energy Commission during World War II?

The Atomic Energy Commission borrowed 65 million ounces from the Treasury stockpile to use in work connected with the atom bombs. The AEC tried to return it in the early 1960s. The Treasury refused, as it was still radioactive. I've never been able to follow up on this story, so I assume that somewhere there's a stash of silver worth over $300 million that's still ticking. As the newscasters are wont to say, "It's your money."

Q: Weren't there some standards set for the amount of wear allowable on gold coins?

In the U.S. Mint Director's Annual Reports you can find some very interesting statistics. Back in the last half of the 1800s the Mint Director devoted several pages to tables and charts showing the allowable wear. The maximum normal wear allowed is 0.129 grains for the $20 gold piece. Extensive tests were run on circulated coins. The measured wear averaged 0.086 grains per year. From this they assumed a loss of 0.5 percent of weight (half of one percent) in 20 years. This assumed circulation but most of the coins stayed in bank vaults for decades so it's difficult to estimate the average life of a given coin.

Q: Has the Mint ever done a study on the amount of metal lost to wear on coins in circulation?

Several studies have been conducted over the years. One of the larger studies was conducted in 1886. From the measurements it was determined that a silver half dollar on average would lose 11 percent of its weight in 100 years, while the quarter would lose about 15 percent of its weight in the same period, reflecting the heavier use accorded the quarter even back then. Breaking these figures down, the average loss is one-ninth of a percent per year for the halves, and one-seventh of a percent per year for the quarters.

Q: Is gold easy to mint? Being so soft, I would think it would be very easy to strike into coins?

Actually it's fairly difficult. The very softness of the metal works against it, causing problems with metal flow into the design elements. When the Mint began striking gold coins in the 1980s they didn't have anyone left on staff that had experience with gold, so they had to learn how to strike it from scratch.

Q: Does seawater affect silver coins?

Silver coins in salt water will start to corrode almost immediately. Many hoards from sunken ships are offered with "salt water" damage. An extended period of immersion will even damage the surface of a gold coin. However, the coins from the SS Central America suffered at worst only minor amounts of damage because of large quantities of iron nearby.

Q: Which takes more pressure to strike - a silver coin or a gold coin?

It depends on the size of the coin, but it may come as a surprise that on average it takes more pressure to strike gold coins than silver. For example, a $20 gold piece with a diameter of 34 mm required 175 tons per square inch of striking pressure. A silver dollar (38.1 mm) required 150 tons, while a half dollar (30.6 mm) required only 110 tons. The $10 gold (27 mm) needed 120 tons, the half eagle (21.6 mm) 75 tons and the quarter eagle (18 mm) 40 tons, which is the same force needed to strike a dime (17.9 mm).

Q: Who signed the bill into law for gold ownership?

The bill very nearly got lost in the uproar. It was sent to President Nixon on July 31, 1974. Nixon then resigned, so President Ford signed the bill on August 13, one day before it would have become law without being signed.

Q: Was the ratio "always" the 16-to-1 between gold and silver, as it was in the 1890s?

The ratio in ancient Greece was closer to 13.3-to-1, varying (with exceptions) between 12-to-1 and 16-to-1 until after World War II. In middle ages the ratio was about 12-to-1, but in the mid 1800s after the California gold discovery it was down to 4-to-1.

A platinum bullion coin.

Q: What did the price of platinum do when gold went over the $850 an ounce mark in 1980?

Very few people know that platinum climbed nearly $200 more, peaking at $1,047 an ounce.

Q: What were the bullion values of $1 and $20 gold pieces when gold went over $800?

A gold chart from 1980 shows that at the $800 mark, a $1 gold coin contained $38.70 and a $20 coin contained $773.99 worth of bullion.

Q: I've seen gold jewelry, coins and medals referred to as "gold flashed, or gold washed." What's the difference?

As far as I can determine, the two terms refer to the same thing, a metal object with a very, very thin plating of gold, less than seven millionths of an inch. For jewelry this is usually a base metal object, but the same process is used to "plate" coins. In most cases the amount of gold involved wouldn't pay the smelting charges to recover it.

Q: What is the complete quotation that is often referred to as the "cross of gold" speech from the Brian campaign?

The sentence reads, "You shall not press down upon the brow of Labor the crown of thorns; you shall not crucify Mankind upon a cross of gold." This quote is from William Jennings Brian's acceptance speech at the 1896 Democratic Convention.

Q: With silver currently so comparatively cheap is there any danger that someone like the Hunts will buy up all the available silver and corner the market like what happened in 1979?

There are still quite a few people around who paid double digit prices for silver back then and who are still waiting and wishing for the market to go back up to the 1980 levels. It isn't our province to give investment advice but I can stress the obvious - There is far too much silver above ground for anyone to corner the market. Very simply, the higher the market, the more that will come out of hiding. Currently the silver producers are going broke or hurting badly.

Q: What is a "United States Bar?"

The official term is applied to a bar of gold or silver that has been refined, assayed and stamped by one of the U.S. mints or official Assay Offices.

Q: Did the Mint make any allowance for silver used as part of the alloy in private gold coins melted down for their bullion content?

The regulations of the Mint specifically noted that, "Silver is considered merely as an alloy of gold coin, except it can be profitably parted (separated) out, and goes for no more than the copper in the same predicament."

Q: What is meant by a "British Standard ounce of gold?"

The British Standard refers to the coining standard of that country, or a fineness of .91666, so a British Standard ounce of gold is one ounce of .91666 fine gold, as opposed to a fine ounce which would be pure, or 1.000 gold.

Q: Is it possible that some of our early silver coins contain gold as well?

Quite possible. Prior to the 1850s methods for extracting gold from silver were very crude and undoubtedly small amounts got mixed into the alloy used for silver coins. The Act of May 19, 1828, addresses that very point because it authorizes the Mint to coin silver submitted by private parties even if it contained small amounts of gold, providing that this be done if the gold could not be economically separated. However, the amounts involved probably would be less than one percent of the total weight of the coin so even with the present price of gold the recovery probably would not outweigh the numismatic value of the old coins. This may well be an outgrowth of the urban legends in several countries centering on gold accidentally dumped into the wrong melting furnace.

Q: Isn't the London daily gold fix really a monopoly?

Every business day representatives of five major gold dealers meet in London twice a day to set a price for gold, based on the market. It is not really a fix, as we Americans understand it, but rather a statement of what would be a satisfactory price to customers. Like a coin reference catalog it is an indication of the market rather than a mandatory price level at which gold must be bought or sold. American gold dealers have tried without success to get the fix point moved to New York.

Q: What's the present status on gold Krugerrands? Are they legal to own?

As it stands at the present time, it is no longer illegal to import the coins. There were (and are) no restrictions on buying or selling or owning the pieces that were already here. For a time the import of the coins was forbidden.

Q: Where was the first discovery of gold made in the U.S.?

The first claim of gold discovery was in 1576 when Martin Frobisher returned to England with a load of 'gold' ore from the U.S. coast. This later was found to be worthless. Further claims of discovery were made in Virginia in 1607-8, but these too were of no value. I also have a listing for gold as being first discovered in 1782 in Virginia but I can't find the source to confirm it. Several sources list the first major find in Cabarrus County, North Carolina in 1799. The Reed Mine there produced $10 million in gold, including a 28-pound nugget. Bechtler struck North Carolina gold into the first $2.50 and $5 coins, but one variety of the coins carried the words "GEORGIA GOLD."

Q: Please explain the term "Spot plus $0.00."

Dealer ads for silver or gold bullion bars frequently will quote a price in this manner. For example a 100-ounce silver bar might be offered at "Spot plus $0.35." This means that you would pay the (daily) spot silver price (currently about $5.00 an ounce) plus 35 cents an ounce, which is the dealer's charge to cover expense and any profit on the deal. Thus, a 100-ounce bar might cost 100 x $5.00 ($500) plus 100 x .35 ($35) or a total of $535. The spot price is the price paid "on the spot" for such metals as gold and silver. Because the price of the precious metals is constantly moving up and down, it is necessary to have a quote for "right now" for a sale, and this is the spot price.

Q: Were any of the items that were stolen from the U.S. Mint collection in 1858 ever recovered?

Not a single piece. It is presumed that all were melted for their bullion content. One of the pieces was a unique $25 California Gold coin made by Templeton Reid. The piece was the only known example of a Territorial gold coin with a dollar sign ($) in the denomination.

Q: What amount of gold was recovered during the 1849 gold rush in California?

The total take in the 11 years from 1849 to 1859 is estimated at $600,000,000.

Q: Is placer gold pure? I want to settle an argument.

Placer gold varies all over the scale, but it's almost never pure. The location where the gold originates has much to do with it. For example, Yukon placer gold ran as low as .625 fine gold. The rest was silver, copper and other metals.

Q: Why are common date gold coins worth more than bullion value?

Common date gold coins are worth a premium over their bullion value because they are coins. An equal amount of bullion in bar or ingot form would have to be assayed to ensure its purity, so it is not as readily exchanged. Common date coins don't depend on the number minted, but instead on the number available in a given grade. Note that this applies almost exclusively to U.S. coins in this country. Gold coins from other countries are usually sold for their gold content plus a small premium.

Q: Did the U.S. Treasury pay full price for the gold bullion that was called in beginning in 1933?

After some debate, Congress authorized the Treasury to pay the going Government rate - $20.67 an ounce - in December 1933. However, by that time the open market price had risen to $35, one of the key reasons why only a fraction of the bullion and gold coins were surrendered.

Q: Just where was El Dorado?

The famed "El Dorado," where 'the streets were paved with gold' actually did exist. It was the 17th century name for Colombia, at the time the largest source of gold in the world.

Q: Did any of the pirates actually coin money?

The Spanish 8 reales were often called pirate money, because a typical cargo would contain a quantity of the popular coin. None of the pirates actually minted any coins. If you were busy stealing from others would you take time to mint coins? A related recurring question concerns a modern-day "replica," which bears the motto "PIRATE GOLD." This perhaps may be the source of the confusing question.

Q: Why were the 1907 $20 gold coins sold by the Treasury at a premium?

The Treasury didn't sell them; the banks sold them. They were released in December 1907 after publicity about the missing "IN GOD WE TRUST" motto. The Sub-Treasuries issued them on an allotment basis to the banks. When rumors began that the Treasury would buy them back, bank clerks charged premiums as high as $35 before the Treasury ordered they be sold at face value.

Q: Please send me a list of all of the U.S. coins that contain gold or silver, and the amount each contains.

I'm sorry but I don't have such a list on hand. The information is readily available in almost any U.S. coin catalog, and in the Krause *Coin Prices* magazine, which appears every two months.

Q: Is it true that the U.S. once controlled most of the world's gold supply?

One figure cited is the U.S. gold reserve in 1944 of more than $26 billion worth. It was estimated to be more than three-quarters of the world's supply of monetary gold at that time.

Chapter 30

GRADING

Grading means literally the exact amount of wear on a coin. After living with adjectival grading for a century a numerical grading system for U.S. coins has taken a lot of the guesswork out of the grading process. Learning to grade coins yourself is your number one priority if you are serious about collecting coins. It's a key part of the "know more about the coin than the person you are buying from" axiom.

Q: What does over-grading a coin mean?

The American Numismatic Association defines over-grading as assigning a grade at least one grade higher than the actual grade of the piece. I would footnote this with the comment that with so many grading firms on the scene a one-grade difference is not at all unusual, so perhaps we need to update the definition to two or more grades higher than the actual, or consensus, grade. Certainly we could start an argument on this topic.

Q: Is there such a thing as an MS-70, or "perfect" coin? I've never seen one offered for sale.

That is a good point, and there are some reasons for it. The only true MS- or PF-70 coins are recent issues, few of which are worth the expense of grading and slabbing, so they haven't shown up in any significant quantities. The ones that do are bringing three- and four-figure premiums. I know of several collectors who order the proof Eagles by the thousands and have culled through them picking out the PF-70s, so eventually there will be examples on the market. Actually, as long as the Mint is mass-producing coins, it can't meet 70 standards on any but a tiny fraction, mostly accidentally.

Q: I have a coin slabbed by ANACS when it was part of the ANA, giving the grade MS-63/65. Couldn't they make up their mind?

The right - or forward - slash (/) in this case gives separate grades for the obverse and the reverse. This usage is by no means universal. Some would use it to mean grades between 63 and 65. The right slash is also used to denote British pounds, overdates, doubled dates, doubled mintmarks, or calendar and regnal year separation.

Q: Is there a correlation between the weight and grade of a coin?

The tolerance allowance makes any figures meaningless. The concept of determining the exact amount of wear by the weight of the coin has one fatal flaw. No two coins weigh exactly the same, unless by coincidence, and the tolerance allowed in the minting process exceeds by a good margin the amount of metal lost to wear.

Q: I need to know the values of some coins I had graded recently. They have a specified percentage of white as well as a numerical grade.

It's virtually impossible to answer your question because we simply don't keep that level of statistics. And, frankly, I don't know what the grading service means by percentages of white. This is an unsettling indication that grading has gone full circle, back to the verbal grading that the numerical system was supposed to "fix." In each case, about the only way to determine the actual value of the coins you specify is to sell them at auction and see what they bring.

Q: How long have we had the general adjectival grade classifications - good, very good, fine, very fine, etc.?

The adjectival grade classifications - sometimes called "verbal" grades - are well over a century old, with most of the basic grades pretty well established by the 1880s. The current numeric grades were introduced in the early 1980s.

Q: In some old ads I see references to "B & D grading." What system was this?

It was a system worked out and published by Brown and Dunn for grading coins using line drawings to detail the amount of wear. It can be considered a forerunner of today's grading standards.

Q: Please explain the "full bell lines" on the Franklin halves?

There are seven lines across the Liberty Bell, three near the rim, and four more just above. A fully struck coin will show all seven lines without any interruption all the way across the bell. The concept was introduced before we got into numerical grading, which for the most part came before the "specialized" grading standards. However, there is still a core group that for one reason or another is not fully dependent on the numbers, that still use the full bell lines, full steps, split bands, full horn and other standards that had more to do with the strike in most cases.

Q: What does it cost to get coins checked by one of the grading services?

Answering this would take far more time than is available, as prices are changed frequently and each company offers a wide variety of time-sensitive or bulk rates. In most cases your best source would be a local coin dealer, who either submits coins, or has the prices at his fingertips for other services. If all else fails, write to the companies for their rates.

Q: Why is there such a wide difference in price between coins with MS-60 and MS-65 grades?

One of the byproducts of numerical grading has been the use of the numbers to justify higher prices. The point behind this is that the closer the coin comes to perfection the more value a single digit grade has. The grade in effect is a measure of rarity, as the higher the grade number, the fewer likely competing coins with that grade or higher.

Q: As a newcomer to the hobby I see a lot of controversy about grading. Why is it so important?

The ability to examine a coin and determine that it is genuine, that it has not been altered and to determine accurately how much wear the coin has received all have a bearing on the relative rarity - and value - of that particular coin. Without specific standards it would be impossible to establish a coin's value. Don't confuse 'condition' and 'grade' as they mean two different things, even though 'condition' is often misused to mean the grade of a coin.

Q: I was told that dealers must use different grades for key coins than for the more common issues. Is there really such a rule?

Anyone who offers that excuse is high-grading your pocketbook. Grades are uniform for all coins of a given series, regardless of their relative rarity. MS-60 means MS-60 whether the mintage is one or one billion. In some series there are variations because of strike quality, but a grade is a grade. My best advice is to learn to do your own grading rather than depending on others.

Chapter 31

HERALDRY

Heraldry takes on an important role in the design of coins. The symbolism in Heraldry can make or break a coin design.

One of several U.S. coins bearing heraldic shields.

Q: What is the heraldic description of the United States shield that appears on our early coins?

The shield, which gave its name to the first nickels, also appears on such coins as the two-cent piece. The official heraldic description reads like this: "Paleways of thirteen pieces, argent and gules; a chief, occupying one-third of the whole azure." Translated, the paleways are the perpendicular stripes or divisions; argent is white, gules is red. The chief is the upper part of the escutcheon, and azure is blue.

Q: A mullet is a fish, but what does it mean in heraldry?

The usual meaning is a pierced, five-pointed star, sometimes used to designate the third son. Spelled as "molet," it comes from the old French and means the rowel of a spur.

Q: What can you tell me about the history of The Great Seal of the United States?

Charles Thompson, the Secretary of Congress, was given the job of compiling designs. Congress assigned three different committees to the task, with the third giving Thompson their ideas. Thompson selected features, wrote a description and sent it to William Barton of Philadelphia, an expert on heraldry. Barton approved the reverse, but modified the obverse. The designs were presented to Congress on June 20, 1782, and accepted. The two sides of the seal appear on the back of the current one-dollar notes. The eye represents the Deity; the unfinished pyramid, the unfinished country. Thompson added the mottos above the two features.

Q: What is a pheon?

It's a heraldic term for an arrowhead or pointer. Pheons were used on some early U.S. notes to flank serial numbers.

Q: Some refer to our early dollar as a "war" dollar. Why is that?

The silver dollars struck from 1798 to 1804 with the Heraldic Eagle design have the arrows in the eagle's left talons, the olive branch in the right. Under heraldic rules this means the eagle prefers war. The "left" in this case refers to the eagle's left, not the viewer's. The feature was repeated on the Trade dollar and on the 20-cent coins.

Crowns come in all sizes and shapes.

Q: What are some of the more common symbols found on coins?

The answer makes an interesting list, and one that you may dispute, or may have alternative suggestions. Topping the list is the cross, followed closely by a crown, then a scepter and orb, a sword, a heraldic animal, a shield or coat of arms, or an effigy of a saint or a ruler. Admittedly, this list ignores some of the symbols of religions other than Christianity.

Chapter 32

HISTORY AND HISTORIC MINTING

I never could see the benefit of my high school Ancient History class. Today I use knowledge from that era almost every day.

The front entrance of the Philadelphia Mint.

Q: How many mints are there now, and how many mints have existed in the past?

There are approximately 70 official world mints. There are perhaps double or triple that number of private mints that are currently operating. Listing all the past mints is simply too big a job. There were dozens in England, dozens more in France, a couple of dozen in Germany, and the list goes on. One source indicates that there were a couple of thousand mints in Greek and Roman times. One problem in counting mints is that there were hundreds, if not thousands of "field" mints, going back to the Roman conquests. These were portable mints that moved with the invading armies, striking coins to pay soldiers, buy supplies and other uses. This practice occurred as recently as World War II, when the Germans used field mints in Poland and other places to strike such things as prisoner-of-war camp tokens.

Q: We see a lot of coins and related items on TV programs these days. Does anyone remember when the first such program was aired?

The late Glenn Smedley quoted Vernon L. Brown as having appeared on WNBC in New York in 1947 on a half hour program, featuring wooden nickels and other numismatic items. This came about as a result of an article on Brown in the Saturday Evening Post. At that time he was curator of the Chase National Bank's money museum. The program hosts were Tex and Jinx McCreary.

Q: Wasn't part of the John Garrett collection destroyed or damaged by a fire?

The great Baltimore fire of 1904 in fact damaged a small part of the collection that Garrett willed to Johns Hopkins University in Baltimore.

Q: What would a coin collector in the Civil War era have found to collect?

First find a collector, as they were few and far between. Those that were collecting had access to a wide variety of U.S. coins and tokens, and world coins, which were still around even after they were withdrawn in 1857 as legal tender. Collectors of that era had little inkling of the knowledge and research that has broadened the scope of collecting to what it is today.

Q: What was the reasoning behind making our first cents so large and heavy, especially when copper was hard to come by?

One of the reasons was that the new country was flooded with not only British half pennies, but also hundreds of thousands of underweight imitations, which for lack of a good coin, passed freely. One source estimated that the situation was costing the country about $30,000 a month in losses, not an inconsiderable sum in those days. The large cent was intended to stabilize commerce by providing a full weight coin from a dependable source.

Q: Have there been any major coin displays at the different world's fairs or expositions held in the U.S.?

The first mention of a coin display at one of the big shows that I found was at the Chicago World's Fair of 1893, also known as the Columbian Exposition. The exhibitor was none other than the U.S. Treasury Department, which had a complete group of U.S. coins and a representative assortment of world coins. If my source is to be believed, the Treasury was but one of 175,000 exhibitors at the Fair.

Q: Why was there a big gap in nickel production between 1876 and 1882?

The principal cause was a lack of need for small change. Literally tons of silver coins were pouring back into the country from overseas and there was also a surplus of nickels. This is one of the very few times, if not the only time, that we had a surplus of small denomination coins in our history.

Q: When General MacArthur was promoted to five-star General, didn't they have to melt some silver coins to make sets of stars for him?

MacArthur was in the Philippines at the time of his promotion. His aides used a number of Philippine, Netherlands and Australian coins to provide the silver, which was cast into stars by a local metal worker. The United Press carried the story in 1944.

Q: Wasn't there a case where a mismatched nickel obverse and reverse caught a spy?

While it sounds like a movie script, it did actually happen. A Russian spy, Col. Rudolph Abel, to conceal microfilm, used a box coin - a hollowed out coin - made from two nickels. The coin was accidentally given to a paperboy. The paperboy discovered what it was when he dropped the coin, which had been made from the obverse of a 1948 nickel and the reverse of a silver wartime nickel with large P mintmark. The boy contacted authorities; Abel was arrested and later was traded for Gary Powers, the U-2 pilot who was shot down over Russia.

Q: Why is the nickel bigger than the dime - or for that matter, why is the half dollar bigger than the SBA dollar?

This is a perennial favorite with young people learning about coins. The dime was a smaller coin because it originally was silver, and the nickel was made larger to go with its base metal status.

Q: Why was the public blamed for the coin shortages in the 1960s and 1970s? How about all the coin dealers with their bags and rolls of coins?

This is the same line of thinking that equates finding a single minting variety in a bag making it a great rarity. Both coin dealers and collectors were blamed for the coin shortages, but they were actually responsible for only a tiny fraction of a percentage point of the coins being held. The true culprit was the public, as millions of people passively hoarded coins. That ashtray or jar full of cents in almost every home was a passive hoard. Adding them up reached an astronomical total that was being held out of circulation.

Q: I've heard there's a stretch of the East Coast called "Coin Beach." Where is it?

It's the popular nickname for Rehoboth Beach, Delaware. The name came from recurring finds of Irish half pennies. They come from the cargo of 400 barrels of the coins on the Faithful Stewart, which sank near shore in 1785.

Q: How long have we had credit cards?

Back around 1100 CE in Cologne, Germany the smallest coin was a denar. One fourth of a denar would buy 20 loaves of bread. To facilitate trade, the first crude credit card was introduced. It consisted of a pair of sticks with notches for each purchase. The customer kept one, the merchant the other until enough sales had been consummated to exchange for a coin.

Q: What's the story on Columbus winning a prize for being the first to see America?

The first sight of land in the new world actually was by sailor Rodrigo de Triana on the Pinta. As is often the case, he was first, but didn't win the prize, as Columbus got the 10,000 maravedis based on his claim of seeing a light the previous evening.

A "double dime" or a 20-cent piece.

Q: Why was the 20-cent coin struck for circulation for only four years?

Actually, it was only struck for circulation in 1875 and 1876. Production for 1877 and 1878 was all proofs, although some of them did reach circulation. The short series was as unpopular as the SBA dollar, for the same reason - similarity in size to the quarter. The reason for the half dollar being larger is more complex, but the principal reasons for the small SBA dollar were the belief that the public wanted a smaller, easier to handle coin, and a reduction in the cost of production.

Q: When did the Columbian Exposition open to the public?
The grounds in Chicago were dedicated on October 11, 1892, which was the 400th anniversary of Columbus' discovery of America. The Expo didn't actually open until May 1, 1893.

Q: When were the American Indians or Native Americans made citizens of the U.S.?
It took a while. To the probable surprise of some, the event took place 80 years ago on June 24, 1924.

Q: What can you tell me about a coin convention that was held at sea?
The event you are referring to undoubtedly is the cruise sponsored in 1977 by Stanley Gibbons Ltd. of London aboard the Queen Elizabeth II. English collectors sailed to the U.S. on the ship, where U.S. collectors joined them for the trip back. The educational portion of the convention featured lectures on coins and stamps.

Q: Why did early day mechanics always have a Mercury dime in their tool kit?
Those were the days of the spark coil, which generated the spark needed to fire the fuel-air mixture, the predecessor of the electronic systems in use today. The dime was exactly the right thickness to set the coil points or to gap the spark plugs.

Q: What did they do with the New York Assay Office after it was closed down?
The building, at 32 Old Slip, on the East River in New York, was sold to a real estate developer for $27,010,000, making it the most valuable piece of Government property ever sold at auction.

Q: In one reference work I checked I noted a comment about "New England" being located where the state of Virginia is now. Is this true?
Our sources say that Captain John Smith did actually rename North Virginia as New England in 1614. At that time Virginia had been divided into North Virginia and South Virginia, but it also stretched from Florida to Newfoundland, so New England was well north of present day Virginia.

Q: Did the Republic of Texas issue any coins?
Texas only issued paper money between 1836 and 1845. As with the Confederate notes, there are many modern copies around. Check the serial numbers against the list of known copies at the ANA Web site at www.money.org or write to me for a copy, including a loose first class stamp.

Q: Have we ever had a true "Ten Cent" coin?
We came close, with the dimes struck between 1809 and 1837, which carried the abbreviation "10 C." However, it was never fully spelled out. The legislation pertaining to the disme, later the dime, used the particular terms, but there never was any legal naming of the coin as a "ten cent" piece. However, between 1809 and 1837 the dime carried the designation "10 C." Although obviously the abbreviation for cents, it was never spelled out.

Q: Were the 1816 cents struck on underweight planchets?
Noted researcher Robert W. Julian weighed a number of that date and found that the average weight was about 166.5 grains, or 2 grains below the scheduled weight, but within tolerance. Finding a group of coins of almost any denomination that average slightly below the given weight is not unusual.

Q: Why were so few coins minted in the U.S. prior to 1805?

It was a combination of several factors. The new mint was struggling with short supplies, especially of bullion and copper, untrained personnel and inadequate machinery. The demand for coins - or lack of demand - was a contributing factor, as it still is.

Q: Were there any companies that paid their stock dividends in gold?

There were two firms in the U.S. and one in Canada. The Homestake Mining Company, which at one time produced 30 percent of the U.S. supplies of gold, used to pay employees with gold coins.

Q: I understand that pay toilets go way back?

In Sardis in Asia Minor archaeologists discovered a large public toilet with a number of coins strewn about dating from 400 to 600 CE, which leads us to believe that the pay toilet goes back at least that far.

Q: Most catalogs list 1793 as the first year that the U.S. Mint struck any coins. Is this correct?

Strictly speaking, the first coins for circulation did bear the 1793 date, although some weren't minted until the following year, a practice that continued for some time to the despair of researchers. The Mint was authorized by an Act of Congress April 2, 1792, and in the first two weeks of July 1792 some 1,500 half dismes were struck. These and four other early coins, the silver center cent, the Birch cent, the disme and the Wright quarter, are usually considered to be patterns. The silver center cents were the first coins struck in the new Mint building in December 1792.

Q: Was wampum used only in the 1600s in the American colonies?

There was limited wampum use after 1700. Actually wampum was still being made in 1850 in New Jersey for trade with the Indians. In 1637 in Massachusetts six pieces equaled an English penny, and remained as legal tender until 1661.

Chapter 33

THE HOBBY PROTECTION ACT

A vital piece of legislation, the Act cooled its heels in Congress for years before finally becoming law. The biggest loophole left in it was the lack of a retroactive policy on copies.

Q: I inherited a coin, which is an obvious copy of a Spanish 2 reale of 1474. Do you know anything about this particular piece?

This is one of several rather notorious copies of rare or valuable coins that were produced and widely distributed in the 1960s. The proliferation of these fakes ultimately led to the Hobby Protection Act, which requires them to carry the word "COPY." In this specific case the Canadian Pacific Railroad Freight Division sent out these pieces with letters in 1968.

Q: Are there rules for copies of political buttons?

The situation is just as bad as for coins. Because the originals were privately produced there were no controls of any kind. The Hobby Protection Act requires the word "COPY" to be incuse in the surface of the coin.

Q: Doesn't the Hobby Protection Act affect clandestine mint strikes, such as the 1913 V nickels?

Legally the way the law is worded they would have to be marked "COPY." However, the Act was not retroactive, so anything reproduced or struck without authority would not be affected as long as it was made before 1973.

Chapter 34

I GET LETTERS

The Internet has put a serious dent in my "snail mail." At the peak of my career as the AnswerMan I was getting some 400 letters a month from readers. My Internet mailboxes often contain that many in a single day. Fortunately I don't have to answer all of them.

Q: I have several questions I'd like to ask, but I'm sure you will put my name and address in your book with the question. If I just sign my initials will you use the questions?

In order to use a question, we have to have a (full) name and address for our records, or the question will not be answered. Perhaps you haven't noticed that I never use names, initials, or any other information about the person submitting the question in my column or in this book, so your fears are groundless. In many instances I prefer to give you an individual answer by mail, so without your name and address I'm powerless to help. Your letter is treated in a professional manner. The contents and your name and address remain confidential and are not sold or traded. Please, give us a name when you write, as initials and nicknames wreak havoc with our computer. And, don't forget to PRINT your name and address, as most signatures are illegible. A significant and growing number of readers are forgetting to include return postage in the form of a loose, unused first class stamp.

Q: Did your Coin Clinic pay for questions at one time?

Not this column, but one of the earliest features paid for "answers." It was a cartoon column called "The Silver Dollar Scholar," which appeared in the *Flying Eaglet* in the January 1956 issue, (one of the early names for what is now *Coins* magazine), and the artist-columnist paid "one silver dollar" for each informative numismatic fact used. Ed Rochette was the author.

Q: I've been waiting for months for someone to ask about (a certain coin) in your column. When are you going to use something on it?

Just as soon as you ask the question I will attempt to answer it. Letting "George" do it is a very common form of procrastination, and evidence of it appears regularly in my mail, so if you have a question don't hesitate to send it in. Frequently I have to disappoint collectors and dealers who have discovered a new minting variety and then waited for someone else to report it. You won't get credit for discovering it unless you report it right away.

Q: Has anyone written to you to tell you that you have too many ads in your newspaper?

For every such letter - and we get quite a few - we get several letters complaining that there are not enough ads. The two sides of this argument probably never will see eye to eye, as many readers buy the magazine especially to read the ads, while an important number are interested only in the editorial copy. We try to strike a happy medium between the two opposing viewpoints, but I need to make the point that without the ad revenue to support the publication, there wouldn't be any editorial copy - there wouldn't even be a newspaper. Subscriptions and newsstand sales are part of the income, but a hobby publication can't survive without ads.

Q: O.K., so I send you a coin. How do I know that you, or a grading service or anyone else will send my coin back?

This seems to be a problem that is self-perpetuating, and one for which there is no pat answer. Unfortunately the attitude is self-defeating as it prevents you from obtaining pertinent information. To put it in perspective, you don't know that you'll get your coin back any more than you know whether you'll get hit by a car the next time you cross the street. You look both ways for cars, and you must exercise caution and common sense in sending your coins to someone. Putting your coins loose in an envelope and trusting to luck is not the answer, obviously. The point is that you are dealing with professionals, whose reputations depend on getting the right coin back to the owner. Mistakes happen, but your chances of losing a coin are very slim.

It is not sensible to refuse to let your coins out of your sight when dealing with professionals. Their own security grading services will not allow you in the room where coins are being graded or authenticated, so this is a fact of numismatic life you have to accept. Thousands of coins are mailed back and forth across the country every day, with only miniscule losses. A substantial percentage of the coin business conducted depends on the mail, so most fears on this score are groundless. One point that most collectors overlook is that the dealer's chance of getting ripped off through the mail is many times higher than the same thing happening to you. The individual bent on larceny has nothing to lose. The dealer can lose his reputation and his business.

Q: The reports that appear from time to time about some old coin being found with a new variety sound fishy to me. How is it possible for things like that to escape detection?

That it can happen is quite probable, and not at all as unusual or suspect as you might think. That it is a "new" variety is another question, since many such discoveries have been made, forgotten, remade, again forgotten or never reported. Or, as often happens, overlooked in the flush of the excitement of the find. I've gotten sandbagged several times with "new" reports that turned out to be listed somewhere else.

Q: Please send me all the information on coins and how to collect them.

You'd be surprised how many letters we get with this type of request. "All" is a big word, and it's also impossible to fill, as it would require a railroad car to hold all the hobby literature. To get the information you need, subscribe to our publications. Check your local dealer for books on coins. Visit your library and see what books they have. There's a good slogan that covers this: "Buy the book before you buy - or sell - the coin."

Q: Any tips for describing a coin when writing to you for help in identifying it?

It saves a lot of time if you have found a similar coin listed, if you would give us the page number, name and the edition (year) of the catalog, and please, the denomination as well as the KM, C or Y number. As you may or may not have noticed, many catalog numbers are not in sequence, delaying identification. Size is always important, as is the apparent metal. Write out all letters and numbers from both sides of the coin and the edge, as well as sending a foil rubbing protected from crushing. You'd be astonished at the number of readers who write in with a description of a coin, medal or token without a hint of what the apparent metal is, with their first question being, "What metal is it struck on?" Since many coins, medals and tokens are struck on several different metals, it is to your own benefit to at least give me a hint as to what the metal looks like.

Q: In a dealer ad I saw, a coin was listed as "1955-P (20) 50 Cents." The price asked was substantially above the catalog value for the coin. Does the (20) in the listing indicate some variety?

The figure in parenthesis indicates that the price is for a roll of 20 of the coins. This is another "secret language" problem.

Q: I wrote to Krause Publications in Iola and got an answer from somewhere else. How come?

Many readers have the mistaken impression that everyone whose name appears in one of the KP publications is in Iola, when exactly the opposite is likely to be true. Our writers are scattered all over. In some cases letters are forwarded to them, but often they are sent to me to answer to ensure that the reader gets a response. Occasionally the letter is addressed to the wrong column or the wrong person. More often than not they come in with nobody's name, so someone has to guess who it's intended for. We have more than 600 people working under one roof, so it's important that mail be correctly addressed to a specific person whenever possible.

Chapter 35

INVESTING IN COINS

Investing in coins is another hot button topic. Every day someone comes along with little or no experience, ready to jump feet first into buying coins for an investment. Bluntly, coins are not a source of instant wealth.

Q: I want to invest in coins. Do you have any specific advice?

This is a question that comes up almost every day on the computer online services and the Internet, as well as from our readers. My best advice is to steer clear of any investments in coins until you have two or three decades of collecting experience under your belt. A standard piece of advice is to know more about the coin you are buying than the person you buy it from. Learn all there is to know about coins before you buy - or sell - the coin. When you do get ready to invest, get all the advice you can, but expect to pay for that advice.

A 1960 Small Date Cent.

Q: I'm told on good authority that the President of the American Numismatic Association described the 1960 small date cents as a "deception." Did he actually make such a statement?

The term was indeed used, although your quote is a bit out of context. In a rather unusual comment on then current collecting interests, ANA President Oscar Dodson made the statement in the 1960 ANA annual report that claims that "microscopic" variations in the date create a "new" variety,.. "In my opinion... is sheer humbug." The term you mention shows up in the last line of his comments, "Any statement that some of these coins constitute a fine investment is, in my opinion, a deception." In all fairness I should note that at the time the coins were the subject of some really wild speculation and Admiral Dodson's comments were obviously addressed to bring the average collector down to earth.

Q: Do you offer the same advice to collectors and investors in coins?

For collectors my comments boil down to one simple piece of advice: collect what you like and enjoy. Advice for an investor is completely different, but often the two are confused. Granted, collectors often eye their collecting with an ultimate profit in mind, but the investor looks at coins strictly as a money making proposition. The investor is interested in the bottom line, not whether owning a particular coin, or set of coins, gives pleasure and enjoyment. Beyond advising potential investors to gain 20 to 30 years experience as a collector first, I don't give investment advice.

Q: I've been collecting cents from circulation for several years. Now I want to buy some upper grade gold coins and silver dollars. How do I go about it?

Frankly, despite the fact that you have some collecting experience, I don't think you are ready for this kind of a switch in collecting tactics or goals. If you want to collect, or invest in top grade gold and silver, you have got to learn enough about these coins and how to grade them to know exactly what you are doing and what you are getting before you buy a single coin. Your checkbook could get you into real trouble without some practical experience to back it up. This question is another frequent one on the online services and the Internet, but most there have no collecting experience at all, or even less than you have. My standard advice to anyone considering investing in coins is to know more about them than the dealer you buy them from. This one piece of advice will keep you out of a lot of trouble.

Chapter 36

KENNEDY HALF DOLLARS

The popularity of the President and the horror over his assassination has given the Kennedy halves a special meaning worldwide. Separating the myths from the history is something of a problem.

Q: Supposedly there was a gap in production of the Kennedy half, but I don't see it in the minting statistics. What happened?

Kennedy halves have been struck with every date from 1964 to the present. However, there was a 16-month period from December 1969 to April 1971 when none were released for circulation. All of the 1970 dates went into proof and mint sets.

Q: Is it true that as many Kennedy halves have been struck as all previous half dollars?

Between 1964 and 1970 about 1.2 billion 90 and 40 percent silver Kennedy halves were struck. In 1971 more than 461 million of the copper-nickel clad Kennedys were struck. From 1794 to 1963 about 1.4 billion half dollars were struck, so sometime in 1971 Kennedy half production eclipsed all the earlier half dollars.

This coin might have been struck after 1964.

Q: Is it true that 90 percent silver 1964 Kennedy halves were struck in 1965 and 1966?

Philadelphia struck 144,182,000 90 percent silver halves in 1965 and 41,674,000 in 1966. The Denver Mint struck 41,793,838 in 1965 and none in 1966. Denver started striking 40 percent silver halves on December 30, 1965. The entire production of 90 percent silver halves went straight to the melting furnaces.

Q: Supposedly most of the 1964 Kennedy halves were shipped to Europe. Are they still there?

That seems to be a popular misconception. The Kennedy pieces were indeed popular in Europe, but the vast majority of them remained here in the United States. Europeans avidly collected those that did reach Europe, as Kennedy had been very popular there as well.

Q: Are U.S. coins much in demand by foreign collectors?

For the most part the market closely parallels the market for world coins in the U.S. Demand is weak for the minor U.S. coins, but it is stronger for the bullion coins. A well-known exception to the lack of demand is the Kennedy half dollar, which saw extremely heavy demand in Europe when it was first issued.

Chapter 37

LOVE TOKENS

Expressing a lover's sentiments has always been an exercise in creativity.
Love tokens have been a popular method and a very popular collectible.

Q: I know that Love tokens are a popular collectible,
but are they only found in the United States?

Love tokens became popular in the U.S. right after the Civil
War. However, they already had gained popularity in
England and Canada for some time prior to that. In England
the practice of shaving the design off one or both sides of a
coin and replacing it with a name, entwined hearts or other
symbols apparently got its start about 1700, or possibly
even prior to that, so they were popular in England at least
150 years before the fad reached the U.S. Before love
tokens there were bent or broken coins.

Q: I have an 1877 quarter in my collection, which has a normal obverse, but the reverse
only has an engraved monogram. What's going on?

You are a prime candidate for the Love Token Collectors Club, an active group of
hobbyists. These were a popular form of lover's tokens back in the 1800s and are avidly
collected. Value depends in part on the "host" coin and the quality and amount of the
engraving. Section 331, Title 18, enacted in 1909, makes it legal. Quite likely the coin
had the reverse ground off in preparing to make it into a love token.

Chapter 38

1964-D PEACE DOLLARS

Talk about a coin with a history. Never released to the public, the rumors about this coin have continued to this day.

Q: I have a question about those 1964-D Peace dollars that were struck in 1965. What would have been the value of the silver in the coins?
In late July of 1964 when the mintage of the coins was authorized by President Johnson's signing of the budget bill that appropriated $600,000 to strike 45 million of the coins, the .77344 ounce of silver in each coin was worth $1.0005, or a slim technicality more than face value. As events would later prove, the coins would have gone first to the gambling casinos in Nevada, which was their principal reason for being struck, and then to the melting furnaces as the price of silver continued to rise.

Q: Please quote the figures on those 1964-D Peace dollars that were struck at Denver?
Our tally shows 30 trial strikes, 76 die adjustment strikes, and 316,000 coins struck in anticipation of circulation. The Mint wound up skirting the issue by declaring all of them "trial strikes" and melted them down, refusing to even furnish an example for the Smithsonian Institution collection. As a result, the Mint doesn't even have a genuine example to compare if one of the coins ever turns up. Eventually some counterfeiter is going to take advantage of this glaring gap in the defenses against fake coins. There were repeated rumors of a quantity of the coins having been taken out of the Mint by employees, and the Secret Service put a lot of effort into attempts to trace such souvenirs, apparently with minimal success. Four planchets for the coins were discovered several years later when a coin press was moved. Apparently a lot of other planchets made their way out of the Mint as well, because the market was flooded with them shortly afterward. Unstruck planchets for the Peace and Morgan dollars up to that time were quite rare. If that many planchets got out, it's logical to assume that some of the coins got out too, but so far nobody has surfaced with one. The Treasury still claims they are "not legally issued," and, therefore, subject to confiscation.

Chapter 39

MARIA THERESA THALERS

The most popular coin in Third World countries, the thalers, has been struck all over the world for more than 200 years.

Q: We know that the dollar traces back to Austria and the later German Jochimstaler, and that many countries later produced dollar size thalers, but are there any recent ones?

One comes to mind, but it is not a coin. In 1978 Sweden issued a medal commemorating the 450th anniversary of the silver Gyllen issued in 1528 by King Gustav Vasa. The medal shows a copy of the die and the coin on one side and has the words SILVERMALM and JOCHIMSTALER on the other. Of course, the Maria Theresa Thaler is still being struck at the Vienna Mint.

Two almost "look-alikes."

Q: Was the U.S. quarter of 1796-1807 copied from the Maria Theresa thaler?

While the quarter design has different hair, there is a fairly close resemblance. However, there is no evidence of a direct link. Robert Scott was the designer of the quarter, and may well have seen the thaler design.

Q: Have there ever been any successful international coins?

If you limited this to modern issues of the early 20th century, the answer would be no, with the exception of the Maria Theresa thaler. But consider that the Persian gold darics were a highly successful international coin, used ultimately in a number of countries, although admittedly under the auspices of an occupying army. Later examples of similar coins are numerous. Today we have the Euro, used by the European Union countries.

Q: Do they still mint coins in an "open" collar?

This technique supposedly went out with high button shoes, but the Austrian Mint is still striking the Maria Theresa thalers in an open collar, which allows the coin to expand in all directions and avoids flattening the edge inscription. The 1980 through 1982 500 schillings were also struck in this fashion.

Reverse of Maria Theresa Thaler.

Q: Can you explain the significance of the different crowns on the reverse of the Maria Theresa thaler?

The crown above the two-headed eagle is the Crown of Rudolph II, signifying in this case the Empress. On the eagle's breast is a shield, surmounted by two crowns. The one on the viewer's left is for the Kingdom of Hungary, that on the right the Kingdom of Bohemia. Inside the shield is the coronet of the Grand Duchess of Austria.

Q: Do you have a list of mintages and mints that have struck the Maria Theresa thaler?

The countries that struck the coin are legion and even the Vienna Mint, which started the modern restrikes probably doesn't have a list of all of them, or of exact mintages. The early restrikes came from Vienna, Prague, Karlsburg, Kremnitz and Gunsburg. The *Standard Catalog of World Coins* lists Milan, Venice, London, Paris, Brussels, Rome, Bombay and Florence. Add to that the Russian mints, which struck the coins rather openly, and some vague reports of a mint or two in Africa that also struck them. The bean counters believe that over 800 million have been struck in all.

Q: Is the Maria Theresa thaler technically a "Konventions thaler?"

Certainly. In the period after the Seven Years' War (1756- 1763) the Konventions thaler was struck in a number of places. The pieces had a standard weight of 28.044 grams and were .833 fine. Many of them bore the inscription "X EINE FEINE MARK," which meant that the coin contained one-tenth the weight of the Cologne mark in silver, the mark (pound) of silver weighing 233.856 grams. Although others survived only into the first part of the 1800s, the Theresa thaler is still being struck to the same standard that was established back in the 1700s.

Q: Did the Netherlands Mint at Utrecht ever strike any of the Maria Theresa thalers?

Add another mint to those commonly listed that struck the coin at one time or another. In 1939 the 's Rijks Munt struck 116,050 of the thalers with the 1780 date, reportedly without any identifying mark to distinguish them from those struck in several other countries. The coins were never delivered (to Austria) and were melted down when the war started. If any of the pieces survive it's quite possible that they actually do have some slight alteration of the standard design, which could be used to pinpoint their origin.

Chapter 40

MEDALS

Often confused with coins, and in some cases deliberately mislabeled as coins, medals are a distinctive class unto themselves. The medal collector faces many challenges.

Q: What is the largest number of busts on a medal?

The Columbian Exposition medal and Medallic Art Company "Shield of Athletes" both have a total of 92 heads. A medal struck in 1903 upon the election of Pope Pius X has the bust of the Pope surrounded by the overlapping profile busts of 62 cardinals forming a ring inside the rim.

Q: What is the significance of a medal, which appears to be made of copper, depicting the frigate Constellation?

The Constellation was the U.S. Navy's first ship. It lies at anchor in Baltimore, where it is a very popular tourist attraction. To finance the restoration of the ship the copper spikes used to build it were melted down and the metal was used to strike 100,000 of the medals. Ownership of the piece entitles you to free admission to the ship for life.

Q: Was there a silver U.S.S. Constellation medal besides all the bronze ones?

There actually were two different silver medals. The smaller was sold only as part of a PNC; a first day cover canceled September 7, 1972, at the special post office aboard the ship. This combination sold for $12. The three-inch, 10 ounce .999 silver medals sold for $95. Only 500 of the latter were struck.

There also were gold plated private issues and one in platinum about 1972. Gold sold at the time for $250. Four of the small national medals were also struck in .999 gold "for presentation purposes" by the U.S. Mint.

Q: What is an "after cast?"

It's the cast version of a restrike—a medal or similar object cast from original dies, but at some later date.

Q: What is meant by a "size 25" medal?

In the early days of medal collecting in the U.S. they were sized in 16ths of an inch, so a size 25 metal refers to one that is 1 9/16 inches in diameter. This was probably done to counter the practice in other countries of sizing medals and coins in millimeters.

Q: Can you tell me anything about an Eskimo Olympic medal?

These were fantasies struck in the 1960s. Three varieties were made with a mintage of 5,000 each. The design had six rings rather than the official five rings of the Olympics. Issue price was $4.

Q: Do you have any information about an error date on the Delaware Bicentennial Medal?

Some 1,000 silver and 5,000 1 1/2 inch bronze medals were made with the date reading July 12, rather than July 1-2. Medallic Arts Company replaced most of the medals but some are still in the hands of collectors. Issue price was $2.50 for the bronze, $20 for the silver.

Q: What's an Ike "Silver Dollar Medal?"
It's a medal dated 1969 that was issued privately. Ironically, despite the legend, it's struck on nickel silver, which doesn't contain even a drop of silver.

Q: Is there a Mint Medal with the St. Louis Arch on it?
The one you are thinking of was struck for the 1964 St. Louis Bicentennial, but it's a private issue, not a Mint Medal. 15,000 were struck in bronze and another 10,000 were struck in silver.

Q: Were any copies made of the Stoney Point Medal for John Stewart awarded in 1779?
This has the distinction of being the only Revolutionary War Medal not restruck at the U.S. Mint. There were several failed attempts in the 1800s.

Q: When did Denver first strike its own medals?
January 15, 1971. Prior to that the medals with the Denver Mint pictured on them were struck in Philadelphia.

Q: I have a coin, which depicts Adolf Hitler, dated 1933, and struck in .900 silver at the Bavarian Mint. What can you tell me about it?
This is a political medal, and not a coin. It was struck at the Munich Mint but not as an official medal, as they did a considerable amount of work for private firms. It is one of the more common Hitler pieces and currently is worth about $35. On the obverse is the slogan, "Ours is the Future." On the reverse it reads, "In the Year of the Change of the German Destiny."

Q: I have a coin (or medal) that appears to be gold plated. What's it worth?
If the piece is a medal from an unknown source, there is no way of telling what metal is under the gold plating without damaging the piece, so I can't be of any special help in evaluating it. Certainly, it will be worth no more than you paid for it, and probably less. The gold plating is very thin and contains at best only a few cents worth of gold, not enough to cover recovery costs. Of course, if the medal was issued in that form, it would probably have some collector value, but would have to be taken on a case-by-case basis. A gold plated coin is an altered coin, consequently it has lost any numismatic or collector value it might have had and in almost all cases is reduced to face value.

Q: I have a medal (coin). What metal is it made of?
This one is high on my list of frustrating problems. While the writer has the piece in front of him, I have to guess. All you need to do to make things simple is to indicate what the metal appears to be - brass, copper colored, silver colored, etc. Very frequently, with a medal for example, the metal may make a vast difference in the potential value of the piece and often will help to identify the denomination of a coin. Make it easy on both of us and include all possible information about your piece rather than make a contest or guessing game out of it.

Q: Is it true that the San Francisco Mint struck gold coins in 1974?
Gold medals, rather than gold coins. The San Francisco Assay Office (correct title at that time) struck its first gold in 44 years when it struck the Cable Car Centennial National Medals. Two examples of the 1.5-inch medal were struck in gold, one going to President Ford, the other to the San Francisco City Archives.

Q: I have a Tombstone, Arizona medal which shows an ore wagon and some numbers on one side - 11/5/00/13/2/29/7. What is the significance of the numbers?

The "00" is the key, as the numbers are from a roulette wheel symbolizing the 100+ gambling dens in the city in the 1880s.

Q: What is the source of the gold Kennedy coins?

Aureus Magnus, a Munich, Germany firm, produced the pieces you have. There is a series of the pieces, but they are not coins, even though they are denominated in several multiples of ducats. The reverses show a six-pointed cross of lilies. The Aureus Magnus pieces are privately issued fantasy pieces or medals. The confusion over whether they are official or not is due to the fact that they have been struck at several of the German government mints, especially Munich. Most of the pieces struck by the firm are listed in our *Unusual World Coins* catalog. The interesting thing about these pieces is that they have a significant market, as current prices for many of the pieces are in the several hundreds of dollars.

Q: Some time back you mentioned there were two different misspelled Hawaiian medals. I've seen one or the other, but never the two listed together.

One is a medal with Oahu misspelled as Ohau. The Maui Chamber of Commerce sold them. The bronze pieces, struck by Wendells, originally sold for $1 each and approximately 40,000 of the 150,000 struck had the misspelling. The second misspelling occurred on the first series Hawaii statehood medals. Nii Hau on the silver and bronze Medallic Art Company pieces was corrected to Niihau, which is the name of one of the islands on the second series of both bronze and silver statehood medals. To add to the interest there are both genuine Medallic Art pieces and fakes. The originals have "STATE OF HAWAII," the fake has just "HAWAII." On the original reverse, "THE ALOHA STATE AUGUST 21, 1959," and on the copy, "ALOHA STATE HAWAII."

Q: I wrote you and asked for information on a medal. I need current information on the piece in each of six grades. Can't you do better than the page from a 30-year-old catalog?

As it happened the information I sent was the latest available, as this was the only book that has been published on this particular medal. This is not at all unusual, as many areas of numismatics have to depend on outdated reference works, which have to be used as a basis for an educated guess as to the current value. The only other course is to spend hours searching dozens of auction catalogs to find any new listings, time which we simply don't have. Expecting to get pricing information for medals or other low volume issues in multiple grades is unrealistic as there simply isn't a readily available source for this kind of information.

Q: I was given a medal, which apparently was struck to honor Consolidated Edison of New York. There's no date on it. Can you give me any information about it?

The piece shows a light bulb, entwined in a ribbon with "100 Years of Electric Service." On the upper part is the New York skyline, surrounded by the words, "New York Salutes Thomas Edison."

The Reverse has "Con Edison/Conserve Energy" in two lines. Edison founded the company in 1882, serving 59 customers on Lower Manhattan. Medallic Art struck the medal, which was sold by Con Edison in 1982 for $16. Curiously my information (and the writer with the question) fails to note what metal the pieces were struck in. Perhaps our readers can fill in that gap.

Q: When did the practice of issuing official Presidential Inaugural medals begin?

The first publicly available medals went on sale in 1929. The first Official medals were for William McKinley's second term in 1901. Prior to that medals were struck for Grover Cleveland in 1893 and for McKinley's first term in 1897, but these were attached to ribbons and considered to be badges.

One source claims the first Inaugural medal was struck in 1877, a date I haven't been able to confirm.

Q: Are any of the Presidential inauguration medals really valuable?

A check of auction records indicates that there are several that have run into five figure selling prices, including the 1941 silver Franklin D. Roosevelt medal which sold in 1979 for $25,000 and a Taft-Sherman 1909 gold medal for $32,000. The John F. Kennedy gold medal is valued at $50,000 by the Kennedy Library.

Q: Where can I find a buyer for the Franklin Mint items that I have?

This is a question that is a regular in the mail, in email and on our telephone, with a number of questions coming from insurance agents who are trying to establish values before issuing a policy. The Franklin Mint frequently refers their callers to us, because we issued a reference catalog of all of their products. However, the last catalog we issued was in 1982 and has long since gone out of print. Ironically there's a better market for the catalog than for some of the pieces listed in it. The products they put out are excellent, high quality material. However, they saturated the market with something that even in much smaller mintages would have to be held for 50 to 100 years or more before it would appreciate significantly. We stopped publishing a catalog simply because there was no real market and no prices we could quote that would mean anything. We do have both buy and sell classified sections for Franklin Mint material, so keep an eye on them.

Q: Is there an aluminum version of the 1933 Roosevelt inauguration medal?

A single aluminum piece is known, surfacing when the estate of John R. Sinnock, the former Chief Engraver of the U.S. Mint, was sold at auction. Medallic Arts made dies for the medal, and it is believed that the aluminum piece was a trial strike made when the dies were turned over to the Mint.

Q: Did Cyrus Field ever get the gold medal that he was awarded by Congress for laying the first Atlantic Cable?

There's a long but interesting story surrounding that medal. Field laid the first successful Atlantic telegraph cable in 1858, but it worked for only a few months. In 1865 he started out again, and laid a 1,200-mile length before it broke and was lost. In 1866 he tried again, and successfully laid a cable from Ireland to Newfoundland, at the same time snagging the broken cable and completing it, so that two cables were in operation. This was hailed as the greatest engineering feat of the era. A medal was struck in 1867 and laid away until it could be presented personally to Fields, but when he showed up for the ceremony, he was asked to wait. In 1869 a copy of the medal was finally presented to him, as the original was nowhere to be found. In 1874 the clerk who had been entrusted with the original came across it in a vault and Field was notified that he could have it for the value of its gold content, at the time worth $600. Field paid the Treasury, and the medal was narrowly saved from the melting furnace.

Q: What are the privately minted medals that I bought back in the 1970s worth?

In almost all cases, recent medals have shown little, if any, increase in value and many have dropped below the issue price. The exceptions, of course, are the bullion medals, which have gone up with the bullion prices.

Q: What was the original source of the 12 signs of the zodiac that appear on so many medals and even some coins?

The signs of the zodiac trace back to the Babylonians. As early as 800 BCE Babylonians had published maps of the stars. Unaware that the earth was tipped on its axis, the early day astronomers had devised a theory that the sun was moving on a long curving trail through the stars. They used this to explain why new constellations of stars appeared in the heavens every month or so. The 12 major constellations were named and from these names came the signs of the zodiac.

Q: Do you have the specifications for the Norse-American commemorative coins?

The Norse-American pieces are medals, not coins. Congress authorized them in the midst of the profligate commemorative coin programs of the 1920s, so your confusion is understandable, and almost universal. Anthony Swiatec researched the medals and provided the following figures. There were 6,000 of the thin planchet silver, weighing 0.36 troy ounce and were 0.065 inch thick. The thick planchet silver had a mintage of 33,750, weighed 0.52 troy ounces and was 0.087 inches thick. The matte proof gold medal had a mintage of 100. A fourth version on a bronze planchet had a disputed mintage of from 50 to 75 and was silver-plated outside the Mint. Other versions exist; including scalloped silver and nickel planchet strikes and a proof medium weight silver, which fits between the thick and thin. Sale prices were an estimated $1.75 for the thin silver and $1.25 for the thick. The price of the gold is also disputed, with $20 and $40 quoted from different sources. The large silver-plated pieces and some of the gold were used as presentation pieces.

Q: I have a medal that depicts a skeleton looking out of the ticket window for the **Lusitania.** *What is this supposed to represent?*

From your description you have one of the Goetz medals struck at the time of the sinking of the Lusitania. The medal was struck after the sinking, but dated before it by mistake, leading to charges that the sinking had been planned. If it is an original rather than one of the numerous copies it might be worth from $25 to $75 depending on condition.

Q: When was the first balloon flight made in the U.S.?

Montgolfer's first ascent November 21, 1783, in Paris got all the publicity. It would be a decade later when Jean Pierre Blanchard made the first successful balloon ascension in the U.S. in 1793. There is at least one medal marking the flight.

Q: Are medal dies always made from hubs as coin dies are?

Sounds like a simple question, but the answer could get quite complicated. The general answer to the specific question is 'no.' If a large quantity of medals are being struck, requiring more than a pair or two of dies, then it would be more economical to use hubs to make the dies. For small quantities, a single pair of dies might do, and there would be little point in making hubs first. Making that single pair of dies could be done in several ways, including the same process (using a reducing lathe) that is normally used to make hubs.

Q: Can you tell me anything about the MacArthur Memorial Foundation Medals?

The Foundation had 10,000 1 5/16-inch medals struck and sold them for $10 donations. A small quantity of 3 1/8-inch medals, which were duplicates of the medal presented to General MacArthur, were available for $1,000 donations.

Q: Do medals require more striking pressure than coins?

They usually do, especially if it's a high relief medal. It is also likely that a large, high relief medal may be struck several times. To facilitate the striking the planchet may also be heated.

Q: I've got a silver medal that I'd like to know more about. Is there any way to determine the fineness?

Your best bet would be to run a specific gravity test on it. This can give you a figure that is very close to the actual fineness of the piece. It involves weighing the coin in air, then suspended in water. If you use distilled water you shouldn't have to worry about discoloration of the medal. You will need a chart giving the weights for various finenesses.

Q: I have an Ike dollar, which has "Commemorating A Great American" around the Presidential Seal on the reverse. What is it worth?

You have a commemorative medal rather than a coin. The 1 9/16-inch medals were issued privately in 1969 at $9.75 for the .999 one troy ounce silver medal, and $3 for the bronze version.

Q: Is there an official White House medal besides the coin?

There is, the medal being first issued in 1972 in a 1 5/16-inch bronze. There is also a limited issue in 40 percent silver, which was not available to the public, but went to the wives and relatives of Congressmen. The bronze medals are currently available from the U.S. Mint.

Q: In comparing some Revolutionary period medals with the coins of that era, I noted that the medals are much more artistic than the coins of that and later periods. What explanation do you have?

The simple answer is that most of the medal dies were done in Paris. The French capitol was the center of medallic art in that period and it would be many years before that leadership was challenged.

Q: Why do so many medals have Latin inscriptions?

Again, there is a simple answer - snobbery. The unspoken purpose was to set apart the educated from the common people. In the 17th and much of the 18th centuries most of the English-speaking peoples couldn't read written or printed English, let alone Latin. While today most of the population is literate, the use of Latin has become a tradition, rather than a blatant divisor.

Q: Was Senator John Morgan of Alabama responsible for getting the U.S. involved in the Panama Canal?

A medal issued by the state of Alabama implies this, but Morgan actually was in favor of a route through Nicaragua. The switch came when the original French company dropped its asking price for its assets in 1901. The U.S. House had voted 308-2 for the Nicaragua route and Morgan remained in favor even after Congress reversed itself.

Q: I'm told there was a silver medal for Mint Director Raymond T. Baker that weighed eight ounces. Is that figure correct?

Baker served as Director of the Mint from March 1917 to March 1922. The medal was issued by the Mint to commemorate his service, and sold for $6. Silver at the time was well below a dollar an ounce.

Q: What is the difference between a medal and a medallion?

Let's add a third term, medalet. The three names refer to size. A medalet is a small medal, usually one inch or smaller in diameter. Then the next larger size is a medal, then the larger ones are medallions, usually three inches in diameter or more. Interestingly enough the term medallion was also applied originally to certain large coins of ancient Greece. The most common mistake is to confuse the names of the largest and smallest, as the U.S. Mint does. Even more common is the confusion between coins and medals (of any size). Only a governing body can issue coins, which are intended as money. Anyone can issue medals, as these are not used as money.

Q: I found a medal with the Confederate flag, and the words "UCV-1899-Reunion-Charleston." What can you tell me about it?

It's a medal struck for the United Confederate Veterans' Reunion in Charleston, South Carolina in 1899. One of the medal specialists in our audience may be able to add more details.

Q: I picked up a couple of calendar medals at a flea market and they got me wondering as to how far back they were made?

Calendar medals, some in the form of perpetual calendars, date back to 1684. They were much more popular before the printed calendar made its appearance. The largest production occurred after about 1750 and continued until the 1860s. They were mainly distributed in the United States and Britain, but examples are found from several other countries as well. They were one of the first popular objects other than tokens used to carry advertising. They make a very interesting collectible. A couple of examples include the 95 mm calendar medal struck in 1967 by the French Mint. The bronze sold for $8.50 or 42 francs, the silver for $60 or 300 francs. There were four different bicentennial calendar medals, a 3 3/4-inch bronze for $25, a gold plated bronze for $45, a sterling silver for $225 that contained 14 ounces of bullion and a 3-inch bronze.

Q: In an old ad I found a medal offered as a "Unimedal?" Any idea what this was supposed to mean?

It's a rather baffling usage, but one source describes it as a term for a small medal or medalet struck a single time, like a coin.

Q: Does the Mint have all the original dies for the medals struck at the Philadelphia Mint?

Many of the old medal dies are still in existence, but there were some peculiar arrangements with some of the early dies. For example, the dies for the Zachary Taylor Mexican War Medal were given to the artist whose portrait was used as a model for the medal. William Garl Brown of Richmond, Virginia painted Taylor while he was still in Mexico. Brown requested the arrangement so that he could sell medals from the dies for his own profit, rather than charging for the use of the portrait. Dr. Robert Patterson, Director of the Mint, agreed but perhaps playing on Brown's ignorance of the minting process, carefully retained the hubs, which had been used to make the dies. The U.S. Mint maintains a large cabinet of hubs and dies for various medals.

Q: With all the interest in the renovation of the Statue of Liberty, wasn't there a medal issued at the time of its installation?

Our source indicates there was such a medal, described as 50 mm in diameter, with the Statue on the obverse, with the words, "Commemorative Monument of American Independence" and on the reverse, "In remembrance of the old friendship between the United States and France by public subscription amongst the citizens of "booth" (correct) nations 1776-1876." The incorrect spelling of "both" reportedly led to withholding of the medal, which was never issued publicly.

Q: Is it true that many of the first Congressional Medals of Honor were recalled?

The medal was authorized in 1862. In 1916 a board investigated 2,625 awards and decided that 911 - about one third - had not been properly earned. If the holder of the medal was still in the Military it was recalled and canceled.

Q: What are the Castorland Medals?

They are medals (actually a pattern half dollar) issued with 1796 dates for the French settlement in the Carthage, New York area during the French Revolution. They come in silver, bronze and copper. One source indicates that most of the pieces offered are restrikes. The originals - which are quite rare - have the UG in FRUGRAM touching, the first A in AMERICANA is lower than the rest, and the 1 in the date is well down into a denticle. Restrikes were made from this die and in most cases show buckling at PARENS on the reverse. The Paris Mint retained the original dies, and made numerous restrikes in a variety of metals. Other modern dies have also been made and used.

Q: Isn't there a Mohammed Ali medal?

There is, with no direct connection to the boxer. It is described as: "A six-pointed green star, with lotus flowers, on a sun with gold and silver rays." It was issued in 1915 by the Egyptian Government in memory of the founder of the dynasty, which ended with King Farouk.

Q: I have a medal, (bar/medallion) struck by (a private mint) back in the 1970s. Can you give me their address so that I can write for more information?

With a few exceptions you are probably out of luck, as most such letters are returned marked "undeliverable." Dozens of private mints mushroomed during the art bar and medal craze of the early 1970s, and as quickly vanished as the fad subsided with the rising price of bullion. The questions are on the increase, but the answers are declining. The private mints that are still in business are welcome to write to me with current addresses.

Q: Somewhere I saw a picture of a World War II medal with K-9 on it. What did the K-9 stand for?

It was a "cute" way of saying canine, or guard dog, which is what the K-9 Corps was made up of. They were frequently used for beach patrols and to guard high security areas on military bases.

Chapter 41

METALS AND ALLOYS

The collector needs to know just what is in a coin. Since most are made of some metal, knowing the basics about the makeup of the alloy is very important.

Q: Please explain why a silver dollar contained more silver than two silver halves, four quarters or ten dimes?

Because our coins contained more than the face value in bullion, the Coinage Act of 1853 reduced the silver content of the minor coins by 6.91 percent but did not change the dollar standard. Ever since then silver minor coins, including the 40 percent silver, have lower total bullion content than the amount in the silver dollars.

The first modern copper-nickel coin.

Q: What can you tell me about the earliest copper-nickel alloy and nickel coins?

The first modern copper-nickel coins were the Belgian 1860 20 centimes. The Swiss issued the first modern nickel coin, the 1881 20 centimes. The Greeks used nickel coins as early as 150 BCE. Coins of Bactria (220 BCE) by King Enthydemus are known with a 78 percent copper - 22 percent nickel alloy. However, the use was apparently accidental, using a native alloy just as it came from the ground. Nickel wasn't identified as a separate metal until 1751.

Q: I've seen the statement that the two-cent coin was introduced to save copper, as it weighed less than two one-cent coins. Could you please comment on that?

The two-cent coin was introduced in 1864, incidentally becoming the first U.S. coin to bear the "In God We Trust" motto. At the time it was proposed, the cent weighed 72.0 grains, consisting of 88 percent copper and 12 percent nickel. But, the same bill that authorized the two-cent piece also reduced the weight of the cent to 48.0 grains and switched it to a copper-tin-zinc alloy. The weight for the two-cent coin was set at 96 grains, or exactly twice the weight of the new cent.

Q: The Mint switched to a copper-plated zinc cent to replace the old brass alloy cent. Is this the first time this has happened?

The plated coin so far as we can find out is the second such coin to be issued. The 1943 steel cents had a steel core plated with zinc, although it was referred to as a "coating" rather than plating, probably as a public relations move. The Mint very carefully never referred to it as "plated" in any of the news releases concerning the steel cents, but apparently decided in 1982 that the public of today wouldn't swallow the same cover-up a second time. The zinc plating on the 1943 cents was applied to the steel strip before the planchets were punched out, leaving the steel core exposed at the edge. The current zinc cent planchets are punched out first then plated by the "barrel" plating method, so that all surfaces, including the edge, are equally plated.

Q: Did the Mint make any allowance for silver used as part of the alloy in private gold coins that were melted down for their bullion content?

The regulations of the Mint specifically noted that, "Silver is considered merely as an alloy of gold coin, except it can be profitably parted (separated) out, and goes for no more than the copper in the same predicament."

Q: What was the first nickel-alloy coin to bear the head of a monarch?

Queen Victoria of England appeared in 1869 on the Jamaica copper-nickel half penny and penny, and a farthing of the same metal with her portrait was issued there in 1880. King Leopold I of Belgium beat her to the punch, however, appearing on the 1860 20 centimes, a less well-known denomination. The 5- and 10-centime coins of 1860 were also struck in copper-nickel but did not bear the bust of the King, instead showing a lion. The first pure nickel coin bearing a monarch was the Italian 1919 50 centisime with the bust of King Victor Emanuelle.

Q: Is it possible that some of our early silver coins contain gold as well?

Quite possible. Prior to the 1850s methods for extracting gold from silver were very crude and undoubtedly small amounts got mixed into the alloy used for silver coins. The Act of May 19, 1828, addresses that very point because it authorizes the Mint to coin silver submitted by private parties even if it contained small amounts of gold, providing that this be done if the gold could not be economically separated. However, the amounts involved probably would be less than one percent of the total weight of the coin so even with the present price of gold the recovery probably would not outweigh the numismatic value of the old coins. This may well be an outgrowth of the urban legends in several countries centering on gold accidentally dumped into the wrong melting furnace.

Q: What is a specific gravity test and what purpose does it serve?

A specific gravity test is conducted by weighing an object such as a coin "dry," then weighing it wet, or immersed in water, to determine the displacement. This gives a ratio of the weight or mass of the coin in relation to an equal volume of water. The specific gravity readings are known for the normal metals or alloys so the results can be compared to determine the exact metallic content of the coin being tested. It's an excellent example of a non-destructive test in that no damage is done to the coin. Striking a coin will make at least a slight change in the specific gravity of most coin metals. For example, a 90 percent silver ingot has a specific gravity of 10.24. A coin struck from that ingot will have a specific gravity of 10.33. The change is due to the fact that the striking slightly compresses the metal, thus increasing the density.

Q: Some time ago you listed several coin metal alloys. Do you have a listing for Koulz's alloy?

Koulz's alloy is classed as a billon alloy since it contains only 26 percent silver, along with 33 percent nickel and 41 percent copper. Any reader help on any coins actually struck in this combination of metals?

Q: Do assays of silver alloy coins show the actual silver content, or the average content?

Mostly they show the average content, as under practical conditions the actual silver content will vary from one part of the coin to another, and from the outside to the center, especially on the older and larger coins, such as the silver dollars.

Q: Is there a white metal alloy called acieral that was used for coins?

This may have been used for some tokens, but not for coins to my knowledge. Its principal use was for auto parts prior to World War II. The alloy contains 91.8 percent aluminum, 6.4 percent copper, 0.4 percent zinc, 0.9 percent nickel, 0.1 percent iron and 0.4 percent silicon.

Q: Could titanium be used as a coin metal?

Like practically every non-bullion metal, titanium has been tested to determine if it could be used for coins. Since it is difficult to machine or work in its solid form, sintered blanks were used. These were made with powdered metal, which was compressed into planchets. However, they did not strike properly and wore out the dies very rapidly. The metal was rejected because of the high costs involved. There have been a few medals manufactured in this metal.

Q: Why aren't there any nickel alloys for coins with greater than 25 percent nickel content other than pure nickel?

One reason seems to be that alloying nickel with other metals into a satisfactory coining metal is quite difficult, because of problems such as excessive gas bubbles in the bars.

Q: The U.S. Mint refers to the alloys used for the cents from 1864 to 1982 as "gilding metal," with a 95 percent copper, 5 percent tin or zinc content. Is this the only alloy known as gilding metal?

One source lists three other brass alloys containing 80, 85 and 90 percent copper respectively; the remainder is zinc, known as "BES gilding metals."

Q: Which was our first wartime coin that had an alloy influenced by the war?

The 1942 to 1945 silver bullion nickels and the 1943 steel cents are likely candidates, but the 1864 "gilding metal" cent is the winner. The 12 percent nickel alloy in use up to 1864 was being hoarded. The large cent came close, during the War of 1812, but held out until 1857.

Q: Are there different pewter alloys?

There are actually a variety of different alloys that come under this general name. They include Babbit Metal, Britannia Metal, Meridian Metal, Pincheck Metal, and White and Pot metal. The one common factor is tin, which is the principal metal. The best pewter is considered to be an alloy of tin, antimony, copper and bismuth, with the tin making up about 80 percent of the alloy. Cheap forms of pewter contain lower amounts of tin and large amounts of lead.

Q: Is there any U.S. coin that contains no copper?

The 1943 zinc-plated steel cent is the lone example. U.S. gold and silver coins contain up to 10 percent copper, with the earliest examples containing slightly more than that.

Q: I have a book from the World War II era that refers to a token struck "on alloy." Is something missing?

At one time the term "alloy" was used to mean a white metal, or Babbit metal, which is an alloy of tin, copper and antimony, so your reference apparently means the piece was struck on either white metal or Babbit metal. More recently "alloy" usually means copper.

Q: Is it possible to authenticate the brass-plated U.S. cents?

It is possible, according to ANACS, to identify the mint-produced pieces, but it takes an X-ray diffraction test, which costs substantially more than the coin's collector value. "Visual" identification, based on color, won't work. They are legitimate, as examples of the brass-plated cents have been examined by the Mint and determined to be genuine. The problem was excessive heat, which caused the zinc core to bleed into the copper plating changing it to a brass alloy plating. They are found with 1983 and 1985 dates, and possibly some others. I would advise caution in purchasing them except from specialist dealers who know what they are, as they can be readily faked. Several have been offered as "brass" cents, which is a misrepresentation.

Q: Does cupro-nickel always mean an alloy with a 75-25 ratio of copper and nickel?

Not always, although most coin references are to this specific alloy. The term originated for an 80-20 alloy used for jackets for military rifle bullets. Old references also list it as "nickel bronze." A couple of countries used the 80-20 alloys for coins.

Q: What was the first use of aluminum for circulating coins?

The earliest use for a circulating coin was in the 1907 British West Africa 1/10 penny and East Africa one cent. The U.S. Mint made an aluminum pattern in 1851, which was probably among the first attempts to use the metal for coinage. At that time aluminum was expensive, on a par with silver. Once a cheap method of recovering it from ore was discovered the price dropped very quickly.

Q: How do you determine whether a nickel is copper-nickel or the silver alloy?

Tests include running a specific gravity or X-ray diffraction scan. The Mint used special coin counting machines, which separated the silver alloy from the copper-nickel coins.

Q: Does the term 'silver coin' always mean that it's solid silver?

Don't read over a description such as that without making sure you understand the terms. 'Solid' silver or gold means only that the piece is not hollow. You need to assume that the silver is diluted with another metal as an alloy, unless it says pure silver. Most U.S. coins, for example, are only 90 percent silver. Offers in the lay press and on TV are likely to slip in similar sounding terms to deliberately confuse you as to what you are getting.

Q: What was the reason for including nickel in the alloy for the first small cents?

The introduction of the small cent in 1857 ended the era of the large cent, which contained enough copper to nearly equal its face value. The addition of 12 percent nickel was intended to satisfy the demand for coins with "real" value, as the nickel metal brought the sum of the metals nearly to face value.

Q: Does the softer metal in an alloy wear faster?

When an alloy is properly mixed the metal wears evenly. It is possible to leach some metals out of an alloy with the proper chemicals.

Q: Are there any U.S. coins with a silver alloy below .900 fine?

The 1942 through 1945 nickels were .350 fine. The 3-cent silver for the first three years was .750 fine. The earliest silver issues from the U.S. Mint were very slightly below .900 fine.

Q: Has magnesium been used for any modern coinage?

Magnesium, which readily catches fire and burns with an intense flame, has been used in some alloys, especially in some of the Jewish ghettos, including Lodz, and in several concentration camps during World War II. Because of its flammable nature, many of the magnesium coins wound up being used as fuel. Magnesium or magnesium-alloy coins have also been used in Manchuko and Laos, and one source mentions a possible Japanese World War II issue. The Philippines began striking their one sentimo beginning in 1967 in an aluminum-magnesium (95-5) alloy.

Q: What was the reason given for removing the nickel from the cent in 1864?

The switch to a bronze alloy came after Mint Director James Pollock reported repeated problems with the 12 percent nickel in the alloy, which made the coins hard to strike, the rising cost of nickel, and the entire dependence on foreign sources for the metal. The popularity of the small size Civil War tokens also was not lost on the Treasury Department. This, of course, didn't stop the introduction of the five-cent nickel denomination two years later.

Q: What is a "French proof?"

The one usage I can find for this term is for the 1865 proof two-cent piece. It is not explained beyond that, so my suspicion is that it resulted indirectly from the fact that the bronze alloy used beginning in 1864 for both the cent and two cent was called "French Bronze," because the French Mint introduced the alloy to coinage some years before. Probably the term began with the 1864 issues, but never reached general use.

Q: Is there any denomination of U.S. silver coins that hasn't been struck in some other metal or alloy?

The only silver coin, which meets these criteria, is the 20-cent piece, struck between 1875 and 1878. The three-cent piece and half dime (or nickel) were also struck in copper-nickel, the dime in clad copper-nickel, the quarter and half in both clad copper-nickel and clad 40 percent silver, the dollar in clad copper-nickel, 40 percent silver clad and gold.

Q: Why will my metal detector scream at tinfoil, but only blip on a coin?

It has to do with the surface area and the reflective power of aluminum foil. This was more of a problem with the older detectors. More recent models can "tune out" foil and can tabs.

Chapter 42

MEXICO

Coinage from our southern neighbor has a colorful and exciting history. Reading about the competition with the U.S. Trade dollar and the wide circulation given to Mexican coins will provide endless pleasure for the fan.

The three common symbols seen on Mexican coins.

Q: What do the sword, scales and scroll symbolize on Mexican coins?

They stand for the three branches of Government. The sword represents the executive branch, the scales the judicial branch and the scroll stands for the legislative branch.

Q: Is there any way of identifying the Mexican coins struck by the U.S. Mint in 1935?

The KM-446 50 centavos were struck at all three mints (Philadelphia, Denver and San Francisco) and at the Mexico City Mint. A total of 60 million of the coins were struck in the U.S. and 10.8 million in Mexico. All of the coins were struck with the "Mo" mintmark, so there is no way to distinguish those from the different mints.

Q: Is it possible that the Mexico City Mint once was in a castle?

Not a castle, but it was in a palace. In 1569 the National Palace was purchased from the family of Spanish conqueror Hernando Cortez, and was used until the present. A new mint was built in 1969, but both worked at the same time, giving rise to a number of interesting die varieties in the Mexican coinage.

Q: When was the last time that Mexican money was legal tender in the U.S?

The accepted answer is 1857 when all foreign coins were demonetized, but they had a quasi-legal status beginning July 1, 1969, in Los Angeles, where they were acceptable in Mexican-run shops on Olivera Street, near the Mexican Embassy. At that time the exchange rate was about 7 1/2 cents for one peso. LA readers might be able to tell us how long the plan lasted.

Q: Why did Mexico place a tax on trade coins?

Apparently the Mexican government was miffed after their trade dollar was removed from legal tender status in the U.S. in 1857. For whatever benefit, the Mexican trade dollar was subjected to a 12 percent export tax. Perhaps one of our financial experts has a more detailed explanation of the reasoning behind the move.

Q: Supposedly there is a Mexican 1866 peso depicting Maximilian that has a die break on the forehead, marking the spot where a bullet entered his head when he was executed in 1867. Any information?

The late Maurice Gould was an intermediate source for the story, but examining photos of coins from two different mints and their descriptions, the reputed mark is clearly an alteration (gash) made in the coin after it was minted. A die break would have stuck up above the normal surface, and none of the specimens reported show a raised area. This puts it in a class with the Kennedy "Dallas dollars."

Chapter 43

MILL, MILLING AND MILLERS

Think of a mill and you think of grinding wheat or corn. The numismatic mill is entirely different and worthy of study.

Q: I'm confused by milled and reeded edges. Can you explain?

The European meaning for a milled edge includes reeded, plain, grained, ornamented and lettered edges. The U.S. usage for a milled coin means one with upset rims. Terms such as milling machine, milled coins, milled edge, etc., have kept collectors going in circles for many years. In general, in the process of making coins, a milling machine is a device which raises the edge of the planchet on both sides so that there will be enough metal there to form the design rim of the struck coin. Another source of confusion is the use of the term 'milling machine' for a machine shop tool, which removes metal with a revolving cutter.

Q: Tell me what 'mill money' is?

Mill money is one of three archaic terms applied to coins. Mill and screw, and milled were also applied to coins struck with milled edges in a screw press. Note that this is the European usage of mill and milling. Italians invented the process.

Q: When did the use of milled coins begin?

The earliest recorded coins with milled edges are in the Augsburg, Germany Mint in the late 1540s. King Henry II of France purchased 3,000 ecus of equipment from Augsburg, and had it installed at the Paris Mint. Coins are known dated 1555 with raised edge letters, from a segmented collar.

Chapter 44

MINTAGE FIGURES AND STATISTICS

Bean counters front and center. A major part of coin collecting is assembling mintage figures. Often obscure data is hard to find and there's always the ever-present problem of missing figures, faulty addition or transposition. I never said it would be easy.

Q: How do you know or prove that the early Mint reports were accurate?
One of the principal pieces of evidence is existing coins that are unlisted in the Mint reports. A number of scholars have made a detailed comparison of the archives with Mint reports. These studies, especially by R. W. Julian, have resulted in revised figures for much of the early mintage. Rather than imply that we are impugning the integrity of the Mint, consider that figures get transposed, incorrectly copied, accidentally deleted, etc. Mistakes get made, despite the best efforts.

Q: Of all the money in circulation in the U.S. what percentage are coins?
The last estimate I've seen is about 10 percent. Along with that you need to consider that the Bureau of Engraving and Printing can turn out enough paper money in 24 hours to exceed the face value output of our four mints for a full year.

Q: Wasn't the 1972-S cent at one time considered to be a scarce coin?
In late 1972 the Mint released figures indicating that only 80 million circulation strikes were produced at San Francisco. This started a frantic search for those coins already in circulation. After collectors rushed to gather up what would have been the lowest mintage since 1955, the Mint backtracked and announced that actual production had been 380.2 million. The missing 300 million was cited as a clerical error.

Q: Do you have an official list of key coins that is published by some authority in the hobby?
There is no official list, or sanctioned list, of key coins. This is primarily due to the fact that any such list would be controversial, for a number of reasons. Historically, key status was usually based on the number minted. More recently the grade, or amount of wear, has become an important criteria. Some coins are common in lower grades and quite rare in the higher grades, which requires footnotes or explanations. The number of coins of a given date and mint that have been retained by collectors also can affect the status of an otherwise qualified key or semi-key coin. In a few cases melting has affected the number existing. With changing collector interests, the list is constantly changing. To my knowledge nobody has (at least recently) compiled a complete list of key and semi-key coins.

Q: Do you have the totals for the value of the two- and three-cent coins struck in the 1800s?
There was $912,020 worth of two-cent pieces struck between 1864 and 1872. The silver three-cent total was $1,282,087.20 and the three-cent nickel $941,349.48, so the total values were fairly closely bunched.

Q: Do you have any totals for the number of coins struck by the United States Mint?

Thanks to Todd Mannebach, a coin dealer in Michigan, I have some interesting statistics. Between 1792 and 1985, the Mint struck a total of 316,098,970,885 coins, in 3,679 different denominations, dates and mints. The total for silver coins was 19,061,646,402 (1,694 denominations, etc.) and for gold, 340,420,942 coins (1,080). Face value of the entire lot was $22,189,189,053,085. As might be expected, the lowly cent accounted for a major portion of the statistics, with 225.93 billion coins, 71.47 percent of the total, and 10.18 percent of the face value.

Q: Is it true that a large quantity of the Type I gold dollars were melted down by the government?

There is some question as to the legality of the melt, as Congress did not authorize it, but Mint Director James Snowdon did melt down 8,000,000 of the coins in 1860, and used the gold to strike the Type III and other gold coins.

Q: Where did all the "nickel" cents go?

Between 1857 and 1864 production amounted to over 200 million coins. However, they were not "legal tender" until 1864, when the cent and two-cent pieces were legalized as payment of debts up to 10 cents. In 1871 Congress authorized redemption of such small change into "lawful" money, intending that they be turned into paper money, but the net result was the redemption of over 80 million of the nickel alloy cents, which were later melted down and used to make nickels.

Q: How many wheat back cents did the U.S. Mint strike?

The figure rounds off at a total of 25.7 billion for the 1909 through 1958 production, or about twice the yearly production in the early 1980s. One would get the impression that most of them are still out there, hoarded by the public. While large quantities have ultimately gone to the smelter, there are still many billions of them hanging over the coin market and keeping most prices low.

Q: How many cents were struck in the first 100 years of the small cent?

Between 1864 and 1964 approximately 44 billion cents were struck. In recent history, that number is struck every three to four years.

Q: How many gold double eagles has the U.S. Mint struck, and how many of them went back to the Mint to be melted down?

U.S. Mint reports show that a total of 174,105,606 $20 gold coins were struck between 1849 and 1933. Of that number, 67.8 million were officially melted down, usually to be recoined, or approximately 39 percent of the total production. This is the largest percentage of any of the gold denominations, the smallest being the $3 gold, with only 6,441 melted out of 539,792 struck, or 1.12 percent. Some $260 to $280 million in gold coins survived 1933; 4.9 million $20, 8 million $10, 10.8 million $5, 12.2 million $2.50. No figure is available for the $1 gold.

Chapter 45

THE MINTING PROCESS

Here's where the specialists shine. Knowing everything there is to know about the minting process is about the most valuable tool in your arsenal. Every collector should have, at a minimum, a basic knowledge of the minting process.

Q: Current punches used to make coin blanks are blunt ended. Was this always true?

In the first cutting machines used to mechanically make blanks, the punches had a sharp edged, slanted face, resulting in many bent and deformed blanks. When more power was available the punches developed into the present blunt form. As you can imagine, when a gang punch with a number of blunt punches is driven through the coin metal strip, it makes a lot of racket.

Q: I know that in current coining practice they use ingots of coin metal that weigh several hundred pounds, but how big were they in the early days?

One source describes the gold ingots used for $20 gold coins in 1856 as being about a foot long, 1 7/16-inch wide and half an inch thick. This ingot would weigh about 60 ounces, so when it was rolled out about 30 to 40 $20 coins could be made. The balance of the strip was sent back for remelting and cast into another ingot with fresh metal. Up until about 1949, the U.S. Mint was using ingots of coin metal, which weighed approximately six pounds. This would allow a strip only a few feet in length, from which approximately 4.2 pounds of coins could be punched. With 156 cents to the pound, this would have meant a maximum of about 650 cent planchets from each piece of strip. In 1949 equipment was put on line at Denver that could handle 400-pound ingots, which became the standard size. From this strip about 280 pounds of planchets or 43,680 coins were produced.

Q: What's the purpose of the rim on a coin?

Two general purposes are generally described. The rim makes it easier to stack coins, and the rim is raised to help protect the central design from wear. Interestingly enough, the upset rim on a planchet also serves two purposes. The raised ridge keeps the planchets from sticking together and jamming the feed mechanism, as well as to focus metal where it is needed for the design rim on the coin.

Q: You've said in the past that it's impossible to strike a smaller coin on a larger planchet. How come there are some U.S. half cents struck on large cents?

The statement stands, because almost all coin presses can't accept larger planchets without help. In the case you cite, the struck cents were first cut down to half-cent size, then restruck as half cents.

Q: How are multi-sided coins struck?

Very carefully. The planchets are punched out in the shape of the coin and then are fed into holders or guides, which hold the planchet at the right position to be struck, or to drop into the shaped collar. The process has of course been mechanized and today they can be struck at speeds approaching those of striking regular round coins.

Q: *Have X-rays ever been used to control quality of our United States coins?*

At the present time X-rays are used to examine coins and help detect counterfeits, but in the late 1950s X-ray equipment was used for the first time at the Denver Mint to control the thickness of the coin metal strip as it was being passed through the rolling machines. The X-ray detector was connected to precise electronic controls, which varied the pressure on the rolls to control the thickness to one half of a tenth of one thousandth of an inch. This equipment was an adaptation of a method used for controlling rolling mills adopted a decade earlier.

Q: *Why aren't coins in as high relief as medals?*

High relief medals are struck with heavy presses, and are usually struck several times. This is extra work that would be very impractical and too expensive for coins. In order to supply the need for circulating coins production is geared to millions of coins a day, while only dozens or at most a few hundred or a few thousand may turn out medals.

Chapter 46

MINTING VARIETIES

My career as a researcher began when I couldn't find answers to my questions. My original specialty was minting varieties, until I branched out into the entire minting process. An insatiable curiosity is a necessary part of your makeup.

Q: Is there any way to tell whether a large raised area on the face of my coin next to the rim is due to a broken die?

These are classed as "major" die breaks, and one positive indication would be a matching area of missing design at the same point on the other side of the coin. The lack of pressure at that point failed to force the coin metal into the design in the opposing die.

A Colombia 1968 5 centavos with a blundered date.

Q: What is meant by a blundered die?

A blundered die, or the coin struck by a blundered die, has some part of the design incorrectly positioned. It may be out of alignment, upside down or lying on its side, etc. Blunders are often corrected, but a blundered die and a corrected blundered die are two distinctly different minting varieties.

Q: Isn't there one of our U.S. coins which depicts Miss Liberty with only three fingers on her right hand?

Take a close look at the first Trade dollars, with dates from 1873 through 1876, and if not too worn you will find Liberty has only three fingers clutching the olive branch. When the dies were revised in 1877, a fourth finger was added to correct the designer's mistake. Oddly, the same thing happened to Andrew Jackson on the $20 notes in the 1934 and 1950 series, as well as some of the late 1928 series, as he is shown on those issues with only three fingers.

Q: How was it possible to punch in an inverted date in a die? Seems like the engraver would have noticed it after the first digit?

There are several instances such as the 1858 half dime. In that era dates were added to the completed die with a logo punch, which had all four digits on a single piece of steel. There were also logo punches, which had just two or three of the digits. This is why on some coins you will find differing gaps between the digits, depending on which logo punch was used, as the remaining digit(s) were added with a single punch. With the advent of the hubbing process used to make the entire die the use of logo punches went out of style.

Q: I have a coin that has parts of the designs of a dime and parts of a cent. Can this happen in the mint?

From your description it's possible that you have a dime, which was struck a second time by the cent dies, giving it a possible value of several hundred dollars. I would suggest having it authenticated by a specialist. For a genuine dual denomination coin, this has to be the sequence, as a cent will not fit into the feed mechanism or the dime dies.

Q: I have a book published in 1975 that lists 25 classes of "error" coins, claiming this to be the largest number in any book. True?

False, and documented proof was furnished to the publisher at the time, but the information was ignored. In 1975 there were at least two other books on the market listing more than 100 classes, and the number in one of them, my Official Price Guide to Mint Errors is now over 400 classes. This fits with my repeated warnings not to depend on outdated reference books or catalogs.

Q: Time to settle an argument. Is a 9/6 date or a 6/9 date considered to be an overdate or not? There's a pretty hefty sum riding on your answer.

My comments are not likely to settle this long-standing hobby argument, but for what it's worth, here goes. Any time you have one digit over another, it is an overdate. If the same digit is punched over itself, this is a doubled date, but not an overdate. The purists have argued that a 9 over an upside down 9 is a repunched or recut date, depending on the method used, and not an overdate. From there the argument degenerates into whether the date was changed intentionally or accidentally. Besides, in the early days it was not uncommon to have a single punch to make both a 6 and a 9. My practice, to simplify record keeping and to make it easy on the collector, has been to call a 9/6 or 6/9 an overdate, regardless of intent, which is usually impossible to prove. An excellent case in point is the 1839/6 large cent, which was from an original 1836 die that was repunched intentionally and used in 1839.

Q: Is it possible to have more than one form of doubling on a coin?

There are at least 28 forms of mint processes doubling from various causes, and it is not at all unusual to have different forms on opposite sides, or even on the same side of a coin. There are numerous examples of coins with hub doubling of parts of the design, with the date or mintmark doubled by repunching. Then add doubling occurring after the coin is minted, such as machine doubling damage, and you can have quite a mixture on a single coin!

Q: I have a particular die variety of an early half dollar. What is the current value for it?

This is a question that is virtually impossible to answer both because there is no indication of the grade and it would require spending several hours or several dollars making phone calls. Tracking the prices of die varieties is a highly specialized area that frequently comes down to a situation where the coin has to appear in an auction before a realistic value can be determined. The potential market for such a coin may be extremely small, so rarity does not necessarily equate with a higher than normal value.

A Jefferson war nickel with a "Dollar Sign" die crack.

Q: What is a "flagpole" on a Jefferson nickel?

You've run afoul of one of the many nicknames applied over the years to various minting varieties. In this case it refers to a die crack from the upper rim to the top of the dome of Monticello. It got the name because the die crack resembled a flagpole on the dome. Sometimes these cracks will continue on down across the coin to the lower edge. On the San Francisco minted war nickels (1942-S through 1945-S) with the die crack running through the S mintmark the variety was sometimes referred to as a "dollar sign."

Q: I have a 1942 cent that has an off center strike with a 1943 date. What is it worth?
Very probably nothing. The publicity surrounding the 1943 cents on brass planchets spawned hundreds of fake "errors," and yours sounds like one of the typical fakes produced then and later. The hard steel cents were found to be ideal for making so called "soft" dies, using the coin as a pattern. These fake dies were used in a variety of ways, including overstrikes on cents of many different dates, dated both before and AFTER 1943. They were also used for making fake bi-denominational coins—cents struck on struck dimes, etc., with some new examples of these turning up as recently as the early 1980s. Many of these fakes are undoubtedly ticking away in collections all over, and eventually may come to light again to haunt the hobby.

A 1983 cent, showing strong doubling.

Q: It's been some time and I need you to please tell me what the 1983 and 1984 cent hubbing varieties look like? (Many readers)
The 1983 hub doubled cent has the ENTIRE reverse design doubled, meaning that everything on the reverse of the coin is doubled. The 1984-cent variety has the lower portion of Lincoln's ear doubled very strongly.

Q: I have a 1941-S cent that has a large date and mintmark. Why isn't there a premium for it?
First of all, there is a large and a small mintmark, but not a large and small date for the 1941-S cent. The principal reason why there is little attention paid to the two mintmark varieties for 1941 and several other years is because the two are found in roughly equal quantities. When one variety is much more rare or more scare than the other, then there is usually a significant difference in price and more hobby attention.

Q: Why do off center strikes or wrong planchet strikes show more design detail than regular strikes?
It's because the striking pressure is concentrated on a smaller area, or perhaps a softer planchet. For example, a Jefferson nickel struck on a cent planchet usually shows all six steps.

Q: Were any of the War nickels accidentally struck on a copper-nickel alloy planchet?
Several of them have been reported over the years. Two that are documented are a 1942-S in the Herstel collection, which sold in 1974 for $11,000. The coin was struck in the pre-war copper-nickel alloy. There is also a 1943-P that Bowers and Ruddy sold in 1974 for $1,450.

Q: I have a coin with the obverse quite a bit off center but the reverse is normal and the coin has a normal edge. How does this happen?
This is classed as a misaligned obverse die. The reverse die can also be offset, usually in a different direction, but the key point is that the coin was struck in the collar. One very common and minor problem in the minting process is a slight misalignment of the die, which allows some of the coin metal to squeeze between the edge of the die and the collar, forming a double rim.

Q: One source lists several varieties of the early half dollars that have only 12 arrows, rather than the usual 13. Is this a variety or not?

The missing arrow, especially on the 1801 and 1802 half dollars, is due to abrasion of the die, which cut away one of the arrows. Walter Breen notes that some of these appear with the arrowhead missing and the shaft still showing, or with the entire arrow missing, but as an abrasion variety they would not have any particular importance.

Q: Are there large and small S mintmarks on the 1979 and 1981 proof coins?

The confusion arose due to one dealer comparing them to various large and small mintmarks that had been used in the past. There is no difference in size for the two dates, but there were different punches for the mintmarks.

Q: What ever happened to that triple struck gold 1904 double eagle?

The piece, which was discovered in 1973, turned out to be an altered coin. Oddly enough, it came out of a "mint sealed" bag found at a Swiss bank.

Q: I ran across a definition for "oversize" coins that I question. What do you think?

One of the reasons for my repeated advice to use technical information about coins that are of recent vintage is this very problem. The definition quoted three or four decades ago for oversize coins was that excessive pressure caused the collar to "expand," resulting in an oversize coin. We know today that this is a physical impossibility, since the collar is a thick, heavy metal plate with a hole in it the size of the intended coin. The collar may crack, or chip, but a force great enough to "expand" the collar would ruin the whole coin press. The actual cause in this case is that the collar was retracted, allowing the coin to expand unchecked, forming what is known as a broadstrike.

Q: How do you tell the difference between the large and small letter Flying Eagle cents without having one of each variety to compare?

Small and large are relative sizes but they do need to be compared, unless there are specific markers on the coin. In this case there is a very obvious marker, as on the small letter variety the A and M in AMERICA are separated. On the large letter variety the AM is joined at the base.

Q: Are the later date half dollars with missing drapery at the elbow from the same cause as the 1839 variety?

The 1839 "no drapery" half is from a design which did not include the drapery. Later dates coins missing the drapery are abrasion varieties, resulting from the shallow design being removed from the die by wear or the normal abrasion that all dies are subjected to if they remain in service long enough. As with all abrasion varieties, they are common, tending to repeat in the same place on many dies.

Q: Are there any Liberty Seated half dollars with misspellings?

The only coin that comes close is the 1859-S half dollar, which has a die break that makes the F in HALF into an E, so that it reads HALE.

Q: I sent you a description of my minting variety and you told me what the coin was. Now a coin dealer says it is something else. What do I do now?

A frustrating question, since I relied on the accuracy of your description, while the dealer has seen the actual coin. But, is the dealer qualified to identify the coin? One of us may be right, or we both may be wrong. Best advice is to seek another opinion, preferably from someone expert on the particular series.

Q: I have a dime struck on a cent planchet that I would like to have evaluated to find out what it is worth.

Several recent questions along this line point up the never-ending need to educate collectors about the details of the minting process. In this case, it means that it can't happen, so the piece is undoubtedly either a fake or as a last resort something that was deliberately "helped" at the mint. There is a very simple law of physics that applies to wrong planchet strikes. The rule is that a coin can be struck on a planchet the same size or smaller than the normal planchet, but it cannot be struck on a larger planchet. A cent can be struck on a dime planchet, but a dime cannot be struck on a cent planchet, or for that matter a planchet for any other current U.S. coin because they are all larger than the dime.

Q: I have been offered a substantial sum for a coin I have, which catalogs for much less. Should I take the money?

There are at least two schools of thought on this, one believing that you should take everything you can get and run. Another view is concerned with the moral and legal technicalities, since when your buyer discovers he has paid too much he is very likely to turn around and sue you, putting the burden of proving that you didn't fraudulently misrepresent the coin on your shoulders. This has been a longstanding problem in the minting variety field because few dealers and collectors know anything about them. It's probably best in the long run to temper your greed.

Q: It's been some time since I checked the proof set listings, so I was surprised to find two types listed for three dates - 1942, 1979 and 1981. Please explain?

The 1942 sets contained either the copper-nickel nickel with small mintmark, or the silver nickel with large mintmark. The 1979 and 1981 sets also have different shaped mintmarks; so all three years have mintmark related varieties. In all three cases the variety or "Type" II is more rare and more valuable.

Q: I have a 1979 proof set with just four of the six coins with the variety II mintmark. Is this more rare than the six-coin set?

It's more common. An estimated 350,000 sets were issued with all six coins with the variety II mintmark, while mintages of the individual coins ranged up to nearly one million. Many collectors have collected a number of sets with different combinations of the two varieties, an interesting variation in itself. Prices quoted have from the start been quoted for a full set of six coins with the same mintmark type, but there are plenty of mixed sets out there. You can figure the rough value of a mixed set by taking the individual Type II coin prices and adding them up.

Q: I have a 1988-P dime that has extensive doubling of the obverse, bust, lettering, date, etc. Is this a doubled die?

I've examined one of these, and had reports of a couple more, but they have turned out to be very heavy abrasion doubling, rather than being a doubled die. The heavy abrasion of the die results in "ripples" in the coin surface, with raised ridges across the ripples roughly matching the outline of the design, but usually separated from it. Other similar forms of abrasion doubling occur around the letters and digits, forming a slope from the edges down to the field. In one case this was so pronounced that it made the mintmark ("P") look like a small letter on top of a large letter. The clad alloy used for dimes is very abrasive and the die faces wear quite rapidly. This damage has to be abraded away with an abrasive to extend die life, so abrasion doubling is a frequent occurrence, with no collector value.

Q: What is a "positional variety?"

The term is applied to a variety created by a difference in position of one or more design elements, such as the date or motto. One example would be a mintmark punched into the die so that it is touching some other element of the design, such as a date digit. Another would be the near and far date 1979-P Anthony dollars and other similar coins.

Q: Is it true that there is a $20 gold piece known that was struck on a cent planchet?

The late Maurice Gould once owned such a coin. To the best of my knowledge it is unique, and I have no idea where it is at the present time.

Q: While searching through quantities of recent cents I've noted several with small areas of the field that are much brighter than the rest. What's the specific cause of this different appearance?

The small bright areas you have found are from repair work to the die. A fine abrasive is used to remove wear and damage from the die surface. If a very fine abrasive is used on the die the area of the coin will appear almost polished. These are very common and have no collector value. It points up another area where collectors and dealers frequently use the wrong term. Circulation dies are abraded, while proof dies are polished. The intent is repair work on the circulating die and to produce a mirror finish on the proof die.

Q: I have a coin that has the date (and most letters) much larger than normal. Is this a large date variety?

It's a frequently overlooked form of the changes that die abrasion can accomplish. In this case an attempt was made to extend the die life by going into the date and letters and deepening and widening them in the die. Die abrasion, thus, can be the cause of both very small, thin letters and large, thick letters.

Q: What can you tell me about the 1965 "double dot" cent?

These were coins with two large dots on the reverse. They were heavily promoted at the time, but were actually of only minor value to specialty collectors. The interest in any dot-sized relief design traces to the official use of dots on Canadian coinage. Die gouges or small die breaks that appear as dots occur frequently on coins, and to have any collector value they must be as large as those in E PLURIBUS on the cent.

Q: Why are there holes in my coin boards for 1922 No-D cents, 1955 and 1972 doubled dies, but not for three- and four-ray 1935 dollars?

In a word, collector popularity. The first three coins and a number of other minting varieties are of interest to enough collectors so that they are included in the coin boards and albums. The manufacturers do regular surveys of their customers to find out which varieties they want included in future issues. If enough collectors want the two-ray varieties it would be considered for inclusion.

Q: Were there any minting variety collectors prior to 1950?

They were few and far between. About the only varieties that were seriously collected were overdates. To put the numbers in perspective, a B. Max Mehl catalog from 1923, lists "Lot 1786 - small cents, mostly of Lincoln, struck off center, fine to uncirculated, mostly of the best. 14 pieces 10 cents."

Q: I have an MS-60 silver coin that has a dark streak across it, apparently in the coin metal when it was struck. Would it help to clean the coin?

Definitely not! All you would do would be to ruin an MS-60 coin. Depending on the coin and the size of the streak, it may well be worth a premium as a minting variety - just as it is.

Q: I have some minting varieties and errors, some of which are worth more than $50 each, which I want to donate for a tax benefit. I have a letter from an organization, which solicits coins for handicapped children. Would this be the best place to send them?

I've never heard of the organization you named in your letter, so I can't comment on their qualifications, but such a group is not likely to have anyone available who would know what your coins are, what they are worth, or how to go about teaching children to collect them. A suggestion to put them to direct use for research and display would be to donate them to The American Numismatic Association or to CONECA. Both are non-profit clubs that can provide you with a receipt to use as a tax deduction. Contact the clubs first for shipping instructions.

Q: I have discovered a coin from a hub-doubled die, but it takes very high magnification to see it. Will it be valuable?

If it takes high magnification to see the doubling on your coin it probably will not be a variety with any significant value. The general rule is that the easier the doubling (or any other minting variety) can be seen, the more value it will have. Generally, if you can't see it with 10 X magnification, it isn't going to be worth anything to collectors. Many novice collectors make the mistake of using a school microscope with 600 or 1200 X magnification, which is far too strong. The maximum practical magnification for most coin work is 30 X to 40 X.

Q: I have an 1839-C $2.50 gold coin with doubled 39/39. Any idea of any extra value?

Walter Breen notes that this is the most common of the three varieties of the 1839-C, the other two being overdates, 39/38. Thus, in this particular case there would be no premium, although usually a repunched, recut or double-hubbed date will bring at least a 10 percent premium.

Q: With billion-plus mintages, the days of coin discoveries in your pocket change are over, aren't they?

I could give you a good-sized list of private collectors who have found very exciting and valuable coins in their change, especially some of the minting varieties of the last decades. There have been over mintmarks (D/S), several major hubbing varieties (doubled dies), the missing P mintmark on the 1982-P dimes and others that have made looking for minting varieties in your change a worthwhile effort—but you've got to learn what to look for.

Q: I have a 1957 dime with four corners or "ears" equally spaced around the coin. What caused this?

Too neat to be a minting variety, so the most likely answer is that you own an altered coin. It is a candidate for the smelting furnace for its bullion content.

Q: You refer to a class of broadstrikes as uncentered. Is that the best choice of words?

Not when you check the dictionary. Uncenter means to "take from the center," while I really mean decenter, which means to be off center, or eccentric.

A 1955 hub-doubled cent.

Q: Were there really 300 million of the 1955 hub-doubled cents struck?

If there had been, the coins would be worth a lot less than the current $33,500 in MS-65. Actually there was but one die involved, limiting the maximum mintage to the approximate die life of one million (or less) coins, so the published reports using that 300 million figure were for once grossly exaggerated. Mintage estimates of similar rarities tend to be self serving, and generally are lower than the actual mintage, although there almost never is an opportunity to obtain any really accurate figures on the numbers of a given minting variety. One commonly used but unsubstantiated figure is that only 20,000 of them were struck. There are a number of myths surrounding the 1955 doubled die cent, and that 20,000 figure is one of them that keeps cropping up even though it was debunked long ago. It probably traces to an incorrect claim by one author that cent die life was only 20,000 coins per die, at a time when the actual figure was closer to half a million. It is much more likely that several hundred thousand of the coins were struck from that one doubled die.

Q: I've found a coin with a minting variety. How many of this particular variety were minted?

There is no way of knowing how many of this or almost any minting variety have been struck as the very fact that they reached circulation shows that they escaped detection and thus counting at the Mint. All we can do is make an educated guess, based on the reports that come in, of the pieces being discovered. Even then they are likely to be a very small fraction of the ones that actually reached circulation. This is because most collectors are secretive about what they have to avoid attracting unwelcome attention from the criminal element. Treat any flat statement of numbers in connection with most minting varieties with the skepticism it deserves.

Q: You mentioned a coin that had considerable value because of a minting variety, but you said most of the coins were worth only a few cents. Would it be worth having my two coins authenticated to see if they are worth more than the minimum figure?

I quoted the catalog value of the coin, a figure that you can check in each issue. While this is not a fixed price that dealers are forced to honor, it does represent the average retail value for that particular coin. Therefore, it would be pointless to spend $5 or $10 or more for each coin to have them authenticated, only to find out that, yes, it is an MS-60 uncirculated coin, which retails for about $1.

Q: As a new collector I'm puzzled by the references to collectors searching through thousands of uncirculated or circulated coins every day. What's the point if you can't sell the coins you find?

A substantial number of collectors got their start in just this fashion, looking through as many coins as they could get their hands on. The first several years I was in the hobby I looked at an average of about 3,000 coins a day - every day. This was back in the early 1960s when you could still find Mercury dimes, Buffalo nickels, Indian Head cents and even Walking Liberty halves in your change. Even so, there was very little market for such coins, because anybody who wanted to spend the time could find the very same coins. Today there is even less chance to find "keepers," but collectors still look because it is excellent training for the eyes, learning more and more about how to grade coins and how to spot those that have been altered or damaged. There still is the opportunity of finding a valuable minting variety too, but the main point is that most collectors who look at lots of coins do so for the potential thrill of discovery, not specifically for profit.

Q: Are hub-doubled die varieties as rare as some of the prices would indicate?

With today's high mintages, there is bound to be some skepticism, but most are at least scarce, and some meet the rarity standards, even though well over a thousand U.S. coin dies with some form of hub doubling have been cataloged. Hundreds of these hub-doubled dies have such minor doubling or show master die doubling so they have little or no collector value. You may find "hub doubling" offered without the explanation that it is master die doubling. Before you buy, learn enough about hub-doubled dies to avoid traps like this. A hub-doubled die is a legitimate minting variety, but a "double" die can be anything such as abrasion doubling, machine doubling damage or other worthless or near-worthless form of doubling. Use "hub doubling" and avoid problems.

Q: My coin book says to watch out for doublers of the 1955 doubled die. How can you run ads for such coins if they are counterfeits?

This reader has run afoul of the secret language of coin collecting. He is either misquoting his coin book or it is one that is badly outdated, as there is no such term as "doublers." The 1955-cent variety is from a hub-doubled die and it is a legitimate minting variety. There are abrasion doubling varieties which are similar but which have only a few cents value, and there are counterfeits, but we do not carry ads for counterfeit coins, as they are illegal to own.

Q: I have an old silver coin which has a cloth pattern lightly etched into part of the surface on one side. Is this a minting variety?

Probably not, as a coin struck through cloth will display a readily visible and distinctly indented surface with the pattern of the weave. One possible cause for your coin could be that the coin was stored in an album with cloth covers, the cloth picking up acids from handling and then coming in contact with the coin. Or it could simply be that it came in contact with a piece of cloth that had acid on it. The oils on your hands are acidic enough to etch your fingerprint on a coin, which is why you should hold a coin by the edge, never by the face.

Q: Were there really silver bars issued commemorating the "double strike" 1955/1955 and 1972/1972 cents?

There were, and just as with many of the reports of the coins, the titles of the bars are wrong. The 1955 and 1972 cents with doubled obverses are both single strikes with hub-doubled dies, not "double strikes."

Q: I'm tired of collecting coins that have multi-billion mintages. Are there any modern rare coins, or should I try collecting something else?

You are certainly not alone in feeling that way, but there are several possibilities in coin collecting that you may not have considered. For instance, collecting minting varieties is a steadily growing area of coin collecting, for the very reason you cite. Collectible minting varieties are almost always far scarcer, with much lower mintages. While collecting multi-billion mintage U.S. coins may be boring, have you thought about world coins? Many foreign circulation and proof strikes have mintages under 1,000.

Q: Is there an official count of the 1972 hub-doubled cents?

Like almost every minting variety there is no official count, because the coins were not spotted before they left the mint. At least nine dies, including one with master die doubling, are known for the date from Philadelphia, plus several from Denver. The die designated as #1 had an estimated die life of 50,000 to 100,000 strikes. Those figures are likely to be rather conservative, as normal die life at the time was about a million strikes per die pair. At one time we listed 18 dies for Philadelphia, but after further study, John Wexler and I determined that several of the listings were stages of the same dies, so the number was narrowed down to nine. The one with master die doubling has doubling, which appears on half of all the 1972 cents from all three mints.

Q: Are there any examples of U.S. coins with a letter on top of a different design element?

One listing I have is for the 1795 half dollar. The engraver cut the Y in LIBERTY over one of the stars. The variety is shown in Overton's book on the early half dollars. This is a relatively rare minting variety, as I know of only a couple of other instances on world coins.

Q: Several years ago a major auction house sold a 1970-S proof quarter struck on a 1900 Barber quarter that had been cut down. What would be the status of such a minting variety?

In a word, "helped." It's merely one more of the numerous deliberate minting varieties, including a 1970-S proof dime struck on a 1930s New Mexico tax token, that was struck and smuggled out of the San Francisco Mint in that year. They make interesting conversation pieces, but they have no place in a collection of legitimate minting varieties.

Q: I have two coins with the same minting variety, purchased from two different (reputable) sources, but with completely different descriptions. How is this possible?

Minting variety "language" is just one area of the hobby where such problems occur. We are a long way from any language standards for the hobby. Ask a dozen experts to describe a coin and you are likely to get 12 different answers.

Q: How many coins on unplated zinc cent planchets have been officially reported?

None have ever been officially reported, if you mean by the Mint. The fact that the pieces have turned up in circulation proves that they escaped detection - and official counting - in the mints. Any numbers that you see are unofficial guesses based on the quantities that appear in the marketplace. This figure usually represents only a fraction of those that occur. It is likely that dozens, if not hundreds of pieces occur each year, given the billions of cents struck each year. One further note, it is possible to remove the copper plating, so authentication of the piece by a minting variety specialist is mandatory.

Q: I've seen stories relating to the unique 1794 U.S. dollar struck in copper. I thought there were two such coins?

There are, but one is a different minting variety than the other. One is a true example of a trial piece as it was struck with an incomplete obverse die, which did not have the stars punched in. This die was never used for striking the circulation dollars, but the piece has the same reverse as the circulating dollars. The other coin is a "regular dies trial piece," struck with a different obverse die and the same reverse die, both used for striking the 1794 dollars. Thus, both pieces are unique, but in their own class.

Q: Why were there so many die defects - die breaks, die cracks, etc., - on the cents back in the 1950s?

This is a composite of frequent questions, and the general answer for a number of minting varieties is that the Mint was going through one of its periods of die steel problems. For instance, you will find that many of the 1954 coins have very poor strikes due to the die steel wearing rapidly, or distorting from the pounding. The 1955 cents especially are noted for the numerous die cracks, chips and breaks.

Q: Is it possible that I have a partially plated zinc cent? I've heard of full, unplated ones, but not partials.

The plated coins are turning up in all percentages of missing copper plating, from 0 to 100 percent, so yours is just one of the group. The catch is that you have to have your coin authenticated so that there's no question of the plating having been removed with acid or by other means. It takes an expert to confirm whether a zinc cent has been altered or if it came that way from the mint.

Q: I found a new minting variety and showed it to a local coin dealer. He offered me several hundred dollars for it, and a fellow collector offered even more. Should I sell it, or do I need to get it authenticated?

The track record for finds like this in an overwhelming number of cases is that neither the dealer nor the collector knew what they were buying, and the coin itself usually turns out to be worthless or worth only a small fraction of the offers. My advice, as for the previous question, is to get the coin authenticated, to avoid the very real possibility that your buyer finds out the true value and sues you for fraud. The temptation to take the money and run is very great, but hazardous. This is a major problem in Internet auctions, where often neither the seller nor the buyer knows what the piece is really worth.

Q: I have several dozen 1999, 2000 and 2001 coins from hub-doubled dies. Where can I sell them?

Unless you are an experienced collector, an unusual quantity of several dates - in this case more than one or two specimens of each date - sets off the alarm bells, because it is highly unlikely that any one collector would be that lucky. The overwhelming odds are that you have the most common form of doubling - worthless machine doubling damage. The solution is to get a couple of the coins authenticated by a specialist to find out what you have.

Chapter 47

MINTMARKS

Mintmarks are important to collectors to identify specific coin mintages. They have only minor importance - other than prestige - to the Mint, so we have to take that into account when discussing their place in numismatics.

Q: Are there large mintmarks on some 1974-S cents?

There are some that are slightly larger than normal, but the difference isn't enough to affect the value of the coin. This is because the cause was excess punching pressure, not the use of a different letter punch as was the case with the 1979-S and 1981-S proof coins.

Q: I have two nickels, which have the same date but different size mintmarks. Are these collectible?

The difference in size of the mintmarks may be due either to a heavy punching of the letter into one die, which will increase the size as the sides of the letter on the punch are tapered, or it may be due to abrasion of the die which can enlarge the letters. In either case there is no extra collector value.

To have collector value the different size letters would have to involve different punches, rather than a single punch used in different ways. There was a 1975-D die with a mintmark, which had been punched in very heavily, making it larger than normal. At the time I reported it to the hobby I described it as a "super D." This does not affect the value, because by definition a large or small mintmark must be from a different punch, which itself is larger or smaller.

A 1922 No-D cent, the result of heavy abrasion of the die.

Q: Is the same cause responsible for the 1922 "No-D" cent and the 1982 "No-P" dime?

Not at all. The 1922 cents without mintmarks are the result either of a filled die (dirt and grease in the letter in the die) or heavy abrasion of the die, which cut the field below the incuse "D." The 1982 dimes came from a die, which never was punched with the P mintmark. Two completely different causes.

Q: Are there any of the Pan Pacific commemorative half dollars without mintmarks?
Abe Kosoff is the source for the statement, "Several die trials were struck before the mintmark was added to the die. They were struck in copper, silver, and two in gold." The mintmark is also missing on some 1915-(S) Pan Pacific dollars and there are trial strikes of the $50 without a mintmark.

Q: I just got my first mint set. Are coins with mintmarks worth more than those without?
It's not very likely on recent coins. You need to read the mintage charts and study the prices in order to tell. On older coins you will often find very low mintages at one of the branch mints with corresponding high values.

Q: I have a cent with a D over an inverted P mintmark. What is the coin worth?
This variety has been reported elsewhere, but after examining a coin from the same die I'm certain that the cause is die abrasion and not a repunch. None of the cent dies get P mintmarks, so it would be very unlikely that there would be one punched upside down, and there is no firm evidence on the coin to back up the supposition.

Q: I read that the Mint claimed that the various large and small mintmarks before World War II were the result of wear on the punch or the die, not the use of different punches. Was that really their answer?
Chief Engraver James R. Sinnock is the man behind that statement. He is quoted as saying in a contemporary letter, in response to a direct inquiry that, "Only one punch was used for each mint during the years I have been here." This would have covered the period from about 1917 to 1940 during which there were both changes in the size of the mintmarks used, and several well documented cases of two different size mintmark punches in the same year, such as the 1928-S cents and dimes. With this and other comments in his letters, it is apparent that Sinnock was not nearly as familiar as he should have been with the die-making process.

Q: Several coins I have carry different size or shape mintmarks. Aren't they all supposed to be the same?
Not at all. The Mint has used a number of different size and shape mintmarks, at one time having special punches for each denomination, including the gold coins. In the 1950s the punches were standardized, with a single punch being used for all denominations, until the larger D punch was instituted for the 1985-D cent. They could have used larger punches on the State quarters, which are too small to read easily.

Q: Do all of the SBA dollars have a mintmark - even the Philadelphia strikes?
The first SBA dollars, struck in 1979 at Philadelphia, carried the P mintmark, as did all the rest struck there until production was stopped in 1982. San Francisco put its "S" on both proofs and circulation strikes, and Denver on all the circulation strikes there. The SBA dollar and the silver war nickels of 1942 through 1945 are the only two series struck in their entirety with mintmarks on every coin. The idea reportedly traced to then Mint Director Stella Hackle who ordered the mintmark added to the Anthony dollars to make the public more aware of the Philadelphia facility and the work that is done there. While this was the public position, the root cause undoubtedly was an effort to attract more attention to the Anthony dollars to get the public interested in using them. The intent at the time incidentally was to just put the mintmark on the dollar in 1979 and at some future date to possibly add it to the other Philadelphia coins. That decision was modified in 1980 when the mintmark was added to all of the coins except the cent.

The "O" signifies the New Orleans Mint.

Q: Why didn't they use an "N" for the New Orleans Mint instead of the "O" mintmark when it opened in 1838?

Although I'm unaware of any official statement on the matter, it is easy to assume that rather than use an "N," which would create a conflict with other possible mint sites such as New York, the "O" was used instead. "New" is considered a prefix, just like East or West, and, thus, Orleans is the principal name of the city. I'm going to guess it was named after Orleans, France.

Q: Won't the Mint's practice of putting the mintmark on the hub eliminate mintmark varieties?

It will eliminate some, but not all. It is entirely possible, as demonstrated on a number of German coins with hubbed mint marks, to get doubled mintmark letters when hub doubling occurs, so don't give up on checking the mintmark.

Q: In the articles you carried reporting the discovery of the 1990 No-S proof cent you mentioned several other earlier dates without mintmarks. I have most of them, so where do I sell them?

Look again, and I think you will find that your coins are circulation strikes from Philadelphia, and not the proof coins, which are struck only at San Francisco. If your coins don't have a bright, mirror field, then they are probably not proofs. The one exception to the all-proof rule is the 1982 circulation dime without the P mintmark, because that is the only instance since they began adding mintmarks to all Philadelphia coins (except the cent) in 1979 and 1980. Circulation strike coins of all denominations prior to 1980 (except the 1942 through 1945 nickels and 1979-P Anthony dollars) were struck without mintmarks at Philadelphia, and cents were also struck without mintmarks at both West Point and San Francisco.

Q: Which coin has the record for the number of mintmark positions?

The half dollar is on top of the list. The 1838 mintmark was on the obverse. In 1840 it was moved to the reverse. It went back to the obverse in 1916, to the reverse in 1917, and returned to the obverse in 1968.

Q: I have a 1945 silver nickel, which has no mintmark. Is this a rarity?

It may be, but it may also be a counterfeit from the same source as the multitude of 1944 nickels struck without mintmarks. Get the coin authenticated, as there are several possible causes for it being a genuine minting variety, as well as other possibilities of its being altered or faked. Francis L. Henning, the man who faked the notorious 1944 nickels without mintmarks, also made several other dates.

Q: What was the effect of the U.S. Mint putting the mintmark on the hub?

The long overdue step was made over nearly a decade, first on the commemorative coins in 1982 or 1983, then the proof coins and in 1990-91 on the circulating coins. Rather than punching a letter into each die, with the location depending on the clear eye and steady hand of the die sinker, putting one on the hub means proper placement on every die, eliminating most doubled mintmarks. We still get an occasional hub-doubled mintmark, but the days of dozens of dies with repunched and over mintmarks are pretty much over. Most otherworld mints have long since gone to this practice.

Q: I have a 1943 cent without a mintmark. Is it worth anything?

Contrary to a Paul Harvey report that "1943 cents without a mintmark are worth $250,000," they are, in almost all cases, worth less than 25 cents.

The Philadelphia Mint struck more than 600 million 1943 zinc-plated steel cents. The vast majority of the survivors are rusted or corroded, making them nearly worthless. Harvey's report was a garbled version of an even more garbled Associated Press story, which grossly inflated the value of a "missing" 1943 cent. The only valuable ones are the two dozen known coins that were accidentally struck on leftover brass planchets from 1942. Thousands of altered dates, counterfeits and copper-plated steel coins flood the market. Test any supposed brass cent with a magnet. If it's attracted it has been copper plated outside the mint and is worthless to collectors.

Q: Is there more than one variety of the blob S that appeared on the 1979-S proof coins?

There are variations, but there is only one variety. So how's that for an ambiguous answer? Actually the facts are that every die for the early 1979-S proof coinage - for all six coins - had the mintmark punched in with the same punch, meaning one variety. This despite the fact that variations in punching pressure and abrasion of the die will change the appearance of the letter, but that doesn't make it a different variety. When that one punch broke, a new punch with a clear S was made and used for a minority of the 1979-S proof coins, the ones with the Variety II mintmark, which carry a premium. Don't be mislead by catalogs which describe the blob as a "filled" S. "Filled" really means that the S is missing from the coin, which is not what the cataloger intends. Easiest to understand is worn or 'blob' S and clear S.

Q: When was the mintmark moved to the obverse of the Jefferson nickel?

The U.S. Mint dropped all mintmarks from 1965 through 1967. When they were restored in 1968 all the denominations moved the mintmark to the obverse to join the cent for uniformity. The first U.S. coins with an obverse mintmark were the half dollars of 1838 with the O directly below the bust.

Q: I just noticed that the cent in my mint-packaged set doesn't have a mintmark. Is this worth something extra?

None of the Philadelphia cents carry a mintmark. The Philadelphia Mint has never put a mintmark on any of the cents that it has struck since 1793. The reports on the 1990 proof cents, which were struck without the S mintmark, have triggered a lot of confusion over the circulating cents. Proof coins have a mirror surface and are normally found only in sets packaged in hard plastic. They are not normally found in circulation, so if you find a cent in your pocket change or a mint set without a mintmark it's a normal Philadelphia cent. All other denominations struck at Philadelphia carry a "P" mintmark. The Philadelphia Mint has not used a mintmark on the cent because cents - also without mintmarks - were struck for a time at San Francisco and at West Point.

Q: I've seen several ads offering 2003-P cents, but I thought the Philadelphia Mint wasn't using a mintmark on the cents?

You are right, and the ads are wrong. All coins except the cent now bear the "P" mintmark, but it is so much of a habit for dealers to list Philadelphia coins with a P after the date that you just can't get them to change. The accepted way to list them is in parenthesis as (P). This is a standard way of indicating a date or mintmark that does not appear on the coin or banknote.

Q: The Mint used arrows to designate a change of weight or standards for our coins. Are there any other such symbols that have been used?

The one that comes to mind is the switch to the oversize mintmarks added to the 1942 through 1945 silver-alloy wartime nickels to distinguish them from the copper-nickel alloy used before and after World War II.

Q: Is there a series of U.S. coins with the mintmark on different sides in the same year?

The 1917-D and 1917-S Walking Liberty halves started 1917 with the mintmark on the reverse. When the design was modified, the mintmarks were moved to the obverse.

A 1912-D or 1912-S V nickel.

Q: Where do you find the mintmark on the Liberty Head, or "V" nickels? I've looked at hundreds and have never been able to find one with a mintmark.

The mintmark is on the reverse between the dot at the lower left and the rim. The principal reason why you haven't found a mintmark is that they only appeared on the coin for a single year (1912) and total production was less than nine million, so they are relatively scarce.

Q: The Philadelphia Mint only used the "P" mintmark for the 1942 through 1945 nickels, and beginning in 1979 on the SBA dollar, and in 1980 on other coins except the cent. Was this true for medals?

The Philadelphia Mint has used a "P" mintmark on some foreign coins, and on some medals struck in other years. The P turned up on a variety of coins (and medals) struck for foreign governments. As early as 1941 the P went on the Dutch East Indies 1/10 and 1/4 gulden and appeared on several wartime Netherlands issues, and for Curacao and Surinam. The American Revolution Bicentennial Medals have a P mintmark.

Chapter 48

MINT MEDALS

Few non-collectors know that the U.S. Mint strikes medals in several categories. The ones most often run into are from the Presidential series. The Mint's medal catalog is an eye opener.

A John Wayne medal.

Q: Which one of the U.S. Mint medals has been their best seller?

One of the top selling medals was the John Wayne medal, authorized May 26, 1979, less than three weeks before Wayne died. In the first year the U.S. Mint received nearly half a million orders for the two different bronze medals. The single gold specimen was presented to Wayne's family on March 6, 1980. That piece contained 15 troy ounces of .999 gold. The Mint does not have accurate total figures for the sale of its medals, as they remain in stock indefinitely and new supplies are struck as those on hand are sold.

Chapter 49

MINT SETS

There are mint sets and mint sets. The distinction rests on who put the sets together and packaged them. A mint-packaged mint set is the ultimate for a collector.

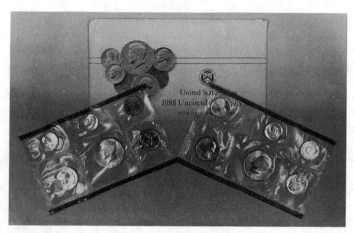

A mint-packaged mint set.

Q: What is the difference between a mint set and a mint-packaged set?

A mint set is defined as a group of coins for one year from one mint, usually including all the coins struck in that year at that mint. A mint-packaged set is the same, except that the government mint specifically packaged it. The key difference is that anyone can assemble (and sell) a mint set.

Q: What constitutes a mint set, just the plastic envelope, or must the brown paper envelope be included as well?

This argument has been going on for a long time, but the best and final answer is that the coins constitute the mint set. Whether the plastic envelope in which the coins are sealed is there, or the brown paper envelope it came in or the box it was shipped in are desirable is a matter of personal choice, but the final value of the set depends strictly on the coins.

Chapter 50

MORGAN DOLLARS

No dear, not the pirate. In this case, the designer whose name replaced "Bland" as the identifier of the dollars struck from 1878 to 1921.

Q: How many dies were used to strike the rare 1895 proof Morgan dollars?

Walter Breen lists a total of five obverses. Authenticators at the American Numismatic Association in 1985 listed four different dies, an unusually high number for the miniscule proof mintage of 880. At least three of the dates on the dies tilt up to the right, so identification must be made by the location of the digits over the denticles. Several of the 1895-O and 1895-S dollars have dates in identical locations, so the position alone is not enough to authenticate the coin. Removing the mintmark frequently alters the branch mint coins.

Q: Is my memory failing me, or did the coin dealers once offer Morgan dollars that had the design frosted after they were struck?

Just as with the 1943 steel cents, the dollars were processed to improve their appearance. Apparently the process was copied from the methods used at the Mint where the design area of the die was sandblasted with the field given a protective covering. This was done to the coins, and, of course, under present standards is considered to be an alteration, eliminating any collector value the piece might have. This doesn't mean that these pieces aren't still around, so never buy a "frosted" coin without checking it closely with a magnifier. Fine grain sandblasting can be easily overlooked with the unaided eye. There are also plated dollars around.

Q: Why were there so many changes, or differences, in the 1921 Morgan dollars from those struck in 1904?

The blame falls on the then Secretary of the Treasury, Frank MacVeagh, who issued a directive in 1910 that all of the models, hubs and dies for the dollar be destroyed. At the time he was going on the presumption that the silver dollar, as unwanted then as it is now, would never be struck again. This meant that when production was resumed in 1921 it was necessary to start at the beginning, copying the dollar design and going through all the steps as if it were a new coin.

Q: Did they make thimbles from silver dollars at one time?

A book printed in 1888 describes the process. Coins were melted, rolled to thickness, cut out with a circular punch and shaped over a metal bar. Most of the readily available coins of that era would have been Morgan dollars.

Q: What was the date of the first strike of the Morgan dollars?

There are two conflicting dates cited. Several sources say that the first strike occurred on March 12, 1878. The Chicago Tribune story, which went into considerable detail, however, said that it was the afternoon of March 11, 1878. When I get my time machine I'll go check.

Q: How come the weird looking lettering for "IN GOD WE TRUST" on the Morgan dollar?

This is an example of Old English, or Gothic lettering, and it was the first time it was used on a United States coin. As to why he used it, the reason is lost to us, so we have to write it off as artistic license by the engraver.

Q: One source says the Morgan dollar is unique because it has the designer's initials on both sides.

The source is wrong on several counts. One example is the Ike dollar, which has FG for Frank Gasparro on both the obverse and reverse.

Q: Any figures on the survival rate of the Morgan dollar?

If you mean the number still in existence, a starter is the fact that the Government melted down more than half of all the Morgans minted. Add to that the number melted to make thimbles, jewelry and other private uses, plus those lying at the bottom of the oceans or otherwise lost, and you can approach a guess as to how many are left.

Chapter 51

NICKNAMES AND SLANG

Samples from the secret language of the coin collector. Enough said.

Q: Why the name "muttonhead" for the Connecticut coppers of 1787 - and didn't it have another name at one time?

My references don't specifically give the reasoning behind the name, but the supposition is that it is because the bust resembles a sheep's head. Actually there were two different "muttonhead" dies. These were believed to be contemporary counterfeits, and at one time were called the "Bradford Head" variety. "Muttonhead" is a term for a stupid person, a blockhead or dolt.

Q: Is there any logic to back up the issues in the U.S. and Canada of 20-cent coins?

There's some "perfect" logic to back both coins - the 20-cent denomination is a decimal coin, as are the other denominations - while the 25-cent coin is not. However, logic fell by the wayside as the public pretty much ignored the "double dimes" as they were nicknamed, and continued to use their favorite quarters.

Q: My family frequently uses the term "brown money." Do you have any idea where this comes from?

It's quite likely that your family tree may trace its roots either to Ireland or, as a second choice, to Devonshire in England. In both places in the local dialect any copper coin was referred to as "brown money," so quite likely the term has been handed down through several generations of your family.

Q: What is meant by a "Louisiana cent?"

The term was a nickname for the French copper sou, which bore the inscription "COLONIES FRANCOISES." These pieces were struck with both 1721 and 1722 dates and were intended for exclusive use in the French colony of Louisiana, which of course at the time included most of the land between the Alleghenies and the Rocky Mountains.

Q: What is meant by a "Controller" coin?

This is a term that apparently got its start in Britain then spread to the U.S. Its somewhat hazy origin indicates it was used in financial accounting, but then became the early day counterpart of what we now call a "key" coin. The key coins and semi-keys, which incidentally were also considered to be "controller" coins in the early days, are such coins as the 1909-S VDB cent in the Lincoln cent series, the 1939-D Jefferson nickel and the 1916-D dime in the Mercury series. In general they are the more rare, or more valuable, coins in a given series, the slightly lesser value or rarity pieces being classed as semi-keys.

Q: What is a "spectacle" dollar?

This term traces to the Orient, where silver coins such as the U.S. Trade dollar were chop marked to indicate they had been tested by a merchant or bank and found to be good silver. Repeated chop marks might result in the center of the coin breaking out, leaving only the rim, vaguely similar to the steel rimmed spectacles of the day, hence the name.

Q: Where does the term "glove money" come from?

Glove money, or a bribe, is an English slang term, which grew out of the custom of sending a pair of gloves to one's legal counsel before a trial. The custom expanded to include the judge or judges who would try the case, and eventually it became a method of discreetly passing a sum of money as a bribe where the coins or notes were enclosed in the gloves. The term persisted long after the gloves were eliminated from the transaction.

Q: What does the term "catchpenny" mean?

It's an old English slang expression for a con game, or a scam for relieving the unwary or ignorant of his coppers. It was used in the American colonies, but has long since fallen into oblivion. A catchpenny is also "Made merely to sell; cheap and flashy; worthless." In other words, the pieces described were some of the numerous cheap imitations of the good coin of the era, made and sold at a discount as a profitable way of making a living at a time when real coins were hard to come by.

Q: What's a junk collector, and is this a legitimate numismatic term?

A certain element among collectors tended to be rather snobbish about other's conception of what was worth collecting. There are several other derogatory nicknames or slang terms which have cropped up in the hobby over the years. This particular term was a sarcastic nickname for those who collected low value or low-grade items. It was included in a glossary listing in the ANA Numismatist in 1945, so it could now be classed as obsolete.

Q: In a story about adventures in the 18th century in the American colonies there is a mention of a coin called a "levy," which I can't find defined anywhere. Can you help?

Levy was a corruption, or local slang for eleven pence, which was the value of the Spanish reale in some areas. Frey lists the term, and says that it was popular in Delaware, Pennsylvania, Maryland and New Jersey. Another source points out that the levy was called a shilling in the northern colonies and a bit in the southern areas. The Spanish reale was called a "nine pence" in New York.

Chapter 52

NOVELTY COINS

The problem children of the hobby. Things done with coins after they leave the mint.

Q: How do they put the cents in the little bottles?

The glass bottles come in two pieces. The coin is placed inside and then the bottom of the bottle is fused onto the top portion.

Q: What is a "capped" coin?

There are two definitions for a capped coin. One was a popular form of "novelty" coins, made by stamping a thin sheet of copper with a design and then wrapping the piece around a cent, much like a bottle cap. L. S. Werner, who donated his dies and a collection of the capped coins to the ANA Museum, made a number of these coins. The second definition is a striking variety occurring when the planchet sticks, and wraps around the die like a bottle cap. They are also known as a capped die strike.

Q: What is a "pop" coin?

A pop coin was a popular name for the novelty coins, which had been altered so that the bust "popped" out, in much higher relief than a normal coin. These have appeared on the scene at scattered intervals since around the early 1900s. A similar slang term, "pop top" coin, means one at the top of the population reports for that date and mint.

Chapter 53

OLYMPIC COINS

In recent years Olympic coins have found a huge market. The older Olympic coins are part of history.

1992 Olympic half dollar.

Q: How far back do Olympic coins go?

The first Olympic coins are attributed to mints of Zeus and Hera at Olympia in 500 BCE. One of the earliest Olympic coins honors a chariot race won by Anaxilas, the ruler of Messana in Sicily in about 480 BCE. Anaxilas issued the coin himself, a silver tetradrachm.

Q: Weren't the original Olympic games limited to women?

The Olympics are traced back to an annual women's foot race. There was a secondary men's race, with the winner named as king. It was a somewhat dubious honor as he was put to death at the next solstice.

Q: Were the Olympics always an amateur event?

Prior to the 4th century CE professional athletes dominated them. The Olympics were banned in 394 by emperor Theodosius because they violated Christian principles.

Q: What is the purpose of the specific colors for the Olympic rings?

The colors are blue, yellow, black, green and red on a white field. These are the official colors for the rings, because one or more of the six colors appear in the flag of every nation on earth. The five rings represent the five major continents.

Chapter 54

OVERDATES

The most popular misconception about overdates and over-mintmarks is that the change was made on the coin. Actually it was the die that was changed, so you need to rethink the minting process.

Q: *Is there an 1845 dime with the 5 over a 3?*

This is one of those controversial coins where there isn't enough left of the under number to determine accurately just what the original date was. Although opinion is divided, the majority opinion seems to be that it is a repunched or recut 5/5, and since the other three numbers are repunched as well, it is currently listed as an 1845/1845.

A 1918-S quarter with design hub doubling, resulting from the use of a 1918-dated hub over a 1917-dated hub. Shows the flat top of the 7 across the top of the upper loop of the 8, with the stem showing in the right upper loop and the left lower loop.

Q: *You once furnished the markers used to identify the 1918/1917-S overdate quarter. Do you still have them?*

Computer memory is a wonderful thing. Q. David Bowers notes that the genuine specimens exhibit die clashes to the left and below Liberty's knee on the obverse, and below America on the reverse. Bill Fivaz also has some detailed information for us. He notes that the die clashes are visible usually only on higher-grade coins. The 7 should show clearly under the 8, with all numbers being of the same height. If circulated, both the 8 and 7 should show equal wear, and 'in relation' to the wear on the other three digits. The conclusive diagnostic, also on lower grade specimens, is a small raised die chip on the pedestal, above the line over the date and just to the left of the lowest star on the right.

Q: *Is there any special reason why the 1918/1917-S quarter overdate is relatively rare?*

One reason given, but mostly overlooked, is the notation that the single die involved in this overdate cracked through the date at a fairly early stage and apparently was taken out of service after only a relatively small number were struck. Since die life in that era was not very high to begin with, this didn't leave very many of the coins to reach circulation. As with all of the other 20th century overdates, this is the result of using hubs with different dates to make the die, so all four digits of the date are affected, even though the piece is commonly listed as a 1918/17-S.

Q: Who is credited with the discovery of the 1862/1 $2.50 gold quarter eagle overdate?
Aubrey E. Bebee is cited as the discoverer. Reports of the find appeared simultaneously in the *Numismatic Scrapbook* magazine for January 1963 and *Numismatic News'* January 7 issue. The overdate shows the 1 as a low relief flat bar at the left side, closing the loop of the 2.

Q: Old timers in the hobby swear that there is an 1804 half dollar. As evidence they cite the mint figure of 160,000 for that year, and the well known 1805/4 overdate. Were the latter coins that were returned to the mint overstruck with a new date?
A hard story to kill, but it's completely untrue. As with the 1804 dollar, the mintage figures were for 1803 coins struck in 1804. The overdate results from a re-punching or re-engraving of an unused 1804 die to make it into an 1805. Contrary to all the old wive's tales about overdates, the change is in the die, not in the coin.

Chapter 55

PANAMA

The Panama Canal put Panama and the U.S. in the same boat. The two countries have had close ties for well over a century.

A Panama 1904 50 centesimos.

Q: Why are the Panama silver 50 centesimos so scarce?

The key reason is that they contained almost as much silver as a U.S. silver dollar (.7235 ounce compared to .7736 ounce in the dollar) so many were melted prior to World War I. A total of 2.8 billion were struck in 1904 and 1905, and on top of the pre-war melts an additional 51 million of the coins were shipped to the San Francisco Mint in 1931, where they were melted down and the silver was used to strike 1-Balboa coins. Those, interestingly enough, contained the same amount of silver as the U.S. silver dollar.

Chapter 56

PATTERNS

Here's another misunderstood area of collecting. Ninety-nine out of a hundred collectors assume that a coin with something "different" on it is a pattern. Where did they all go wrong?

1877 half dollar pattern.

Q: What's the difference between a pattern and an experimental piece?

A pattern is a piece representing a new design, motto or denomination, struck in the intended metal but not adopted for regular coinage in the dated year. An experimental piece is one struck with any dies to try new metal or alloy, new configuration, different denominations for a metal or alloy already in use, or a change in the form of the planchet. If it is in some other metal, then it is an experimental trial piece and if it is in a pattern in another metal then it is a pattern trial piece.

Q: What's the story on the 1883-dated pattern coins for Hawaii?

1883-dated patterns were struck for the 1/8th dollar, and 1884-dated patterns were struck for the quarter and half dollar. The 1/8th dollar was struck in gold, nickel and bronze. The quarter pattern was struck in platinum, gold, oride, brass and bronze. The halves came in platinum, gold and bronze. Despite the dates, someone who had access to the dies that were stored there apparently struck these patterns at the Philadelphia Mint in the early 1900s. One could wonder if it was the same person who struck the five 1913 nickels.

Q: An old reference book, besides the copper-nickel cents, mentions several dates, such as 1865, 1877 and 1881 where cents were struck in nickel. Why aren't they listed with the other cents?

For all three years - 1865, 1877 and 1881, there are examples of pattern cents struck in nickel and in other metals, so the reference in your book is to the patterns and not the regular strikes. It was not unusual for the lay press at that time to mistake patterns for coins, and they often confused even the supposed experts.

Q: Is it true that besides the 1883 no-cents nickels there were also 1882-dated versions as well?

Very little information or recognition has been given to Barber's "prototypes," which he designed and had struck in 1881 and 1882. Breen describes them as patterns, which is correct. Pollack lists both 1881 and 1882 patterns, but only the 1882 reverse matches the 1883 circulation strikes, which had UNITED STATES OF AMERICA and E PLURIBUS UNUM next to the rim. Breen and Judd say that several of the 1882 patterns circulated and were found in worn condition. Pollack states that there is a different arrangement of the stars on the 1882 pattern obverse, but a detailed comparison of photos fails to bear this out.

Q: What is the three-headed figure on the Massachusetts half cent?

It's actually a half-cent pattern, and is unique. The three-headed figure is that of the two-faced god, "Janus," as he was sometimes depicted.

Q: What's the history of the pattern 1907 $20 Indian Head gold?

The pattern, with the same design as the $10, disappeared after St. Gaudens' death in 1907. It reappeared in the early 1930s in the hands of a collector, who had obtained it from the estate of Chief Engraver Charles E. Barber who died in 1917. It went through a number of owners before being sold to King Farouk of Egypt. It was returned to the U.S. in 1954. A-Mark purchased it from the Dr. J. E. Wilkinson collection, and later loaned it to the U.S. Mint to display at the restored San Francisco Mint in 1976.

Q: Does anyone collect wallpaper patterns?

No doubt, since there are collectors for just about everything. None have come to our direct attention, but perhaps readers might know someone with this hobby. There ought to be examples with coins on them as well as there was at least one pattern showing bank notes.

Q: Please, a bet that needs to be settled. I argue that the Mint never struck a pattern for the $50 gold coins of 1855. My friend says the Mint did strike a $50 pattern. Who is right?

The bet is off as you are both right, given the two statements. The Mint didn't strike a pattern for the $50 gold coins in 1855, but it did strike such patterns in 1877, and two of the gold patterns are now in the Smithsonian Institution.

Q: What is the story on the 1868 large cent?

The pieces are considered to be test strikes, as they were made using leftover hubs from 1857, the last year of large cent production. They were used in anticipation of a new 10-cent coin, for which the dies had not been completed in time. Examples are known in copper and in nickel. Patterns, using the large cent obverse and a reverse similar to the large cent but with "TEN CENTS" in the center, were also made in the same metals. Both the cent and 10-cent pieces are dated 1868.

Q: Is there a U.S. gold pattern set that has the same design on all the pieces?

There is a single set of gold patterns, all with the same William Barber obverse, struck in 1872. It contains the $1, $2.50, $3, $5, $10 and $20 gold pieces. The set was purchased in 1973 from Dr. J. E. Wilkinson by Paramount International Coin Corp.

Q: Did the U.S. Mint ever make a pattern for a gold quarter like the California gold issues?

The smallest denomination gold coin pattern was for a 50-cent piece struck in 1852.

A $4 Stella.

Q: Old references state that the Stella weight is 108 grains, but that the restrikes weigh 103 grains. Is this correct?

That is incorrect, as the weights of the originals and the restrikes are the same - 108 grains.

Q: Stella is a pretty name for a girl. How did a coin wind up with that name?

Stella is the Latin word for star, and was applied to the $4 pattern coins. The Stella was actually a pattern for a coin intended to match several foreign gold coins. Congress failed to approve the coin, but a number of the patterns got into circulation. The Stellas were struck using a different fineness, .857 rather than the normal .900 fine. The letters and figures on the Stella indicate the amount of the three principal metals in the coin alloy - six grams of gold, 0.3 grams of silver and 0.7 grams of copper, for a total weight of seven grams.

Chapter 57

PEACE MEDALS

Remember, "Bribery will get you anywhere?" These were early bribes given to the Native Americans, now popular collectibles.

Q: Isn't the Zachary Taylor Native American Peace medal considered to be the most rare of the original strikes?

One source indicates that only 37 of the original medals survived the melting pot, making it a candidate for the rarity claim.

1877 Van Buren Indian Peace Medal.

Q: Are their counterfeits of the Indian "Peace" medals?

As with any valuable collectible there are fakes. A Native American from Nebraska is known to have made a tidy sum with copies of Washington medals dated 1789 and made of pewter and silver-plated copper. These fakes are also collected, and have become relatively valuable, although not to be confused with the modern reproductions struck and sold by the U.S. Mint. The Civil War had been over for a year when the last Peace medal was presented to Chief Hoo Ke Up of the Blackfeet in 1866. The early missionaries and fur traders issued private medals of this type, but the U.S. Secretary of War controlled such private issues later on, and in 1844 rescinded authorization of any further private issues. The government stipulated that the private issues had to be called ornaments and not medals. Since they weren't labeled most would call them medals. The earliest example of an Indian Peace medal is French, issued in 1693. Religious Indian medals were struck even earlier.

Q: Are there any Indian Peace medals that depict President John Adams?

Our sources indicate that since there was a surplus of Washington pieces, these continued to be distributed, and none were made for Adams.

Q: I know the U.S. government issued a lot of Peace medals, but how about Canada?

Canada issued far fewer Indian Peace medals, but they did issue a few. The Canadian pieces were usually smaller than the U.S. Peace medals.

Chapter 58

PHILADELPHIA MINT

The "Mother" mint. Now in a relatively modern building (the fourth), the Philadelphia Mint has a long and obviously colorful history.

Q: What were the first coins struck with the new steam-powered coin presses in 1836?
According to the Mint Director's report, "all of the copper coins were struck," beginning with successful tests on March 23, 1836. This would mean the cent, and apparently the half cent, although only proof half cents were struck that year. The first half dollars were coined with steam power on November 8, 1836.

Q: The first Assayer at the U.S. Mint in Philadelphia was actually a convicted criminal, wasn't he?
Albion Cox or Coxe avoided debtor's prison in New Jersey by grabbing a quick ship to England. Later he returned to the U.S. before assuming the office of Assayer in 1793.

"Old Peter" or a Longacre eagle.

Q: Is the Longacre eagle on the Flying Eagle cent really "Old Peter?"
Old Peter was a pet eagle at Philadelphia Mint that was killed by the machinery. However, he was not Longacre's model. Most historians agree that Longacre used a modified version of Gobrecht's eagle instead.

Q: What was the historic construction material that was used for the second Philadelphia Mint building?
Although they weren't used for the original construction, steel I-beams were used for the first time in the world during a remodeling project in 1848. The original building was constructed in 1833.

Q: What was the cost to build the second Philadelphia Mint?
The second Mint was constructed in 1833. Costs included $173,390 for machinery and buildings, $35,840 for land and paving, and $28,270 for other improvements. In very marked contrast, the Calcutta, India Mint, which also was built in 1833, cost $1,138,000.

Q: How long has the Smithsonian Institution's collection of numismatic items been in existence?
The Smithsonian Institution collection dates back to 1793 when the United States Mint at Philadelphia began saving an example of each type and date coin struck. The original Mint collection was enhanced by various means - some dubious - over the years, as a number of significant items were missing from it and were obtained by trading coins with private collectors and dealers. After the end of World War I the Mint decided to get out of the museum business and turned the collection over to the Smithsonian Institution.

Q: Were the banks the only ones who could get coins from our first mint in Philadelphia?
At that time the public could get coins directly from the Mint, just as the banks did. R. W. Julian noted a third source of coins, one that has escaped most attention. The customhouses at important harbors along the coast were also getting copper coins from the Mint and distributing them in their local areas.

Q: What happened to the Tiffany glass mosaics in the old (third) U.S. Mint at Philadelphia?
They were moved to the new (fourth) Mint in 1969. They are described as seven favrile glass objects d'art originally produced for the main entrance to the third Mint, which began operation in 1901. They depict steps in the production of Roman coins. The current value is probably well over the million dollar mark as they were appraised at $420,000 in the 1970s.

Q: Out of curiosity, what does it cost to build a mint?
The most recent U.S. Mint building was the Philadelphia Mint, which cost $39.4 million to build in 1969. The cost was raised sharply to accommodate the equipment for producing clad coinage strip. Even without that expense, it would probably cost well over $500 million now.

Q: Wasn't the present Philadelphia Mint (the fourth, constructed in 1969) intended to continue proof coinage?
Up until 1964 the Philadelphia Mint had struck almost all the proof coins issued. However, the coin shortage, capped with the failure of the roller die press, caused a change in plans. The special mint set production had already been shifted to San Francisco, which also had successfully struck proof coins for Panama, so the decision was made to convert San Francisco to proof production.

Q: Where was the Canary Cage and what did it have to do with coins?
The nickname was applied in the 1850s to the weight room at the Philadelphia Mint. The term would probably be politically insensitive today as it referred to the 50 women who worked in the room, weighing coin planchets and adjusting the weight with files.

Q: When was the last time that only one mint struck all of the circulating coins of a particular denomination for that date?
Unless I missed something, the last time this occurred was when the Philadelphia Mint struck all the Franklin halves in 1955 and 1956 - including the proofs. 1965, 1966 and 1967 coins were struck without mintmarks but at all three mints.

Q: Was the steam coin press the first use of such power at the Philadelphia Mint?
Steam was used as early as 1814 to power the rolling mill and a punch press used to make planchets. The problem was that at the time there wasn't a foundry in the U.S. that could build a steam engine large enough to meet the power needs of the Mint.

Q: How did our first mint roll out the coin metal to the proper thickness?
This was definitely a case of horse power. Prior to the adaptation of the steam-driven equipment our first mint in Philadelphia in 1792 used rolls powered by a team of horses to roll out the copper ingots into strips of metal about 2 1/4-inches wide, from which the planchets were punched. The horses were quickly replaced with oxen when it was found they couldn't handle the job.

Chapter 59

PLASTIC COINS

Plastics are everywhere, even in our coins. During World War II the Mint got serious about issuing plastic coins to save vital war material. Ironically, plastics suddenly were in short supply, which shelved the idea.

A 1942 experimental plastic cent.

Q: Did the U.S. Mint ever make any plastic coins?

In 1942 there were a number of secret experiments by commercial firms working for the Treasury Department, in Connecticut and Tennessee, using crude plastics. However, plastics quickly became a critical war material, so no action was taken on the plastic coins. There was an attempt to get an authorization bill through after the fact, but the idea was dropped.

Q: Was there more than one size or thickness of the plastic 1942 cents that the Mint made while they were experimenting with substitute materials?

Specimens of at least six different thicknesses and weights are known, ranging from 8 to 57 grains in several different colored plastics. All were the same diameter as a normal cent. One of several private manufacturers made these under contract and not by the Mint itself. The dies used were provided by the Mint, which apparently used a set to strike the experimental zinc-plated steel examples with the same date.

Q: What's the story on this plastic 10-franc coin of the West African States?

That's a good question. The piece seems to be an excellent copy, the one noticeable difference being the lettering on the reverse, "G.B.L. Bazor" on the plastic piece. The "logical answer" is that this is a piece of play money. If so, someone went to considerable trouble to make a detailed copy. My suspicion, based so far only on a hunch, is that this was one of a set made in 1959 to introduce the new coinage to the merchants and the public, similar to practice coins made and used by several other governments. The only fact supporting this is that the 10-franc was the first of the new coins to be introduced in that year, the 5-franc the following year and the 1-franc in 1961. Perhaps one or more of our readers has the facts needed to put this piece in its place.

Q: I have a piece that I have been unable to identify. It is a plastic oval, which has "KIDDY/ 6d/CASH" on one side. On the other side are the words, "HONG KONG," a crown, and the initials SRF. Any idea what it might be?

This may come as a disappointment, but your piece is a plastic token, a piece of play money, using the British symbol for pence.

Q: I have a piece that is plastic, with a large 50 on one side and another 50 on the other, along with a ship, which is nearly identical to the design on the New Zealand 50-cent piece. Is it play money, or what?

Play money, but an official issue! You have one of a set of plastic coins, matching the denominations of the decimal coins introduced in 1967, which were distributed by the New Zealand Government for practice purposes before the new coins were released. 600,000 sets were passed out at the time.

Q: You mentioned the official plastic coins that New Zealand had struck to smooth the way to decimalization. Didn't Australia have the same thing?

They were the same, but different. In that country a major oil company (Esso) produced the sets of model coins for use in their own facilities, with one side bearing designs similar to the real coins, as was the case in New Zealand, but on the other side the Australian pieces carried the company logo. Similar private issues were also made in Britain.

Chapter 60

PRIVATE MINTS

The private mints went boom, then busted. Hundreds of mints never survived the end of the silver art bar fad. The survivors depend on official sounding names to survive.

Q: Isn't it illegal for these "official" sounding private "mints" to offer coins at five or ten times what they are worth?

There is no law on the books prohibiting excessive charges, and it cannot be held to be misrepresentation. These firms spend plenty of money on legal talent to make sure they are within the letter of the law, even if just barely.

Q: Were there any private mints in the U.S. in the 1800s and early 1900s?

The principal private mints were The Scoville Manufacturing Company of Waterbury, Connecticut, The Dunn Airbrake Company of Philadelphia, The Gorham Manufacturing Company of New York City and Providence, The Denver Novelty Works in Colorado, and Camacho Roldan & Van Sickel of New York City. Attempts to start a private mint indirectly led to confiscation of the genuine 1969-S hub-doubled cents by the Secret Service.

Chapter 61

PROOF COINS

How many times do we have to say that proof is not a grade, it's a special method of manufacture.

Q: Isn't it a good idea to open and check proof sets received from the Mint?

There's no premium and a potential serious loss in dealing with an unopened box. It was a fad back in the 1960s to leave the boxes unopened, but con artists filled them with rocks and resealed them. It's always a good idea to check for damaged or defective coins, holders, etc. Of course, you also want to check for valuable minting varieties too. In the 1950s and early 1960s many U.S. dealers would refuse proof sets or mint sets which had been removed from their original government packaging - at the same time that they offered plastic holders for sale. This fad in the 1980s was the "in" mode in Europe, especially with some German dealers. The enlightened word, however, is to buy the coin, not the box or roll. The best advice is an old Yankee expression - "Never buy a pig in a poke."

Q: What is a matte proof surface?

It differs from a mirror proof in that it is applied to the already struck coin. The coins are variously sandblasted or pickled to produce the roughened surface. Some may have had the planchets treated as well, but the effect of this on the struck surface is dubious. Europeans prefer matte proofs to the mirror proofs most U.S. collectors are familiar with.

Q: Why didn't they put the Ike dollars into the proof sets in 1971?

The principal reason for the lack of a dollar proof in the set was that dollars had never previously been included in proof sets, so it would have run against tradition. The Ikes were added to the proof sets in 1973, jumping the price from $5 (for the 1972 set) to $7. The same thing happened with the 1973 mint sets, with the added dollar, increasing it from $3.50 to $6.

Q: Why do some earlier proof-only coin dates command higher prices than years in which there were both proofs and circulation strikes?

Many collectors want a coin for each year and mint. Proof-only issues usually sharply limit the number available, with a corresponding boost in the price.

Q: I was told to buy proofs, as "then you won't have to worry about grading." Now I'm beginning to wonder?

With good reason. Proof is not a grade, to begin with, but proofs are graded, and the ANA grading standards cover grades from impaired proofs up through proof-60 to proof-70, so you need to learn to grade proofs just like other coins.

Q: Are proof dies used to strike circulation coins?

We know that proof reverse dies have been sandblasted, and then used at San Francisco and Denver in 1980 and 1981. The sandblasting would remove all traces of the proof die surface. Refurbished proof dies were used to strike some 1969-D, 1970-D, 1971-D and 1972-D quarters, 1998 and 2000 one-cent coins and 1999 one-tenth and one-fourth ounce gold Eagle bullion coins.

Q: Are all the 1916 proof coins matte proofs?

The McKinley gold dollar proofs are all brilliant, mirror proofs, while all the other proof coins of that year are matte or satin finish.

Q: Has the Denver Mint ever struck any proof coins?

Besides some of the modern commemoratives, the Denver Mint is known to have struck a very small number of proof or specimen gold coins when it officially opened in 1906.

Q: Since the grading standards are the same how can some uncirculated coins be worth more than proof coins?

The first fallacy here is that proof and mint state coins are graded by the same standards. Mint state coins are graded from MS-60 to MS-70. Proof coins are graded Pr-60 to Pr-70. Same numbers, different prefix, but considerably different grading standards. As but one general example, there are no bag marks on upper grade proofs. When it comes to different values, a key element in pricing is the number minted. In many cases, especially recently, more proofs than uncirculated coins have been struck. Even given the normal premium a proof expects over a matching MS coin, where there is a major difference in mintage, the MS coin is going to be worth more. In some earlier instances, more proofs were saved than circulating coins, so the few MS examples from say the 1860s or 1870s are worth far more than the proofs. In some cases uncirculated coins were made with the same dies, after they had been used to strike proofs. The only difference is that the dies show some wear. Early proofs were made much differently than they are today and many early coins that are called proofs are not really that "good" of coins. Granted, where the choice is between a single specimen of a proof and an MS coin, the proof gets the nod, but there are very few cases until recently where proofs and MS coins are evenly matched in any significant number.

Q: Are all U.S. proof coins struck with impact presses?

The one record I've seen indicates that a hydraulic press was used in 1893, but the majority has since been struck with impact presses.

Q: While looking at photographs of several Trade dollars, I noticed that both the 1884 and 1885 Trade dollar proof dates are different from the earlier dates. Isn't that unusual?

This is but one more of the mysteries surrounding the two proof Trade dollars. For whatever reason - a broken logo punch, or perhaps the punch was destroyed at the supposed end of the series in 1883 - the date was punched into the dies for both years with a logo punch that was normally used for the $20 gold double eagles. The usage suggests the possibility that both years were struck at the same time.

Q: Is there such a thing as an "original" 1916 proof set of U.S. coins?

The 1916 set consists of two coins, the cent and nickel. There were individual proofs of the quarter and half and the Commemorative McKinley gold dollar, but they were not issued with the sets. All the references I can find indicate one known original set, in the Lester Merkin Auction of 1968 and later in the Bowers & Ruddy Kensington sale of 1975. Readers may know of others.

Q: Did the Denver Mint strike any proof Olympic or Statue of Liberty coins?

Denver struck a handful of proofs in the 1905 through 1907 period, including 40 proof tokens marking the opening of the Mint, but it did not strike any proof versions of either the 1984 Olympic or 1986 Statue of Liberty coins. Denver did strike proof versions of the 1996 Olympic coins.

Q: I have written several times to the Mint, suggesting that the proof cents should be struck in copper (brass) rather than the copper-plated zinc used for circulating coins, but have never received an answer.

I can't answer for the "no answer" but I can answer the proposal. The regulations require that the proof coins be struck in the same alloy as the circulating coins. One significant variation from that theme - the 40 percent silver Ikes and Bicentennial coins - was struck under special authorization. Now we have silver proof sets, but the proof cents remain the same alloy as the circulating coins.

Q: Are the copper-plated zinc cents prepared any differently when they are struck as proof coins?

It's not generally known that besides getting an extra cleaning bath the proof cent planchets get a double thickness copper plating. The reason is that without the thicker plating the copper tends to separate from the zinc core, due to the double strike the proof coins get. Evidence of this double strike problem shows occasionally on circulation cents that show separation of the copper plating in the date and mintmark area or between the date and the rim.

Q: Did the U.S. Mint decision not to issue a proof set in 1965 have any effect on the Canadian sets of that year?

The unexpected decision caught the Canadian Mint by surprise, as hundreds of U.S. coin dealers and collectors descended on the Ottawa and Toronto post offices, in a two-day period, mailing almost 900,000 orders by January 4. A total of 2,904,352 proof-like sets were sold.

Q: A couple of the proof sets I received from the Mint have plastic fragments in with the coins. Should I send the sets back?

I would doubt that would be necessary. The debris is inert plastic, from the case, so it should pose no real problem or any threat to the coins.

Q: I have come into possession of a set of 1955 proof coins, which contains the cent through the half dollar, all without mintmarks. Were other proof coins struck at any of the other mints that year?

You have a complete set of 1955 proof coins in the set. Philadelphia was the only Mint striking proof coins at that time, so that set is also complete. Proof coin production, for the minor denominations, was switched to San Francisco in 1968. Since 1984, all of the Mints have struck proof commemorative coins at one time or another.

Q: I notice in some of the proof set listings that the abbreviation "Pres." is used. What does this mean?

This question is coming in in increasing numbers from beginning collectors. "Pres." stands for Prestige Set. The Mint began issuing these sets in 1983. They include the regular proof coins, plus a proof Olympic dollar in 1983 and 1984, a proof Statue of Liberty dollar in 1986, a proof Constitution dollar in 1987 and a proof Olympic dollar in the 1988 Prestige Set. Proof coins used in the Prestige Sets have separate mintage figures from the other proofs.

Q: Is there any record of who got the first proof Ike dollar?

The first proof Ike was shipped on the anniversary of Ike's birthday, October 14, 1971, to C. L. Manning of Lincroft, New Jersey. The first 40 percent special uncirculated coin went to Clarence L. Harris of Columbus, Kansas.

Q: Now that the Mint has gone back to silver for part of the proof coins, will that make the base metal proofs worth more?

I seriously doubt it. You are looking at annual mintages that ranged up over four million sets a year, meaning that there will be a tremendous backlog of these sets in the hands of collectors for years to come. It's much the same situation as noted in previous questions, except that the attrition on proof sets is much less than for circulating coins. In other words, since they are collector coins, they tend to remain in the hands of collectors or dealers and are better protected from the natural causes that reduce the number of circulating coins. The opposite may even occur, with the silver proofs driving down the price of the less desirable base metal proofs.

A 1906-D $20 proof.

Q: Are there any Branch Mint proofs?

Yes, from New Orleans, Carson City, San Francisco and Denver, says Breen. That includes the 1838-O half-dollar proofs. They are the first branch mint proofs listed by Breen in his Encyclopedia, where he says, "Not more than 20 were struck." He accounts for 11 known. Apparently there were none from Charlotte and Dahlonega. The first official mintmarked proofs were the 27,600 1942-P silver 5-cent proofs. Currently the U.S. Mint is striking proof commemoratives at Denver, Philadelphia, San Francisco and West Point.

Q: Were there two different proofs for the 1936 cents?

There are two varieties of 1936 proofs - satin finish and mirror finish, and a number of both wound up in circulation, so they are found with wear. The early dies were only partially polished, lacking the mirror finish, so they are often mistaken for circulation strikes. Key to tentative identification is the sharp edges of the rims, and unusually detailed bust. The 1937 proof comes only in the mirror version. Both years will show mirror surfaces on the edges as well.

Q: Were any U.S. proof coins struck between 1917 and 1935?

A goodly number of proof coins were struck, especially of the commemorative half dollars. Most are quite rare however. For a listing, see Walter Breen's *Encyclopedia of U.S. and Colonial Proof Coins.*

Q: What is a clad proof?

This usually refers to the 40 percent silver and copper-nickel proofs of the Ike dollars. Although 40 percent silver proofs are clad, the term is usually used for the copper-nickel proofs.

Q: I have a couple of proof coins that are worn, as if they had been in circulation. How do you classify them?

"Once a proof, always a proof," to paraphrase an old saw. A proof coin remains a proof, as proof is not a grade, regardless of what happens to it. A circulated or damaged proof is classed as an "impaired" proof. This hasn't always been the case, as an old auction catalog lists a coin as follows: "Was a proof, now uncirculated."

Q: Are there really three kinds of Ike proofs?

No, there are only two. They are the clad copper-nickel, and the clad 40 percent silver. The confusion may arise because there are also Special Uncirculated 40 percent silver Ikes. To get 40 percent, the core was .209 silver and .791 copper, with the clad layers of .800 silver and .200 copper. The only other proofs struck in two different alloys were the 1942 nickels, which were struck in copper-nickel and in the 35 percent silver alloy adopted that year.

Q: I have an 1881-O coin that is a proof, but I can't find a listing for it.

If it's a Morgan dollar, there are no proofs known for the date and mint. The coin may be proof-like, or close to proof condition, and thus worth a premium, but it would need authentication to determine if it actually is a proof.

Q: I'm arguing that all proof coins are struck by hand, but my buddy says not. Who's right?

Currently the U.S. Mint strikes proof quarters and halves singly, but cents, nickels and dimes are mechanically fed. This means that the planchets for the quarters and halves are manually placed between the dies, while the smaller planchets are fed automatically. All proof coins are struck at least twice, the larger coins three and four times. By the way, if you were arguing that they were struck by hammering the dies, that went out nearly two centuries ago. As posed, the coins are not struck by hand, as the action of the press is automatic once the button is pushed.

Q: I have a Buffalo nickel and a Peace dollar that are coated just like a proof coin. What can you tell me about them?

The Mint does not coat proofs. Anything on your coins was added after they left the Mint. Some old-time collectors lacquered their coins, so you may have pieces out of an old collection.

Q: I read somewhere that proofs weren't struck until the 1800s. Is this correct?

Sorry, but the information is wrong. Proofs were struck in England in the 1600s. There were other European proof coins, and some of our own coins of the 1790s were classed as specimens or proofs. Probably the first proof "coins" were medals. Most historians trace the proof process of using polished dies on polished planchets to Italy in the late 1400s or early 1500s. The Italians were the inventors of the screw press, which for the first time enabled medals and later coins to be struck with enough force to bring up the design completely. Complicating the tracing of the history of proof coinage and medals is the fact that most Europeans preferred a surface which would correspond more closely to a matte finish than the polished proofs we are most familiar with today. The technical art of coining and medal making depended more on obtaining very high relief for a more natural appearing design than the flatter strikes of the medieval period.

Q: When were the first U.S. proof sets offered for sale?

Breen quotes an 1858 notice by J. R. Snowden, offering sets for sale, but George F. Jones, in the *Coin Collectors Manual of 1860*, says that cased sets were sold as early as the 1840s. A set of minor coins with a face value of $1.94 sold for $2.02.

Chapter 62

PROPOSALS AND SUGGESTIONS

If all the proposals for coins were strung end to end, we'd be swamped. Some ideas were good. Some were very, very bad.

Q: Didn't the Mint propose a change in the alloy of the nickel a few years ago?
The proposal was contained in a study commissioned by the Mint, but never officially endorsed, which would have changed the proportion of the 75 to 25 percent Cu-Ni alloy to 93 to 7 percent to use the scrap from the clad coin metal strip. The same study recommended the mini-dollar, (the only major change actually instituted) and elimination of the cent and half dollar.

Q: Has there ever been any official action toward doing away with the cent?
Treasury Secretary William Simon in a report to Congress at the end of his term recommended eliminating the cent and the half dollar, and reducing the size of the (Ike) dollar.

Q: Did the personal views of Thomas Jefferson affect striking foreign coins at the U.S. Mint?
Yes, they probably did. In 1789, in rejecting a proposal by a person from another country to mint U.S. coins, he is quoted as saying, "The carrying on of a coinage in a foreign country is without example."

Q: I don't like any of the current cataloging systems for coins so I have constructed my own system, which I feel is much easier to use. How do I go about exposing it to the hobby so that it will replace the other systems?
The best way is to write a book using the system. If you can find a publisher, and the public likes your system and starts to use it, it will find its place. Many systems have been proposed, and few are universally accepted, so don't get your hopes too high. The most common complaint is that we already have too many cataloging systems. I was one of the few fortunate ones, as my classification systems for minting varieties and paper money varieties were turned into cataloging systems by the collectors.

Q: When was the first proposal made for a small-size (Anthony) dollar?
The suggestion came in the famous Research Triangle Institute report of September 15, 1976. Mint technicians supported the idea in a separate report.

Q: The State of New York didn't authorize any coins in the Colonial era, but weren't some struck?
There's a lot of history involved, so I'd recommend reading *Breen's Complete Encyclopedia of U.S. and Colonial Coins* for the background. Summarizing, the State coat of arms was used on some coins, but none were authorized. Most of the examples were struck in England. The Brasher doubloons actually were patterns for a proposed New York State coinage.

Q: What was the scheme to begin our coinage with unusual denominations?

Robert Morris, Minister of Finance, proposed a group to match circulating notes of the states. In order to match, the so-called 'unit' was designated as 1/1440th of a dollar. Privately minted patterns were struck, paid for by tax money, but the concept was quickly scuttled in favor of the decimal fractions of the dollar.

Q: What ever happened to the "commercial dollar?"

It turned into a Trade dollar on the way to the Orient. The original proposal and patterns were labeled commercial dollars, but in 1872 the first Trade dollar patterns appeared and in 1873 the design was adopted.

Chapter 63

RATION TOKENS

You had to have lived during World War II to remember how important these little tokens were to the public. Now they are collectible.

Q: My grandfather used to tell a story about problems with those little round red and blue OPA tokens being used in vending machines during World War II. Were they a serious problem?

The vending machine industry hated them with a passion, as did the bus lines. The pieces would jam the machines or fare boxes, and each time that happened a repair man had to open it up to remove the jam. In some of the cruder vending machines they would actually work as a dime.

Q: What's the story on collecting the OPA red and blue tokens?

Two questions in the same mail on these, so they are by no means a "dead" collectible. There are 30 letter combinations known on the reds, the scarcest being MV. There are 24 blues, with WC and WH the hardest to find. The government originally ordered two billion of them, 1.1 billion of the red, used for meats and fats, and 900 million of the blue tokens, which were good for processed foods. The initial plan was to make them the size of a quarter, but because the vulcanized fiber used to make them was in short supply, the size was reduced to less than that of a dime. The size reduction more than doubled the number obtained from the same amount of material. The tokens cost the government $1.19 a thousand to make. I believe that tons of them were destroyed after the war, when they were no longer needed, as it was probably not practical to recycle the material. The system was put into effect on February 27, 1944.

Q: I have an OPA red ration token, which is much thinner than normal, and appears to have been painted on one side. Was this some special form of these pieces?

Sorry, but you have an altered piece. Not too long after they were issued, sharpies discovered that splitting the pieces in two and by applying a red dye, paint or even lipstick, they could use the two halves to purchase twice as much. Counterfeiting of the paper ration coupons was rampant, so it's not surprising that the fiber tokens were involved too.

Q: Is it true that the old OPA tokens wound up being used in Europe after World War II?

The ration tokens, which were used in the U.S. during the war, became surplus when the war and rationing ended, and the remainder were sold to Yugoslavia, where they were used in Displaced Persons camps.

Q: I have a red OPA token from World War II rationing, which has been struck off center. Do you have any idea of its value?

By chance I have an ad for several similar pieces, which gives an idea of retail values. Your piece is probably worth around $5 to $7.50.

Chapter 64

REEDING

Reeds and reeding are two terms special to the coin-collecting hobby. They remain undefined in any standard dictionary. The closest are lands and grooves, terms used in gun making.

Q: Are there coins with the wrong number of reeds?

Unfortunately there has been very little research in this area. We do know that reeding was standardized in 1964. Prior to that there are several listings, including the 1921 Morgan dollars with abnormal (157) reeding, (Normal is 188), the 1876-CC quarter with a normal 119, or those with 153 fine reeds. Almost without exception New Orleans dimes have 103 reeds while most contemporary Philadelphia struck dimes have 113, or for those between 1855 and 1860, 121 reeds.

A 1921 Morgan with abnormal reeding. The wide, thick reeds are compared with the dainty narrow reeds of an 1880-CC dollar.

Q: In checking my new gold coins I notice that there are some blobs of gold between the ends of the reeds and the rim. Is this something unusual?

If the blobs are between the ends of the reeding, and extend toward the reverse rim, they are probably metal that was scraped out of the reeding as the coin was ejected from the collar. This will frequently occur with reeded coins, and probably will not affect the value of the piece.

Q: Were all of our silver coins reeded?

There were five exceptions. The 3-cent silver, 5-cent silver (1942-45) and 20-cent coins all had a plain edge. The early silver dollars and half dollars had a lettered edge. These latter coins frequently are overlooked.

Chapter 65

REFERENCE BOOKS AND CATALOGS

It bears repetition. "Buy the book before you buy - or sell - the coin."

Q: I have an older copy of a popular coin price guide that lists a "1908-S VDB Cent." Is it of any value to collectors?

This particular printing mistake or typographical error might get you a dollar or so extra, but not likely any more than that. I checked the copy in our library and it has the same mistake so it's very likely that it occurred in all of the copies. A more recent issue of another guide left out three whole years for one denomination, so mistakes do happen. We published an issue of *Numismatic News* with one page dated 1857, which I have in my collection, thanks to a sharp-eyed reader.

Q: Which would be the best cataloging system, one that has a single number for each year or one with a group of numbers for each year?

Most cataloging systems for coins use a group of numbers so that there are enough to cover any varieties that might show up.

Q: Why is there so little older literature on the minting process?

The Mint and the Treasury Department considered any information about how coins were made as valuable to counterfeiters. English mint workers at one time were required to take an oath not to reveal anything about minting coins to outsiders. Even so, there were a few articles and pamphlets published. In my personal reference library I have a quite interesting pamphlet on the minting process, which was published in 1895. The Mint's attitude about releasing information has swung wildly in both directions over the years.

Q: Why doesn't a certain reference work list the 1970 mint set with the so-called "small" date cent? It lists the 1960 set.

Why indeed. Krause does not publish the book, so we can't speak for the editorial policy. There seems to be a curious comprehension gap when it comes to published reference works, as hardly a collector understands that issuing price guides is a very highly competitive field. This question is about like going to a Chrysler dealer to complain about how a Ford car is built. Neither they nor we can do anything about our competitors - except to put out a better product.

Q: How big a library does a collector need to have to effectively pursue this hobby?

This is like the old argument about the number of angels that can dance on the head of a pin. The answer depends entirely on what you collect and how you collect it. You might be able to get by with a single book, or you might need several thousand if your interests are wide ranging. The key to the answer is that you need all the information you can get to be an effective collector.

Q: You have the wrong price on (a certain coin). I just saw the same coin listed in (a competing price guide) for $100 more.

I'd suggest getting a copy of *North American Coins and Prices*, which we do publish, and which we are responsible for. We get a similar group of questions from those who accept some other reference as gospel and automatically assume we are wrong if we disagree with their price quotes. We make mistakes, but so do the "infallible" references, so keep that in mind when you prepare to jump to a conclusion. It isn't just the collectors who are unaware of reality. I recently overheard a dealer seriously suggesting that we should "State that our prices are a certain percentage of those in a (competing publication)." I wonder how the dealer would feel if he had to announce that "My prices are 25 percent higher than the dealer across the aisle." We believe we have the best pricing information available. If we didn't we'd get out of the reference publishing business.

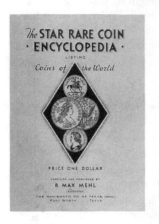

One of B. Max Mehl's catalogs.

Q: What is a copy of The Star Rare Coin Encyclopedia *by B. Max Mehl worth?*

From the number of Mehl catalogs still around (as common as 1934 Federal Reserve Notes or Barr notes) you would think he had a multi-million press run. Almost everyone saved their catalogs, which have not appreciated significantly in the 80 years since they were published. Prices very roughly range from $5 up to $15 to $20 for early ones that are in pristine condition.

Q: Was the Red Book the first guide or catalog of U.S. coins published by Whitman?

Whitman Publishing got into the publishing area of the numismatic field in 1941 with a *Handbook of U.S. Coins*, which was designed primarily for coin dealers, and ultimately became known as the Blue Book. The first *Guide Book of U.S. Coins*, or the Red Book, was produced and published in 1946 with a cover date of 1947. Top condition examples of that first edition bring several hundred dollars from collectors and even later editions from the 1940s and 1950s are bringing good prices.

Q: Why did the Guide Book get nicknamed the Red Book?

The Red Book was by no means the first book to be known by the color of its cover, and probably won't be the last. One of the popular coin guides of the 1960s was *Strauss' Monthly Yellow Coin Book*, the same publisher putting out a Black and White Coin Buying List. Whitman had its own Blue Book, the dealer version of the Red Book, and there have been many similar publications, which used some color of the rainbow to trade on the popularity of the Red Book.

Chapter 66

SALES TAX TOKENS

Samples of a little-know era in U.S. history, sales tax tokens were, to say the least, controversial.

Q: Did the Treasury Department ever take any of the states that issued sales tax tokens in the 1930s to court?

Apparently not. Although the tax tokens looked like money, traded like money and really were a form of money, the states managed to get away with issuing them, even though the federal law is specific in stating that anything that close to being "real" money was illegal. Treasury Secretary Morganthau rumbled and grumbled and wrote a lot of letters, but never actually enforced the law. For those of you who wonder where our current state, county and city sales taxes got their start, it was those "emergency" laws of the 1930s that are still on the books in revised forms. The earliest state sales tax reportedly dates back to 1920, but I haven't been able to determine which state.

Q: What can you tell me about the state tax tokens?

Tax tokens were issued during the 1930s as a means of paying the fractional (mil) sales taxes imposed on purchases. After various problems, including trouble with the Treasury over issuing "private" coinage, the idea was dropped. The pieces are collected by a significant number of collectors, and there is even a national club devoted to their collectors. Values in most cases are minimal as they were produced in large quantities. Thirteen states used metal tax tokens if you include the World War II years. They include Alabama, Arizona, Colorado, Illinois, Kansas, Kentucky, Louisiana, Mississippi, Missouri, New Mexico, Oklahoma, Utah and Washington. Ohio used a paper token, and there were several cities that issued tokens, usually in mils. (1/10th of a cent.)

Q: Did the U.S. Government try to issue coins to thwart the efforts by the states that had issued sales tax tokens?

Treasury Secretary Morganthau repeatedly warned the states that were issuing sales tax tokens in late 1935 that they were illegal and promised (or threatened) that the government would issue a half cent coin and a one mil coin for general circulation. President Franklin D. Roosevelt reportedly designed the two coins, the half cent with a hole in the center and the one mil coin on a square planchet. The House Coinage Committee, however, saw it differently and bottled up the Secretary's bill to enable the issue of the two coins, forcing the Treasury to watch what would become a total of 13 states that eventually issued sales tax tokens.

Q: Fact or fiction? Were all of those state sales tax tokens of the 1930s illegal issues?

Fact, and some red faces when the Senate Banking Committee was politely informed back in 1937 that there was a 1909 law still on the books which prohibited tokens "with a value of less than $1." This also was the case with the streetcar tokens, the "good fors" and other similar pieces of the era.

Chapter 67

SAN FRANCISCO MINT

Talk about history! Whole books have been devoted to the San Francisco facility and its several permutations.

The old San Francisco Mint.

Q: What did it cost to restore the Old San Francisco Mint?
Restoration costs for the four-year project ran to over $5 million. This compares to the original building, which only cost $2,130,512 to build in 1874.
The then Mint Director, Mary Brooks, took considerable pride in the fact that not a cent of tax money was used for the job, as the funds were obtained from "reimbursable numismatic funds."

Q: Could San Francisco strike coins after the 1906 earthquake?
The Mint building and machinery were not seriously damaged, but the quake disrupted the gas supply so it was impossible to strike any coins. Instead, the San Francisco Mint acted as the banker for the city until the private banks were able to re-open.

Q: Why wasn't the 1979-S SBA dollar included in the mint sets for that year?
The decision to produce the SBA dollars at the San Francisco Mint for circulation wasn't made until late in the year. By that time it was too late to change the packaging.

Q: As a beginner, I'm puzzled by the many references to "scarce" or "rare" San Francisco coins. If I read the mintage figures right, aren't there a lot of "S" coins which have higher mintages?
You are right. A handful of truly rare coins struck at San Francisco have, over the years, magnified the "S" mintmark to an often-unwarranted indication of scarcity for much larger mintages. You won't go wrong by making your own comparisons of mintage figures, although as you become more expert, you will find other factors affecting value as well. Another possible cause for the legend is the fact that S-mint cents rarely made it to the eastern part of the U.S. where there were many more collectors.

Q: What was the first coin to be struck in quantity at the San Francisco Mint when it moved to its current building?

The San Francisco Mint began striking coins on October 22, 1937, in the new building, striking first the 1937-S dimes.

Q: Did the U.S. Mint at San Francisco automatically revert to the status of an Assay Office when it closed in 1955?

The San Francisco Mint ceased producing coins March 31, 1955, and closed down, but it officially remained in the status of a Mint until the passage of Public Law 87-537 on July 11, 1962. That law changed its status back to that of an Assay Office. Public law 89-81, Title II, Sec. 201, dated July 23, 1965, authorized striking coins at San Francisco. The facility began striking coins September 1, 1965, after supplying planchets to the Denver Mint during the coin shortage. The first coins struck were 1964 dated cents - without a mintmark. The San Francisco Mint was officially converted back to Mint status in 1988. An earlier bill to change the status died with the 1982 Congress. There had been several previous attempts.

Q: Didn't the U.S. Mint have a special method of handling gold coin strip that was too thin so that proper weight planchets could be punched from it?

The method was described as "doctoring" the strip by making it concave. When a planchet was punched from the curved strip, it would have sloping sides, the underside being large enough to bring the weight up to normal. This process apparently was only used at the San Francisco Mint.

Q: Why is San Francisco sometimes labeled as the "Forgotten Mint?"

In the San Francisco Mint's lengthy service it has been shoved back and forth between status as a mint and status as an Assay Office and was often officially ignored. One indication of this is the fact that the first Secretary of the Treasury to ever visit the San Francisco facility was David Kennedy on October 1, 1970, well over 100 years after it went into service.

Q: It seems odd to me that the San Francisco Mint didn't strike any quarters in 1949. Can you check on it to find out what happened?

The Mint assigns production at the different mints as coins are needed. The 15 million struck in 1948 apparently were enough to meet the needs of the western region through 1949, so no quarters were struck at San Francisco that year. If you check back you will find that this happened several times for different denominations. There's nothing sinister about it, just common sense. There is no law or regulation forcing the Mint to strike coins every year. The number struck is based entirely on the number on hand and the projected usage and demand.

Q: I thought San Francisco only struck proof coins after it reopened in 1968. Why do I see listings for what must be circulation strikes?

San Francisco struck circulation strikes as well as proof coins from 1968 to 1974, but not all denominations in each year. They did strike cents for all of those years. They struck both 40 percent silver and copper-nickel clad proof Ikes and 40 percent silver special uncirculated Ikes. Both circulation and proof strikes were made of the Anthony dollars there as well.

Chapter 68

SLOGANS, MOTTOS AND CATCH PHRASES

Everybody likes a slogan. Countries use them to make their identity clear. Lots of Latin adds to their prestige.

E PLURIBUS UNUM on a "V" nickel.

Q: Which minor coin was the first with the E PLURIBUS motto?

That honor goes to the Liberty head, or "V" nickel, introduced in 1883. It's interesting to note that early coins carried the E PLURIBUS UNUM motto without any specific law requiring it. The requirement was made law in 1873 and the nickel was the first minor coin affected.

Q: Would you please translate the motto that appears on the Rosa Americana coins?

The motto is "Rosa Americana Utile Dulci" - "American Rose, the Useful with the Pleasant."

Q: Did the slogan "Value me as you please" originate during the Civil War?

The slogan goes back a lot farther than that. Dr. Samuel Higley of Connecticut issued tokens from 1737 to 1739 with the slogan. Higley had been making three pence tokens that were the size of the halfpenny tokens then in circulation. After complaints, he changed the dies, adding the slogan and changing the denomination to a Roman III. There was a Hard Times and a Civil War connection, as the slogan was repeated on some Hard Times tokens and later was used on several Civil War tokens.

Q: Is our 'Trust in God' peculiar to U.S. coins?

God is mentioned on many coins of the world. One has only to note the DG, or Dei Gratia (By the Grace of God) on almost all English coins. Similar recognition of a deity is found on the coins of most European countries, such as France and Germany. Many Arabic coins mention Allah.

Chapter 69

SO-CALLED DOLLARS

They look like dollars, but they are private issues. Since they are often referred to as dollars, the best face on it is to call them so-called dollars.

Q: What is a Referendum dollar?

Technically they were referendum souvenirs. Joseph Lesher of Colorado struck the pieces, which first sold for $1.25 and later sold for $1. His premise was that the public could "vote" on whether to accept both them and the concept of free silver.

Q: Then what is a Pedley dollar?

Like the Referendum dollar, the Pedley pieces were really souvenirs. The Pedley-Ryan Company of Denver attempted to promote investment in silver in 1933 with a dollar-size 430-grain silver piece, which sold three for a dollar. The silver came from the Denver Mint, but only about 1,000 sold in seven varieties before the idea was dropped.

Chapter 70

SPACE MEDALS

There are enough medals and coins out there with space themes that they have become one more specialty collection among the hundreds of possibilities.

Q: Are there any bronze medals available for the XS-1 plane that broke the sound barrier back in 1947?

There was only a single silver medal struck for Chuck Yeager, the pilot, in 1975, and no bronze versions. There may be privately issued pieces, but I don't have a listing for them.

Q: I've heard rumors of a very large platinum medal struck to commemorate the first lunar landing. Can you give me any details?

The piece in question apparently is the 76 mm platinum medallion struck by American Mint Associates of Media, Pennsylvania in 1969. The list price was $5,000. It was one of a set, including a palladium, silver and bronze, all the same size. The palladium sold for $1,000, the silver for $50 and the bronze for $12.50. The pieces depicted the moon landing of Apollo 11, and were colored with baked-on enamel.

Apolla 11 commemorative medal.

Q: Are there two different sets of Apollo 11 medals from the Franklin Mint? How do you tell them apart?

The original set was minted in 1970, mistakenly billed as made from silver, which had been around the moon. When the mistake was discovered the sets were recalled. A new mintage with the correct silver was made, which has a bar, or horizontal line, above the F mintmark. 1,269 of the original sets were not returned, and 3,698 sets were replaced.

Q: Some special medals went on the Apollo 7 flight in October 1968, but who designed them?

Two hundred twenty-five .925 silver and 16 14-karat gold medals were carried on the 11-day flight. They were designed by one of the three crewmen, Maj. Don Eisele, and struck by the Robbins Company of Attleboro, Massachusetts.

Q: Weren't there also medals struck from metal from the Gemini VI mission?

These interesting space medals keep turning up, moving the "earliest" space flight medals, which incorporated metal carried on the flight, back to 1966. The gold (18.5 grams) and silver (10.75 grams) medals were made with bullion carried on the December 15 and 16, 1965, flight. The source I found did not indicate who struck them, or the mintage. Any more that our readers can report?

Q: What country first honored the Apollo 11 moon flight?

Guinea issued a 1969 proof set, with a 250-franc coin honoring "Man on Moon."

Chapter 71

SPECIAL MINT SETS

The child of coin shortages, the Special Mint Sets filled the gap between the last of the 90 percent silver coins and the beginning of proof coinage at San Francisco.

Q: I have a 1965 quarter that appears to be a proof with a shiny surface. Could it be a pattern?

That is very doubtful. The most probable source is a coin intended for a Special Mint Set. Many of these sets were broken up at the time and spent because there was little interest in them. The coin may also have been "whizzed" to give it its appearance, or even plated. You'll need to have a specialist examine it.

Q: Was there some connection between the Carson City Mint and the 1965-67 Special Mint Sets?

All of the coins for the Special Mint Sets were struck at San Francisco. The only connection with Carson City was the loan of a heavy-duty press, which was shipped to San Francisco to strike the coins.

Q: What were the original issue prices of the 1965, 1966 and 1967 Special Mint Sets?

The prices for all three years were $4 each.

Q: Do you have the official description of the Special Mint Sets that were issued in 1965-67?

The Mint put it this way: "Consisting of one coin of each denomination minted (1, 5, 10, 25 and 50 cents). Although not of proof quality, the coins are struck one at a time from specially prepared (polished) blanks on high tonnage presses, with a higher relief and better appearance than coins of regular issue." As far as I know the "higher relief" has never been documented.

Q: Were any 90 percent silver coins found in the Special Mint Sets?

Despite the fact that the 1965 sets were made while the silver coins were still being struck, there have never been any reports of one containing a silver coin. Actually, the Special Mint Sets were struck at San Francisco, which was not striking the silver coins.

Chapter 72

STORAGE

Probably the topic of more questions than most parts of the hobby, proper storage is a vital part of collecting.

Q: I have an old coin tube with a coin stuck in the bottom of it. Any suggestions for removing the coin without wrecking it?

I still have a couple of tubes with coins stuck in them from my early collecting days. You might try carefully filing a groove in the bottom of the tube and up the sides allowing the plastic to split when you twist the tube. Readers may have some other suggestions.

Q: Some time ago you noted in answer to a question that the flaps on plastic flips (or paper coin envelopes) should not be tucked in. Do you still advise this?

I do, although I probably said in the same breath that, "they are not designed to be tucked in." I recently ran across an ad from the late 1960s for a plastic flip, which specifically said that the flaps could be tucked in, "if required." The problem here is that tucking in the flap makes it extremely difficult, if not virtually impossible, for all but the most dexterous to open the flap on a plastic flip, and I defy anyone to open a paper coin envelope with tucked flap without tearing it. More important, the tucked-in flap allows the coin (especially a small coin) to work its way past the flap and escape, something that can't happen if the flap is folded over the outside of the envelope. Despite the maker's claim in this ad, the advice about tucking-in the flap is flawed.

Q: I'm told the capsules containing the 1984 Olympic coins are not airtight. Should I remove the coins and put them in airtight containers for long-term storage?

Historically, an original container will add something to the value of a coin, but in almost all cases the cases or boxes were very limited in number. For mass-produced coins of the current era, the coin itself is what has the value, so whether or not it is in the original container has no effect on the value, but the use of an airtight container will have a significant effect on long-term storage.

Q: Are the 2x2 cardboard holders made with a safe plastic? I've heard that the cardboard dust is bad for coins.

Most 2x2 cardboard holders use an inert Mylar film, which is safe for coins. The cardboard dust is a problem, but more one of appearance, as the cardboard is usually a very low sulphur paper, which is less likely to cause harm to the coin than contact with air-borne contaminants.

Q: I have a sealed Mint bag of Denver cents, dated November 11, 1982. Would the coins be the small or the large date variety?

They very probably are the small date. Denver stopped striking the zinc large date cents late in October. It would be best if you took them out of the bag and used a neutral solvent to clean off the oil and dirt. Bags are at the bottom of the list of storage media and in all too many cases wind up as a bitter disappointment for the bag's owner because they offer such poor protection for the coins.

Q: I find it difficult to get proper storage materials for my medal collection. Any help?

Medals are a problem because of the variations in diameter and thickness. I can't recommend any specific product or service, but getting some custom-made holders may be the solution. I'd suggest writing to some of the firms that produce holders, and describe your needs. The material must be neutral, rugged (because of the size and weight) and as airtight as possible.

Q: Is Mylar "always" safe for coins?

Pure Mylar is safe, but if it contains any impurities it may cause problems. Also, because it is very brittle, it should never be used for shipping coins through the mail. I've seen dozens of coins that have split out of their flips in transit, or even just by dropping them in the flip. Mylar also will scratch coins if they moved about frequently within the flip. Many dealers still use flips with PVC for temporary storage or mailing, so if you buy coins that come in flips, remove them at once unless the flips are Mylar. If this is all you have, reinforce all four sides with tape before shipping coins. It's best when shipping one or two large coins to tape the flip, holder or envelope to a thin piece of cardboard, and even better to run tape on all four sides of the holder.

Q: I have a book on coins that recommends aluminum foil as a safe storage medium for bulk quantities of coins. Is it really safe?

Absolutely not. Back in the 1960s it was suggested as being safe, but my experience and that of a number of readers who have commented on its use is that it has the potential to seriously damage your coins, especially in a humid or damp atmosphere. The book apparently is based on previously published, but outmoded, information. My standard recommendation is to use only those products SPECIFICALLY designed and tested for coin storage. Using household expedients like aluminum foil and plastic wrap are classic examples of taking the wrong approach to safe coin storage.

The same goes for cellophane and waxed paper envelopes intended for stamps. They are not designed for coins and won't hold up.

Q: I bought a mint-sealed bag of coins via a local bank. Wouldn't the coins automatically grade MS-65?

It's very likely that a significant number won't grade over MS-60. How the bag was handled is going to play a significant role, as rough handling will reduce many of them to below MS-60 standards. One tip is to get the coins out of the bag as soon as possible and into storage media, such as inert plastic tubes, that will protect them. Bags are one of the worst possible storage medias because they offer no protection at all for the coins.

Chapter 73

TERMS, ABBREVIATIONS AND DEFINITIONS

More hobby language. Learn the terms and you will be a step ahead.

Q: Aren't the abbreviations on the Fugio cent rather odd?

In today's world, we're not used to oddball abbreviations for the states, although there is still a conflict between the old abbreviations and the two-letter ones required by the post office. Back then, they probably didn't raise an eyebrow over: N. Hamp, Massac, Connec, R. Island, Delaw. Also N. York and Pennsy.

Q: What does the "S.M.V." abbreviation mean on some of the California gold pieces?

It stood for "Standard Mint Value," an attempt to indicate that the coins were full weight. Others had "W.M.V." for "Warranted Mint Value."

Despite the claim, most of the private issues actually contained less than the required or stated amount of gold.

Q: Am I missing something? A friend looked at my coins and told me I don't have a collection. What does he mean?

It's difficult to answer this question diplomatically, but the probable reason for your friend's comment may be that you have a quantity of coins that you have yet to organize in any recognizable fashion. A collection is generally considered to be a number of coins that have been arranged in some logical manner, following either a traditional or non-traditional pattern. For example, a set of cents, with the dates and mints represented for a specific period of time, could be considered a collection. A tube randomly filled with coins of that same period probably would not fit the definition. In general unsorted, unconnected coins would be presumed to be an accumulation rather than a collection. A collection entails work on your part, above and beyond filling a jar or a shoebox.

Q: Do the narrow and wide date terms mean there is a difference in the width of the date?

That's correct. The terms are applied to dates that have the digits close together or far apart.

Q: Please explain "old tenor" and "new tenor."

Tenor refers to a standard for coinage or paper money. Walter Breen tells us that "old" tenor gold coins of the U.S. are those struck before June 30, 1834, and silver coins before April 1853. Oddly, "new" tenor was not applied to later coinage, but was used for some issues of Colonial paper money.

Q: In answering a question you described a coin as "worthless." Isn't it always worth face value?

I always assume that people understand I'm talking about the collector value of a supposed variety on a coin and not the coin itself, which is "always" worth face value. The rest of the sentence is that the coin is "worthless to collectors, as it has no collector value."

Q: On the 1792 half dime, what are the two abbreviated words?

On the half dime dies prepared by Birch, the abbreviations are LIB and PAR, standing for "Liberty, Parent - of Science and Industry."

Q: What do the initials F.T. and R.T. stand for?

They are the abbreviations for the flat top 3 and round top 3. The flat top has a straight or flat upper bar, while the round top has a curved arc. Among the listings using this designation are the U.S. 1913 nickel patterns. The Canadians use this designation for the 1893 10-cent coins.

Q: What is an effigy?

This is a term, which while technically correct, usually isn't applied to a coin or medal. Of the several definitions, the appropriate one reads, "A representation or image, especially sculptured, as on a monument."

Q: What is a pellet on a coin?

The best description is that it is an elongated dot, used as an ornament in the design, or as a "stop" between words or lines of an inscription.

Q: What is coin glass?

This was a popular item during the late 1800s, the objects bearing impressions of several coins in the glass. They were especially popular during the 1892-93 Columbian Exposition. The Central Glass Company of Wheeling, West Virginia produced the glassware in 1891, using actual coins as molds. The Secret Service stopped production. Later copies were made simulating coin designs and designs of foreign coins.

Q: What is a "shell card?"

The embossed shell cards consisted of a cardboard disc in a thin metallic shell. The metal bore a stamped design and a printed ad was placed on the cardboard. Shell cards were issued from 1866 to 1876, and are relatively scarce.

Q: What is the difference between an abraded die and a polished die?

The hobby has long used the term polished die for any repair work done to the die. More properly, proof dies are polished, while most circulation or business strike dies are repaired with an abrasive, so they are classed as an abraded die. This avoids the obvious problem of describing a rough, striated surface as "polished."

Q: How did we wind up with "dollar" as a denomination?

It was a gradual transition, from thaler to daler, daalder, and various other coins of northern Europe that were copied from the thaler in other languages. The Spanish 8 reales were referred to as "milled dollars" from sometime preceding the establishment of the U.S. denomination, and most sources say that our dollar was "patterned after the Spanish Milled Dollar." As to spelling, it traces a roundabout route through Denmark, where the "daler," "dalar" or "rixdaler," was the Danish version, and when the English began using the term, they started with "daler" and made "dollar" out of it.

Q: What was the purpose of Trade coins?

They were made and issued by a number of countries, although the Mexican and U.S. Trade dollars probably got the most publicity. They were used mostly for trade with the so-called "Third World" countries from 1850 up to the end of World War II. The term is also used for privately issued tokens used in promotions.

Q: What is a hallmark?

It's a manufacturer's or artisan's mark, which guarantees the bullion content, weight and fineness of a silver or gold object. The use of hallmarks traces to 1327 when the Guild of London Goldsmiths was chartered. In the same year a law was passed in England requiring silversmiths to use hallmarks.

Q: What is the Numismatic Literary Guild?

The Guild is an organization for authors, writers, editors and publishers in the numismatic field. The NLG holds an educational seminar, usually on the topic of writing articles or books on numismatic topics in conjunction with the ANA each year, and a "bash" which is an evening of entertainment. If you have had any articles or other material published in the field of numismatics, then you are eligible for membership.

Q: What is meant by a "title" collection?

Not a blue blood, but the principal collection in an auction, which the auction is named for to identify it – as, for example, the Garrett Auction.

Q: What is Territorial Gold?

This was the name applied to privately issued gold from territories, which later became part of the U.S., most notably from California.

Q: Have we always used Uncle Sam as one of our national symbols?

Uncle Sam didn't come along until later. The first national symbol was 'Brother Jonathan' in Colonial times, based on Connecticut governor Jonathan Trumbell, who was one of Washington's important advisors.

Q: What is meant by "blanching" a coin?

This is a common minting process for silver coins, especially billon pieces, which contain less than 50 percent silver. The planchets are dipped in an acid solution to leach the copper from the surface. This increases the silver percentage, giving the planchet and coin a whitened surface, which gives it the appearance of being struck on a higher percentage silver planchet.

Q: What part of a coin is the exergue?

It's that part of the design below the main design on the reverse of a coin that carries details such as the date and place of minting. It is sometimes separated from the main design by a raised line.

Q: Exactly what does a "bust" mean? Is it the full figure?

A bust is defined as the head, neck and upper trunk of a person's body. Webster describes it as "head and shoulders."

Q: I thought cobs were irregular shapes. What about the evenly round cob coins from Mexico City?

You are right, cobs, which were made from metal sliced off the end of a bar, were noted for their irregular shapes. The round cobs were special presentation pieces given as gifts to high officials. They draw a substantial premium over the regular cobs. But, counterfeits abound, so be careful.

Q: At a coin club meeting I overheard a reference to "slicks," but didn't get a chance to find out what was meant. Can you help?

Any silver coin which has had the design worn to the point of being unrecognizable is considered to be a slick. This applied especially to the Barber dimes, quarters and halves, which seemed to have gotten an unusual amount of wear. During the height of the silver boom in the early 1980s silver buyers heavily discounted such coins because they had lost a significant part of their weight of bullion. The term probably also was applied to the worn Mercury dimes and the "V" nickels and other well-worn coins.

A well-worn slick.

Q: What is meant by a professional numismatist, and how do I become one?

A professional numismatist is anyone who makes a living from the coin hobby. Usually it refers to coin dealers, but others, such as journalists, researchers, writers, authors, etc., can also be professionals. You become a professional by starting out as an amateur and learning all you can about the hobby until you reach the point where you know enough to be able to charge for your services.

Q: What does it mean in a coin description when it mentions "mounting removed?"

It was a very common practice to turn coins into jewelry. One way of doing this was by soldering some sort of mount, or a link, which would allow the coin to be attached to a bracelet, necklace or some other item. The mounts usually were added with silver solder to silver coins and were brazed to gold coins. This, of course, damaged the edge of the coin, even when skillfully removed. Once a coin has been fixed into a jewelry mount it usually reduces the value, especially if the repair work has not been skillfully done. Always check the edge of a valuable coin closely, even if it means getting it out of a slab.

Q: Do billion and billon mean the same things in other languages?

In most languages billion refers to a number while billon designates an alloy containing a low amount of bullion. One key point, billion doesn't mean the same amount in all countries. Some consider a billion to include 12 zeros, while others use it to mean a number with only nine zeros.

Q: What does the "condition" of a coin mean?

This is another example of a term that is typically misused even by experienced collectors and dealers. "Condition" is meaningless, because it is an individual judgment that is undefined. Your "good condition" could be my "terrible condition." We all need to stop using "condition" when we really mean the "grade" (exact amount of wear) of a coin.

Q: Do clash marks affect the value of early coins?

Usually they do not. Clash marks are the result of damage to the dies. This occurs when a planchet fails to feed between the dies so that the dies hit each other, the sharp edges of the design outline cutting into the face of the opposing die. Such damage was frequent in the early days of minting, so it rarely affects the value. Modern coinage presses are equipped with brakes, which can stop the press in a single cycle to prevent the press from striking if a planchet hasn't fed into the coining chamber between the dies. To have value to modern collectors die clashes must be heavy and show a significant portion of the design of the opposing die.

Q: What is the technical name for the triangular arch under the roof of the Monticello building on the Jefferson nickel?

It's called a pediment.

Q: What is meant by minor coinage? The dictionary definition doesn't seem to fit any more.

The times have changed, and minor coinage has changed as well. The old definition was any fractional silver coin of less than the unit (dollar) size. Until World War II minor meant those not containing silver or gold. It has since been broadened to include any fractional coin of any metal.

Q: What is a cartouche on a coin or medal?

It is usually an oval or oblong area either decorated with a design or outlining an inscription.

Q: Could you please explain some of the abbreviations that you use in your coin price charts, such as CLPFT1, PFT1 or PFT2?

The abbreviations have different meanings on different coins, so it's difficult to find room for all the footnotes that are needed. PF stands for proof. For the 1979 and 1981 proof coins in all six denominations there are two different mintmark punches so they are listed as T1 and T2 (Type 1 and 2). CL means clad, and refers to the clad proofs of the Ike dollars, as opposed to the 40 percent silver proofs. For the 1976 Ikes there are two types, with different style lettering, so here the CLPFT1 means the thick round letters used on the first Ikes of that date on a clad proof.

Some others: SMS - Special Mint Set of 1965-67; 3 Pc Lib - The three-coin set of Liberty Commemorative coins; Box - Probably the boxed Ike special uncirculated and proof dollars; Pres - Prestige Set - proof sets with added coins since 1984; CDPF - (copper-nickel) Clad Proof - may also be Silver clad proof; and Slabs - Plastic cases used by the grading services to hold coins after they have been graded.

Q: What is meant by the term "chasing?"

Chasing is a term used in the art of engraving, meaning to clean up, add to or repair a design on metal using various engraving tools. One of the regular jobs at the Philadelphia Mint is checking every die and making any minor repairs that are needed to correct minor flaws induced in the hubbing or annealing process.

Q: Is there a weight called a "blank?"

Harrison Manville is our source for such a weight, used by the early moneyers, amounting to a fractional part of a grain. There was also an Anglo-Gallic billon coin of Henry VI called a blank.

Q: A relative has one of the 1925 Norse-American Centennial medals. Who was "Opus Fraser," named on the medal?

To answer this question we need to know a bit about art. In this case Opus is not a name. It is Latin for "a creative work." This means that this medal is a creative work of James Earl Fraser, designer of the Buffalo nickel. Fraser signed his work either with Opus or "F," standing for Fecit, another Latin word commonly used by artists and sculptors, meaning, "He (or she) made it."

Q: What's the difference between a holey dollar and a dump?

As the name implies, the dollar has a hole in it. The dump is the former center of the dollar that was punched out. Spanish dollars and other coins were punched into two parts because it helped keep them in local commerce and the two parts could be valued at more than that of the original dollar. A second definition for dump is a lump of metal usually struck with oversize dies.

Q: What is a suction mark on a coin?

This is both an obsolete and a meaningless term. It was based on the false assumption that dies "sucked" molten metal when they retracted from the strike. Another term for the same "effect" was "die pull." Since coins are struck on solid pieces of coin metal, this nickname has pretty well died out due to more information on the minting process becoming available. However, some other nicknames from the same era, such as 'cud' or 'shift,' still have a life of their own.

Q: What is meant by a business strike coin?

Coins intended to circulate in commerce are described as either circulation strikes or business strikes. The two terms have the same meaning, with business strikes probably tracing to the banker's use of the term for their business customers.

Q: What is a "Fillet head?"

The term is used with the meaning of a hair ribbon, worn by Miss Liberty. The design was used on the early half cent and cent.

Q: Isn't "blank planchet" what is known as an oxymoron?

An oxymoron is a combination of two terms, which have opposite or conflicting meanings. Blank planchet is a term, which has hung on in the coin hobby for quite a number of years, but perhaps I can deal it a deathblow with some information that Del Romines furnished. A blank in metalworking terms (used by the Mint) is a piece of metal as it is punched from the strip of coin metal. It becomes a planchet when it has passed through the upsetting mill, which raises the edges on both sides of the piece. Coins are struck on planchets, not on blanks, at least, not normally. Good terminology would be either unstruck blank or unstruck planchet.

Q: Is "flan" a term for a planchet, or object, upon which a coin is to be struck? Some of my friends disagree with this definition.

Flan is commonly used in the U.S., and perhaps other countries, as a term meaning a blank, or planchet, which has not been struck. Flan is a French term, and used by France (and Canada) to mean an unstruck planchet. However, the English usage of the term is to describe the struck coin. It's interesting to note that we in the U.S. are not the only ones to fall into the trap of describing a planchet as being "metal," a failing which ignores some of the other materials (plastics, ceramics, etc.) which are or have been used for coins.

Q: What's the source for the term "Pieces of Eight?"

It was the nickname for the Spanish peso or 8 reales, so named by pirates in the 16th and 17th centuries. At the time the reale was worth 12 1/2 cents. Curiously a check in several dictionaries showed no mention of this pirate connection.

Q: What exactly is a Hard Times token?

They were pieces mostly the size of a large cent, which were privately struck in the period from 1833 to 1844. They are popularly assumed to have alleviated the shortage of small change. However, they played a more important role as political tokens, bearing all manner of sarcastic and downright mean-spirited comments about opponents of the other parties.

Q: What is the purpose of a die trial?

Very literally it means to try the die. The resulting coin from a trial strike usually was struck on soft metal to demonstrate the design, without causing harm to the die. The die adjustment strike is often confused with it but occurs during the installation of the dies in the coin press.

Q: What is the real meaning of specie?

Specie is another name for coins, although in most cases it is limited to gold or silver coins. My sources don't trace it back to any particular time or place. One reference mentions its use in the 1830s, but apparently it goes back a lot farther than that.

Q: What is, or was, "Mickey Mouse" money?

There are two meanings. It was the snide nickname for Japanese invasion currency for the Philippines. Today we have to define the source, as there actually are notes issued by Walt Disney Productions with Mickey Mouse on them.

Q: What is meant by the term "inedited?"

It shows up in the dictionary as meaning not edited or published. In other words a new or first report of a coin, published for the first time. The term 'unpublished' pretty much means the same thing.

Q: What are ancient coins?

Ancient is a standard term in the hobby, applied to coins struck before 500 CE. It's interesting to note that many of the novice collectors getting into the hobby through the Internet seem to consider any coin struck before 1970 as "ancient."

Q: What's the source of the term "coin?"

There are many possibilities, two that I have found. One is Irish the other is English. A prince by the name of Cunobeline (Shakespeare's Cymbeline) ruled eastern Britain from 5 to 40 CE. His name was also spelled Coynobeline, from which came coyne, used until the 16th century when the spelling changed to coin. The ancient tribes of Ireland used the term coyn'ye or coyn'e for tribute demanded from residents by a tribal leader and his cohorts. The Oxford English Dictionary gives us a wealth of information about "coin," including such odd spellings as "quoyne" and "qwyne." While we still use the word to mean the striking of coins, its original usages also included the die; the image produced by the die and even the mint itself was called a coin. Root source is the Latin, cuneum or "cuneus," which means corner or wedge. Wedge in turn was once a term used to describe an ingot of silver. Perhaps the most curious form is one of the originals of coinage, spelled "Knownnage."

Q: I've often seen references to token coinage. What do they mean by it?

Very simply, any coinage is considered to be a token coinage when the face value exceeds the intrinsic value of the metal it contains. At present all of the U.S. circulating coins fit the token coinage definition.

Q: Do "incuse" and "intaglio" mean the same thing?

Not at the technical level. An intaglio design is in relief, but is recessed below the face or field level. The best example of this is the Pratt designs for the U.S. gold $2.50 and $5 coins of 1908 through 1929. An incuse design is "hollow," extending down into the coin surface, such as the "F" designer's initial on the Buffalo nickel or the dates on the 1984 Olympic dollars. Common - but incorrect - usage is incuse for coins and intaglio for paper money plates. If you remember that incuse is the opposite of relief - a raised design above the field - then you are on pretty safe ground.

Q: What does a slash (/) or right slash stand for?

Usually it means "over" something, such as an overdate, a doubled date, an over mintmark, or a doubled mintmark. Earlier usage was also to represent British pounds sterling. A right slash is also used to separate the calendar year from the year of reign on Arabic and other coins. It is also used between dual grades. It also means a virgule, denoting words on separate lines. The original term was "right stroke," meaning a mark made by a single movement of a writing instrument.

Q: What is the meaning of the term "brassage?"

Its meaning is connected to that of seigniorage - a charge made for coining, "usually the difference between the face value and the intrinsic value of the piece." Seigniorage is defined as the difference between the face or circulating value and the cost of the metals plus the brassage. There seems to be a bit of conflict in the definitions, but if we consider seigniorage as the "profit" involved in minting, then the conflict resolves.

Chapter 74

$3 GOLD

An odd denomination with a purpose. That didn't make it popular, so it went the way of the Dodo bird.

Q: I have an 1854 $3 gold piece which has a piece of slag imbedded in the obverse field in front of the nose. A dealer told me it was worth much less than a normal coin in its grade. Is this correct?

The coin is likely to be worth more than the normal numismatic value, but not to a regular coin dealer. You need to find a dealer who specializes in minting varieties and errors.

Q: Which was the stated purpose of the $3 gold coin? Was it to buy rolls of 3-cent coins or 3-cent stamps?

The stamps win out in this case.

Wheat, corn, cotton and tobacco.

Q: Is there any special significance to the components of the wreath on the $3 gold coins?

There is, because the wreath consists of the three major crops grown by the English settlers - wheat, corn and cotton, plus the native tobacco.

Q: I have an 1856-S $3 gold with a small S mintmark. Is it worth more than the other varieties?

There are three mintmark varieties for the S - small, medium and large. However, the values are the same for all three.

Q: Was the $3 gold coin popular with the public?

Those of you who dislike the Anthony dollar will know the answer readily. The $3 was disliked because it was easily confused with the $2.50 and $5 coins.

Q: What's the story on the gold $3 with a bust of Abraham Lincoln with the motto "GOD AND OUR COUNTRY?"

Maurice Gould attributed the piece to "Merriam, but not a mint product." To add to the confusion the reverse was from an 1867 pattern die made by the Mint. Three or four pieces (weighing 76 grains) are known and there is one unique piece weighing 100 grains. This would have to be classed as a privately issued fantasy piece.

Chapter 75

TOKENS

Tokens make up one third of the main trio of numismatic collectibles. Tokens are just as likely as medals to be mistaken for coins.

Q: I have a set of four coins of the 1860s, which have had the reverse ground off and the symbols of the four card suits engraved on them - hearts, diamonds, spades and clubs. Any idea what they are supposed to be?

My guess would be that they were used as markers in a card game to indicate the trump suit, possibly a variety of bridge, but perhaps a reader may have a better answer.

Q: Do you have any information on a "two bit" piece of "whale money," from Nantucket Island?

A Nantucket businessman, Harry Howard, had $7,500 worth of two bit (25 cents) and four bit (50 cents) pieces of the whale money made during the coin shortage of the mid 1960s. The pieces circulated freely on the island at the time, and coin dealers sold the pairs for $4.95 until the Secret Service finally put a stop to them.

Q: Can you tell me the facts concerning a "Souvenir Coin of Admission" that I own, handed down by my great grandfather who attended the 1904 Exposition in St. Louis?

You didn't indicate which variety you have, the round or the octagonal. Both were struck by the Louisiana Purchase Souvenir Coin Company, a group of promoters who had no official connection with the Exposition and no authority to strike such a piece. The pieces, mislabeled as coins, were sold for 50 cents each, the claim being that the buyer could exchange them at the gate for a ticket and a chance to guess the number of paid admissions to win a $50,000 prize. After somewhat less than 25,000 of the round pieces were sold, the promoters ordered the octagonal pieces, but before delivery disappeared, leaving the pieces to be bought up by souvenir and coin dealers. The Treasury Department was asked to rule on the presumed illegal use of "coin" on the pieces, but ducked the issue. Current value is probably in the $75 to $100 area, depending on the variety and condition.

Q: Are there any tokens that are redeemable in gold?

Arlie Slabaugh lists a Philippine token, from the Lackawana Manufacturing Company, good for $2 in gold, and a Harry C. Kahn & Son piece valued at $5 in gold. They were issued before gold was recalled in 1933, the Philippine piece dating to around 1900. Also there is a rare Alaskan piece with a nugget attached, good for $1 in merchandise.

Q: How did the tokens issued in Alaska get the nickname "bingles?"

Longtime reader and Alaska token expert Dick Hanscom says that the bingle name occurs in Alaska literature prior to the arrival of the minister Rev. Bert J. Bingle on the scene. It is traced to the sound of jingling tokens in the pockets of early residents. The Alaska Rural Rehabilitation Token of 1935 was one of at least three which bore the nickname. Merchant H. W. Nagley issued bingles in Talkeetna in 1920 and a B. N. Nauman issued another Talkeetna token. Rev. Bingle conducted services along the Alaskan Railroad between Fairbanks and Seward, and later was the publisher of the first newspaper in Palmer, Alaska.

Q: The 1864 law, which banned tokens, outlawed metal or its compounds. How about hard rubber?

Hard rubber was not specified, but the law said, "coin, card, token or device." The language was fairly vague, but nobody challenged it in court. Today a similar law undoubtedly would start a flurry of lawsuits.

Q: I have a token, which has what appear to be four lines of partial letters on each side, and no other design. Any idea what it is?

If your token has two little studs, (or two little holes) at the 3 and 9 o'clock positions on the edge, then you have a "spinner" token. If the token is spun, the letters "merge" and you can read the message on it.

Q: I picked up a gold medal honoring the Alaska Pipeline. What was the fineness of the piece?

My records list a set of 12 for an original price of $3,600 but don't show the gold content. Thanks to "Jim" we found out that they were 22 karat (.9167 fine). Each of the medals contained one ounce of gold. A similar set of one ounce silver medals sold for $360. Dick Hanscom tells us that there was also a series of quarter-size tokens struck in 10-karat gold, containing about 1/20th of an ounce of gold, which sold in the early 1970s for $25.

Q: What's the best place to get some information on a token I have been unable to identify?

For specific information, write to the Token & Medal Society, David E. Schenkman, P.O. Box 366, Bryantown, Maryland 20617. When you write, print out all of the lettering on both sides (and edge) of the piece as well as making a rubbing, and as for this column, include return postage. If David can't answer the question he'll pass it along to a member who perhaps can help. His email address is turtlehill@olg.com

Q: I've started a collection of "lucky cents," those pressed into aluminum holders, but I haven't found one with a 1943 steel cent. Do they exist?

They do. Token and medal expert Arlie Slaybaugh said a number of years ago that he had been unable to locate an encased 1943 cent. It may have been that the steel core was too difficult to successfully press into the hole in the aluminum token. One issue I'm aware of is one that Krause Publications issued in 1988 for the Pittsburg (Steel City) ANA convention. If you find another one, let me know about it.

Q: I have a peculiar piece with a 1958 Minnesota Centennial design on one side and "IRON NICKEL/VIRGINIA MINN." on the other. The problem is, the piece looks to be struck on some light metal, not iron?

The piece came from the Iron Range country of Minnesota, but was in fact struck on aluminum, a somewhat better material for tokens than iron, which will rust rapidly. The pieces sold for 10 cents each at the time. The mintage figure does not seem to be available.

Q: Didn't George Raft, the movie star, once appear on a gambling token?

In the late 1960s, although barred from personally entering England, Raft was part owner of the London gambling establishment, the Colony Club. The club used his name extensively in its advertising and when it came time to order new gaming tokens, they were produced with Raft's face on one side and the club building on the other. Recognizing that they would be kept as souvenirs, and adding to the club profits, it was a smart business move, but if I recall correctly, the club failed shortly afterward.

Q: Would you say it is important for the beginning collector to know the difference between a coin, a token and a medal?

This is some knowledge that is also important for the experienced collector too, because mistaking a token or medal for a coin can waste hours of your time fruitlessly looking for a token or medal in a coin catalog. An uncomfortably large number of the letters that come to our numismatic publications and dozens of new collectors and commercial firms on the Internet display a lack of knowledge of the difference. This is one of the first things you would (or should) be likely to learn. A coin usually is dated, has a specific value, and is a legal issue of some governing body. A token usually is a private issue, which may show a value, but shows no indication of official sanction. A medal is usually issued to mark some occasion or honor some person, but carries no value and may not be dated. In all three there are exceptions, but the descriptions are deliberately generalized to highlight the specific differences. To add a bit of confusion, one old numismatic dictionary has this to say about a medal: "A term for a coin, not struck for currency."

Q: Mexican, Central and South American plantation tokens are well recognized in the hobby. Shouldn't the plantation label be applied to early American coins and tokens?

That's a very good point, and one that has been overlooked by most hobby historians. The precedent is based on the fact that the British commonly referred to the colonies - in North America and elsewhere - as plantations. The concept probably would not meet with much favor at this late date.

Q: There's a major dam not far from Las Vegas. Which is it - Boulder Dam or Hoover Dam?

This takes a bit of explaining. The dam started out as Boulder Dam, because it is in Boulder Canyon. Some 11 years after the 1936 completion it was officially renamed the Hoover Dam, in recognition of President Herbert Hoover who signed the original dam legislation in 1928.

There is a copper token with a picture of the Hoover dam on one side, and Herbert Hoover on the other, dated 1874-1967. It's about the size of a cent. Beyond the fact that the pieces retailed for 35 cents each (3 for $1) I can't be of much help. The dates are those of Hoover's birth and death.

Q: Are there any coins depicting Noah's Ark?

I'll need reader help on this, as I don't recall any coins. However, there's at least one English token of the 1600s that features the Ark.

Q: What can you tell me about a "Boyd's Battery" token?

These tokens were frequently sold as Civil War sutler's tokens, but they were not patented until January 17, 1876, so they had nothing to do with the Civil War. They actually were part of a quack cure-all belt that strapped around the waist.

Q: What is a "Lucky Tillicum" token?

These were tokens struck on nickel by the Patriotic Products Association in 1933. Tillicum is an Indian word for "lucky piece." The tokens had a bust of Franklin D. Roosevelt with a map of the U.S. on the reverse, with the sun above, and the 1933 date on the sun. The legends read "LUCKY TILLICUM / REBUILD WITH ROOSEVELT" and on the reverse, "PROSPERITY / FOLLOW THE ROOSEVELT TRAIL." Apparently a second version has the U.S. Capitol on the reverse. These sold originally for 35 cents in bronze and 75 cents in silver.

Q: Why is it so difficult to obtain accurate mintage figures for tokens and medals?

Few artists are familiar with how to run a business so numbers made little difference. Because there are no government controls as there are for coins, the mintages are often misstated to enhance their rarity and value. Medals are frequently mislabeled as coins when offered on the Internet, which is a form of misrepresentation. Only a government can issue a coin.

Q: What was the original source of the "Ships, Colonies and Commerce" slogan on Prince Edward Island tokens of the early 1800s?

The slogan is credited to Napoleon, who after the battle of Ulm predicted correctly that British ships, colonies and commerce would eventually cause his defeat.

A transportation token.

Q: Please define "Vecturist."

It's what a transportation (streetcar, ferry, rail, etc.) token collector is called. The tokens themselves are called vectures, according to the American Numismatic Association dictionary, one of the few places the term is listed.

Q: Love tokens I know of, but are there funeral tokens as well?

Just like the love tokens, the funeral tokens are engraved on coins, which have had one or both sides smoothed off, and were then decorated with black enamel. Among other allied private engraving efforts are christening tokens. Readers may know of other special pieces?

Q: Is there a U.S. coin that has all of the Presidents appearing on it?

An automatic "no" to that one. There are tokens or medals with group portraits, at least some of which were advertised as "coins," but none of them are coins, and none are official issues.

Q: I have a token that I found in a dealer's junk box, which says: "Ft. Warren Canteen/10 Cents." Where was Ft. Warren?

This was a military post in Wyoming. The pieces are fairly scarce, and depending on condition should be worth from $10 on up, so it's a nice junk box find.

Q: Is there a Civil War token that has some Morse code spelled out?

There is a listing for an undated token for S. W. Chubbuck, of Utica, New York, a manufacturer of telegraph equipment in the 1847 to 1863 period. The piece has the complete Morse code alphabet with the dot and dash symbols on the reverse.

Q: What can you tell me about the Angels Flight Railroad?

It was billed as the world's shortest railroad, which traveled up a 33 percent grade in 315 feet. It was still operating under new ownership in the mid-1960s. It was built on Bunker Hill in Los Angeles in 1901, and carried 100 million passengers in its first 50 years. There are Angels Flight Railway tokens of bronze, brass and aluminum, "Good for one ride in 1932," but they were issued by a private collector, and thus are fantasy pieces. The real Angels Flight Railway disclaimed any connection with them. Perhaps readers can tell me if there are any genuine tokens.

Q: Where can I find some information on an 1864 Civil War token with an Indian head on the obverse, "NOT ONE CENT" on the reverse and a "C" apparently as a mintmark?

These pieces are replicas. They were struck in 1976 from dies that were first used in 1974 to strike replicas by the Columbus Mint. The 1974 replicas were correctly stamped with the word "COPY" in incuse letters on the obverse. However, the 1976 strikes, made by someone else, were in violation of the Hobby Protection Act because they were not stamped as copies.

Q: Isn't there a Civil War token, which suggests problems similar to the recurrent Pentagon procurement contract scandals?

There is a token that reads, "Millions for the Contractors - Not One Cent for the Widows."

Q: In an attic I found a "coin" dated 1873 with "James and French Have it / Clarksburg, OH." It has an Indian head and 13 stars on the obverse. What is it?

Token expert Russ Rulau provided the answer, as this is a tricky piece. First, it is a merchant's store card, and not a coin. He identified it as a Civil War piece, which accidentally received the wrong date. It is listed with the Civil War tokens by Fuld, as 170B-1a, and would currently have a value of $40 or more in XF condition. Rulau also commented that it is the kind of piece that is almost never found in a button box, or a trunk in the attic, so you are quite lucky.

Q: Does the slogan "IF ANYONE ATTEMPTS TO TEAR IT DOWN, SHOOT HIM ON THE SPOT" have to do with the "Dixie" or the South?

The confusion comes from the author of the slogan, Senator Dix of New Hampshire. The token with this slogan was called a "dix." It had nothing to do with Dixie, reputed variously to come from Dixon of Mason & Dixon fame, or the "dix" or 10-dollar note of New Orleans. It was definitely an anti-southern slogan at the time. A popular variety of this token has "Spot" spelled as "Spoot."

Q: Did any of the Civil War tokens actually carry a denomination?

The law forbade private coinage, so most that indicated a denomination used the "not one cent" or some similar evasion. An exception was the "1 Cent" token issued by F. A. Plum of Troy, New York, which not only clearly stated the value, but also was stamped on hard rubber rather than metal.

Q: How many privately issued tokens were made during the Civil War period?

The best estimate I can find is that there are about 13,000 different store card and patriotic varieties. A grand total of 50 million pieces were struck before they were outlawed in 1864.

Q: What did it cost a merchant to get a Civil War store card made?

An ad for the firm of Murdoch, Spencer and Stanton in Cincinnati quotes $10 for the first thousand and $8 for each additional thousand. Since the cards circulated as cents, once the dies were made the merchant could make a 20 percent profit on them.

Q: Why were the numerous Civil War tokens banned by the Government in 1864?

One of the principal reasons was that some merchants refused to redeem the tokens they had issued. Ironically, after banning the tokens for this reason, the Government proceeded to issue coins that also were not redeemable.

Q: Why are most of the Civil War tokens dated 1863, with only a relative few dated 1864?

Congress outlawed the tokens on April 22, 1864. The law did not address those already in circulation, but prohibited any new issues. As a result a few were minted with the wrong date to evade the law.

Q: When did the Federal Government finally put the various private mints out of business?

The matter dragged along until the multitude of Civil War tokens forced a decision. On June 8, 1864, the law was signed which outlawed all private minting. The previous law had banned only the making of copper coins by private mints.

Q: We hear a lot about the Civil War tokens used in the north. Were there any southern Civil War tokens?

They certainly don't get the publicity that the northern patriotic and store card tokens get, but there were some 50 varieties of southern tokens.

Q: What's the difference between a "patriotic" token and a "store card" token?

The terms, as applied to the multitude of Civil War tokens, separate them into two classifications, the patriotic with slogans supporting the nation ("Army & Navy") and the store cards, which carried advertising messages.

Q: Was there any one city that produced most of the Civil War tokens?

Cincinnati, Ohio claims credit for the largest number of varieties produced by any one city, with the firm of Murdoch, Spencer and Stanton believed to have produced more than 2,000 varieties of the "copper cards."

Q: Were there any anti-war tokens issued during the Civil War period?

Not many, but there were a few, usually associated with sympathizers for the South. One had the slogan, "Horrors of War/ Blessings of Peace."

Q: Did Abraham Lincoln appear on any of the Civil War tokens?

A logical choice of design, but appearing on less than a dozen pieces, with almost all of the Lincoln tokens considered scarce to rare.

Q: Were all of the Civil War tokens the same size as the small cent?

By no means. Many were patterned on the dimensions of the old large cent.

Q: Are there any of the Civil War tokens with Hebrew inscriptions?

There are at least two, probably more. One listing I have shows two varieties of a FELIX DINING SALON, 256 Broadway, New York, which have the word "Kosher" in Hebrew letters.

Q: I've found a reference to "elastic metal" as a material on which a Civil War token was struck. Please explain?

This was another term applied to vulcanite, ebonite, or just plain hard rubber, patented by Charles Goodyear in 1851.

Q: I have a vulcanite token, which is cataloged as black, but mine is black on one side and brown on the other. Is this a special variety?

The two-color tokens, such as you describe, are the result of exposure to sunlight, or cleaning, and are not "as made." According to the experts experiments with vulcanite tokens have produced brownish or two-color tokens in this way.

Philadelphia coin dealer's store card.

Q: I've been told that the way to tell the difference between a Civil War patriotic token and a store card was by the edge. Is this a true statement?

There is a kernel of truth, but only a very small one. The vast majority of the patriotic tokens have plain edges. For the store cards, about half have plain edges and the other half are reeded.

Q: As I understand it, there is but a single Civil War token with the Star of David on it. Is this true?

Virginia Culver said that Carl Diem of New York issued a 32 mm token with the star, which is believed to be unique.

Q: What was the first true merchant's token to be issued in the United States?

William and John Mott of New York City issued the first tokens that fall in this class in 1789. There are several varieties, with an eagle on the obverse, and a clock on the reverse.

Chapter 76

TRADE DOLLARS

Dollars made for trade with other countries. Simple, but the U.S. Trade dollars were controversial from the moment they were first issued.

A chop marked Trade dollar.

Q: How many of our Trade dollars actually went to China?

According to one source some 30 million of the coins wound up in China. Congress passed a redemption law for the coins on February 19, 1887, but it specifically excluded those coins that had been chop marked in China. This effectively isolated more than 25 million of the coins, which had been chopped as soon as they arrived, but an estimated two million that had not been marked were returned and turned in for standard dollars or smaller coins. As far as trade was concerned it was something of a "bust." The Mexican silver "dollar" or 8 reales dominated trade in the Orient in the 19th century and no amount of promotion of the U.S. Trade dollar could overcome that lead.

Q: Do you have a date for the striking of the first Trade dollar?

The first Trade dollar was struck on July 11, 1873.

Chapter 77

TYPE COINS

There are a multitude of ways to collect coins, and more than enough specialty areas. Collecting by type is one of the more popular methods of enhancing a collection.

Q: What's the difference between a type and a variety?
A type coin is a coin that is representative of a particular series or denomination, usually one that is obsolete. The term is also used for current coins to a lesser extent. For example, type coins for the Lincoln cent would be one of any date or mint with the wheat reverse and a second coin of any date or mint with the memorial reverse. A variety signifies a change of design, either intentional or accidental.

Q: In dealer ads or on price charts, when it says, "Type I or Type II," or varieties with numbers, does that always mean that it refers to the mintmark?
Definitely not. While one of the more popular "types" are the two mintmarks on the 1979-S and 1981-S proof coins, the listings usually are based on some other part of the design being changed. Gold dollars for example are commonly listed as Type I, II or III. Each is a different design, or different size. If you check in the annual *North American Coins and Prices* price guide, the different types and varieties are listed and are usually explained.

Chapter 78

THE UNITED STATES MINT

Although it nearly didn't survive its early years, today the Mint is a major business enterprise, which besides making circulating coins does millions of dollars worth of business in collector coins.

Q: Were there any more date freezes after 1964?

There was another attempt a decade later, in 1974. Treasury officials were completely convinced that coin collectors were to blame for recurring coin shortages. Their solution to the problem was to urge Congress to approve another date freeze like the one from 1965 through 1967. The blame actually fell on the public, which tended both to hoard coins and to resist all attempts to keep coins circulating. For every one coin that a collector saved there were probably thousands that were being held by the non-collecting majority. New collectors still ask why there are no 1975-dated quarters.

Q: Has there been any other incidence of the removal of mintmarks from our coins other than the 1965 through 1967 period?

The U.S. Mint announced that as a result of a study, which indicated that mintmarks served no useful purpose and instead resulted in a 30 percent increase in demand for cents, they were going to remove the D mintmark from cents struck in 1980 at the Denver Mint. The announcement caused the usual collector uproar and under pressure from Congress the plan was dropped.

Q: Isn't there another government seal that is similar to the English language version of the Treasury seal?

The seal of the U.S. Customs Service is identical except for the wording "Treasury - U.S. Customs Service," since it is a branch of the Treasury.

Q: Which U.S. coin has been the most consistent?

Probably the nickel. It has remained about the same size and the same weight since its introduction in 1866, with only one temporary change in alloy from 1942 through 1945.

Q: I know there were coin shortages in the 1960s and in the mid 1970s. Have there been any recent coin surpluses?

From the days of the first U.S. Mint in the 1790s, there have been chronic shortages of small change until well into the 20th century. There was a surplus of small change in the 1870s because large quantities returned from overseas, and in 1977 the Mint laid off workers because of a surplus of cents.

Q: What are the locations for over-the-counter purchases from the U.S. Mint?

The list I have may have been changed, but I show sales offices are located at the Main Treasury Building, 15th and Pennsylvania Ave., Washington, DC, Union Station in Washington, DC; the U.S. Mint, Independence Mall, Philadelphia, Pennsylvania; the U.S. Mint, 320 W. Colfax Ave., Denver, Colorado, and the San Francisco Old Mint, 88 5th St., San Francisco, California.

Q: Were any essais made of the coins struck at the U.S. Mint for French Indochina from 1920 to 1922, and 1940 and 1941?

There are none listed in the Mint records or in the *Standard Catalog of World Coins*. Both the Paris and Heaton Mints struck some of the 1920 through 1922 coins, and may have struck essais.

An 1814 cent.

Q: Why are there so few top grade 1814 cents?

Almost the entire output - 357,830 - was used for the Mint payroll, so nearly all of the cents struck that year circulated. Can you imagine the uproar if the Mint attempted to pay its employees with newly minted cents today?

Q: Was there a specific date when the first Lincoln cents with the Memorial reverse were first issued to the public?

The new reverse was approved and announced by President Eisenhower on December 20, 1958. The coin was struck at both the Denver and Philadelphia Mints, and distribution was begun on Lincoln's birthday, February 22, 1959, a relatively short period of time between approval and actual distribution.

Q: Please fill me in on which Mints struck which versions of the 1984 Olympic coins?

For the silver Olympic coins, the only proofs were those struck at San Francisco - which also struck uncirculated versions. For the gold coins, the only Mint striking uncirculated coins was West Point (W) and the PDS pieces are all proofs, but West Point also struck proofs. The proofs can be distinguished from the uncirculated pieces by the mirror finish, and the sharper edges on the rim and design.

Chapter 79

VENDING MACHINES

We don't realize how much of our economy depends on vending machines until they run afoul of a new issue such as the downsized Anthony dollars.

Q: Why is so much weight attached to the vending industry's opinion of coins?
Billions of dollars in coins go into vending machines, telephones, jukeboxes and other coin-operated devices every year, so coins must be made to work in them without major modifications. Vending machine needs can be credited with the switch to copper-nickel clad coins in 1965 and the scuttling of the 1974 aluminum cent, as well as several other changes in our coinage.

Q: Other countries have used aluminum and aluminum bronze coins. Why not the U.S.?
The biggest stumbling block has been the vending machine industry, which claims with some truth that aluminum alloy coins are too light to operate many types of coin mechanisms and that they are difficult to separate from slugs. Aluminum is by far not the easiest metal to strike into coins either.
There are also medical arguments, as aluminum is hard to detect on X-rays.

Q: What's wrong with so many of the dimes that I see lately? Most of them look like they melted or got struck funny.
Chalk up another collector who is beginning to look more closely at his or her coins. As a point of reference, most dimes since 1965, when they switched to copper-nickel clad, have been pretty low quality coins, simply because the nickel alloy is extremely abrasive and wears the dies very rapidly. Being the smallest coin doesn't help either, as this seems to increase the wear problems. If you compare them with quarters you'll see generally much less wear on the bigger coins. A close look at some dimes will show very heavy wear and repair work, distorting the lettering severely at times. As for how they are being struck, several readers have sent in examples with high wire edges caused by the metal squeezing between the die and the collar, some edges thick enough to hang up in a vending machine or coin counter.

Q: What is the status of the trial pieces for the SBA dollars, which were issued to vending machine companies for test purposes?
Only a couple of these have turned up, including one that I photographed back in 1980. At that time the Mint said flatly that the Secret Service would actively pursue such pieces, a switch in policy from past cases such as the 1913 "V" nickel. The pieces were round with a raised rim, with 11 interior sides and a hump in the middle on both sides. I haven't checked lately to see if this is still true. The piece I examined was clad, but I understand at least one in a different alloy has turned up.

Q: Wasn't the vending machine industry behind the push for the Eisenhower dollar in 1971?
The vending machine industry has gotten involved in the issue of several coins, including the Ike dollar. They were very active in 1969 and 1970 lobbying for the new clad dollar, but when it was finally issued they lost interest and few machines were converted for the Ikes. Curiously the industry followed the same pattern for the Anthony and Sacajawea dollars, pretty much ignoring them after they were authorized and issued.

Q: When was the first vending machine patented in the U.S.?
The first U.S. patent issued for a vending machine was for one that dispensed postcards, in 1886.

Chapter 80

GEORGE WASHINGTON

Anyone not familiar with George, please raise your hand.

Q: I have a George Washington medal that is brass, half dollar size, and dated 1955. The legend reads: "Hickock Father of the Year Award." On the reverse is an eagle, with: "A lifetime of Good Luck to Dad."

The Hickock Belt Company produced these. I believe as a Father's Day promotion, with one of the pieces going with each belt sold. I'm not sure at this point whether they celebrated Father's Day as far back as 1955, but if not, it was another sales promotion.

Q: Didn't George Washington almost wind up on the nickel?

Breaking the long-standing prohibition (based on Washington's wishes) against using Washington on our coins, Washington patterns for the two-cent coin were produced in 1863, and in 1866 a pattern was struck for the nickel. Pattern dies were also made in 1909 for a five-cent coin.

Q: What is a grate halfpenny?

This is a token with the bust of George Washington, with a fireplace grate on the reverse and London 1795 below. There are several varieties.

Q: I'm interested in finding some history on the American Numismatic Society's George Washington medals struck for the New York World's Fair. Do you have any idea what the issue price was?

The ANS had the medal struck in 1939 to mark the 150th anniversary of the inauguration of Washington as President. The 2.5-inch bronzes were sold by subscription for $5 each and the same size silver medals were sold for $10. Russ Rulau catalogs them currently at $110 for the silver and $50 for the bronze, so they have maintained their price relationship for more than half a century.

Q: Why was Washington picked for the U.S. Capitol?

Congress decided on July 16, 1790, to move from Philadelphia to a spot on the Potomac River, which had been picked by George Washington. The principal significance of the location was that it was halfway between Maine and Georgia.

Q: Didn't George Washington have the advantage in getting men for his army during the Revolutionary War?

Although it didn't do them much good, there were actually more Americans on the British side. Washington, at the peak of his command, had only about 8,000 troops out of 2.2 million people. The British were able to out-recruit, but were unable to win the war.

Q: Is there any significance to the "Roman Emperor" fantasy cents with Washington depicted as a Caesar?

One source considers them satirical pieces, made by Obediah Westwood in revenge for Washington's refusal to give coinage contracts to the Birmingham, England private mints, and his opposition to portraiture on coins. They were not released until the 1830s, after Washington's death.

Q: They teach in our schools that George Washington was the first leader to be known as the Father of his Country. Is this really true?

Not by a long shot, and about two thousand years. According to historians the title was first accorded to the Roman leader, Julius Caesar.

Q: How did George Washington's Medal of Merit become the Purple Heart Medal?

It was a "badge" of merit, rather than a medal, and of cloth, purple and heart shaped, with the word "MERIT" printed on it. The award languished, but the design was later incorporated into the Purple Heart Medal, awarded to those wounded or killed in combat.

Q: Is it true that George Washington visited only one foreign country?

With the possible exception of Canada, the only recorded trip was to the British island of Barbados. You have to remember that this was an era where many people never ventured more than a few miles from their homes at any time in their lives. Barbados issued a $250 gold coin in 1982 to mark the 250th Anniversary of Washington's birth.

Q: What was the first coin to bear the picture of a U.S. President?

The early dollars nearly had George Washington on them, but it wasn't until 1900 that the Lafayette Commemorative dollar was issued, with the conjoined heads of Washington and Lafayette. The first circulating coin was the Lincoln cent.

Q: Is there a special connection between the Laura Gardin Fraser bust of Washington, which was rejected for the Washington quarter with some other coins?

The Fraser design is based on the bust by French sculptor Jean Antoine Houdon in 1785. The bust was also used for the 1900 Lafayette dollar, and similar Houdon statues of Ben Franklin and Thomas Jefferson were used for the half dollar and nickel. The Houdon statues, or copies, have appeared on several banknotes and stamps for both Franklin and Washington. Houdon did a bust of Lafayette, but Chief Engraver Charles Barber ignored it and copied the design from the bust by Caunois.

Chapter 81

WEIGHTS AND MEASURES

One more important area where knowledge is king. Weighing a coin is the best available - and non-destructive - test for many problems.

Q: Can you trace the origin of "troy" weight?
The term comes from the city of Troyes in France. It was a major trading center with its own weights and measures. The primary weight in the Troy system was the grain, defined as, "A grain of wheat, round, dry and from the middle of the head." Want to bet there were plenty of arguments about meeting those requirements? There were still wide variations in larger quantities. For example, it takes 5,760 grains to make a troy pound. Other measurements had similar roots. The yard was the length from the tip of the King's nose to the tip of his finger. The foot? You guessed it - the length of the King's foot.

Q: What is the difference between a troy ounce and a normal ounce?
If by normal you mean the avoirdupois pound of commerce, then one troy ounce equals 31.1035 grams or 480 grains and equals 0.91 avoirdupois ounces, which contains only 437.5 grains. There are 12 troy ounces in a troy pound, 16 ounces in an avoirdupois pound. The troy pound contains 5,760 grains, while the avoirdupois pound equals 7,000 grains, so a troy ounce and a pound are both smaller.

A gold American eagle.

Q: What is the "real" or total weight of the one-ounce American eagle coin?
The coin, which contains one ounce of gold, weighs 33.9305 grams, of which 31.103 grams is gold. Diameter is 32.7 mm.

Q: Is there a quick way to approximate a troy ounce?
You probably have the right items in your pocket. Make a simple balance beam scale with a ruler or similar piece, and then put ten pre-1982 cents on one end. They weigh approximately one troy ounce. This is a handy way to check the purported "gold" coins, such as the Blake $20 copies, since if they were genuine they would weigh just under a troy ounce.

Q: I'm told there is a difference in the thickness of the Ultra, High and normal relief St. Gaudens 1907 $20 gold coin. Does this mean there is a difference in the weight or the amount of gold they contain?

All three varieties contain the same amount of gold, although the Ultra thickness is listed as 4 mm, the High relief at 3 mm and the regular issue at 2 1/2 mm.

Q: Why do we use grains rather than grams to weigh our coins?

The grain weight system was selected originally when the first U.S. Mint was established and the coinage system was set up, so all coin weights are still officially given in grains, even though for numismatic purposes we commonly use both systems.

Q: What does the U.S. Mint use as a standard of weight to determine the proper weight and fineness of its coins?

The Mint uses an exact copy of the British troy pound, which was made in 1827. The brass copy weighs exactly the same as the original - 5,760 grains - and was kept in a locked box, with one of the keys retained by the Director of the Mint, the other by the Superintendent of the Philadelphia Mint. From this standard working weights were made, and these are what were used in daily weighing at the different mints. The U.S. Assay Commission, as one of its annual duties, compared the working weights to the official troy pound to make sure that the correct weights were being used. The weight is still on display at Philadelphia. Not too well known is the fact that the Mint was the forerunner of our National Bureau of Standards. The Mint also required thermometers of extreme accuracy, and liquid measures as well. The model weights and measures were a function of the Mint until July 1, 1903, when Congress legislated the Bureau of Standards and made it part of the Commerce Department.

Q: What did the private $50 gold coins struck in California weigh?

The weight was about 2.78 troy ounces with about 2.5 ounces of that being pure gold. One source incorrectly gives the total weight of the private "slugs" as 2.5 ounces, and 2.418 for the Pan Pacific $50, but in both cases that was the gold content. The correct official total weight for the Pan Pacific $50 is 2.6875 troy ounces, or 83.592 grams or 1,290 grains. The weight is exactly five times that of the then current $10 gold eagle.

Q: Many years ago there was a report that the Mint was stamping worn or mutilated coins in some way and returning them to the owners. Can you trace this down?

The original report of this appeared in the July 1909 Numismatist which reported that the New York Sub-Treasury was stamping light weight or slightly mutilated silver coins with a large letter "R" to indicate that they were refused, or rejected. The same report indicated that the Sub-Treasury was only accepting coins worn smooth as bullion at a rate of 30 cents on the dollar. Do any of our readers have any further information on this stamping, or an example of one of the stamped coins?

Q: Did the price of copper affect our early coinage?

It had a substantial effect. The first copper purchased for the new Mint cost 16 cents a pound. In late 1792 copper rose to 26 cents a pound, and even at that price was nearly unobtainable. To compensate, in 1793 the weight of the cent was reduced from 264 to 208 grains. In 1795, again for the same reason, the weight was dropped down to 168 grains, as copper prices reached 36 cents a pound. Copper prices hovered around 40 cents a pound in the 1850s, forcing an end to the large cent.

Q: Why are U.S. coin measurements given in millimeters when we are all used to inches? It seems as if you are trying to confuse people.

There is a very logical reason for using millimeters, as they are parts of a meter, and the meter is the official standard of measurement of the U.S. government. Despite the reluctance of Congress and the public to follow through, the U.S. has been officially on the metric standard since 1883 when the National Bureau of Standards declared the meter the official standard for all government transactions. At that time the inch was officially defined as being 25.4005 millimeters. Stick to inches if you wish, but the decimal-based metric system is far more accurate and easy to use. As but one example, the English inch is a different length than our inch; it is actually 0.00012 mm longer.

Q: What was the original source of the karat weight?

The karat, a metric weight of 0.189 grams, originated as being equal to the weight of a carob seed or bean, the carob also known as St. John's Bread. As with other "standard" weights, the carat, or karat weights, vary in different places, currently being accepted generally as 0.20 gram, or 1/5th of a gram.

The U.S. standard was not adopted until 1913, fixing the weight of one carat as equal to 0.200 of a gram. Prior to 1913 the Amsterdam carat was 0.2057 of a gram, in London 0.2053 and 0.1972 in Florence. This is the same standard used in weighing gemstones.

Q: How do I go about converting carats of gold to fineness?

Pure gold is 24 carat, so the scale figures out like this: A single carat is .0416 fine, 12 carat gold is .500 fine, 18 carat gold is .750 fine. Most gold jewelry is figured in carats so using these figures it is a simple matter to determine the full weight of the piece, dividing by the fineness to figure the amount of gold that it contains. Many coins are 22 karat gold, thus with a fineness of .9166. The Gold Stamping Act of 1976 specifies that all jewelry made and sold after October 1, 1981, must be within 0.3 percent of the specific stamped content, or about 1/14th of a carat, according to the Gold Institute. While this is not a guarantee that what you buy is correctly labeled, it does give you recourse if you find that the product was mislabeled. One of the popular methods of describing fineness up until about the late 1940s was the use of fractions of a carat, which was divided into 32 parts. Thus a coin's fineness might be described as 21 and 19/32 carat gold, which corresponds with the now common and easy to use .900 fine.

Q: Were our silver coins made in an exact weight ratio to denomination like the gold coins?

Even if we ignore the several earlier fluctuations, the answer is "No." The last 90 percent silver coins were struck in 1964. Ten dimes contained a total of .7240 of an ounce, while four quarters or two halves contained .7236 of an ounce, all less than the Peace dollar, which contained .7736 of an ounce of silver.

Chapter 82

WEST POINT MINT

The youngest of our mints, West Point comes with its own special history.

Q: What can you tell me about the Mint at West Point?
It began as a U.S. Silver Bullion Depository. It was built in 1938. The first shipment of silver to West Point consisted of over 1.2 billion bars, amounting to some 1.2 billion troy ounces. A 1973 law authorized "any" facility for striking coins. Presses were moved in and the facility began striking cents - up to 1.5 billion a year. In 1988 its status was upgraded to a full-fledged Mint.

Q: Did the West Point Mint strike any foreign coins with the W mintmark?
No, but West Point did strike all of the Panama 1974 one centesimo coins. The W was not used until the 1984 U.S. Olympic coins.

Q: Quite a number of years ago didn't you make the statement that the West Point W was not likely to appear on coins struck there?
My answer to the question was, "Not likely." However, the answer was to a question asking specifically about the W appearing on the cents that were being struck there at the time. The W has appeared on a number of commemorative coins struck at the West Point Mint, but not on the cents.

Chapter 83

WOODEN MONEY

Name a solid material and it has probably been used as money at one time or another. Wood has been a popular material for tokens and even some medals.

Q: I came across a wood (in Alabama) from the 1997 Cabin Fever Party at Silver Lake Lanes. Can you give me some background so I can catalog the piece?

We do get around. The Cabin Fever Party is an annual event put on by Krause Publications for its employees, to shake us out of the winter doldrums. It's based on the premise that if you're stuck inside all winter you get sick of the four walls and need a change. Krause Publications, Iola, Wisconsin, issued the wooden tokens. Silver Lake Lanes is a bowling alley about 3 1/2 miles south of Iola, near the town of Scandinavia.

A Cabin Fever "wood."

Q: Can you tell me how much wooden money the Tenino, Washington Chamber of Commerce issued back in the 1930s?

Tenino claims to be the first place in the world to issue wooden money printed on slices of spruce or red cedar. The first issue came out in 1932, and was given to bank depositors who pledged a quarter of their bank balance to back the issue. By the end of 1933 a total of eight separate issues had been made, totaling $10,308, of which only $40 was ever redeemed. In 1989, as a state centennial project, Tenino again issued wooden money, charging $3 a set, with the proceeds going to support a local museum. There is also an issue dated 1932 from Blaine, Washington.

Q: Are there any wooden nickels from the U.S. denominated in a foreign currency?

There are wooden nickels and dimes issued in Holland, Michigan. "Een" (one) guilder and "Twee" (two) guilders. There are two varieties of each, on light and dark wood.

Q: I have a couple of pieces of what appear to be wooden money, with carved figures of Roman emperors on one side. They are about two inches in diameter. Are they coins?

They are pieces from a popular board game of the 16th century, called "Eckdame," or literally, "corner girl," somewhat similar to our modern checkers. The intricately carved pieces were close copies of Roman coins and occasionally other appropriate subjects, and are popular collectibles in Europe.

Q: A veteran collector of wooden money told me that at one time they used wooden coins in the slot machines in Nevada. Did the coin shortage really get that bad?

I'm afraid his story is part fact and part fiction. There was an incident involving wooden coins back in the 1950s that may be the basis for his story. The Sparks, Nevada Chamber of Commerce put out 10,000 wooden coins which were the exact dimensions of a silver dollar and it didn't take long before some of the more enterprising citizens discovered that they would work "as is" in some of the slot machines, and needed only a little reworking to operate some of the others. The problem resulted in an amendment to the Nevada gambling laws which provided for a six-month jail term and a $500 fine for using anything but a United States government minted coin in a gambling device. This law has since been repealed.

Q: Has wooden money ever reached the status of legal tender?

In at least a couple of instances it has. Details are sketchy, but the Austrian city of Hadersfeld issued wooden money at the end of World War I. During the German inflation period following the First World War, wood was just one of a multitude of emergency materials used for money.

Q: How far back do wooden "nickels" go?

Wooden money traces back to the Byzantine Empire (395-1425 CE).

Q: Have wooden nickels ever been illegal to own?

Yes, and no. The Treasury Department has at one time or another confiscated some wooden nickels, which were considered to be in violation of Federal law, but the majorities are perfectly legal. The key provision that is most often violated is assigning cash value to the pieces and allowing them to be redeemed anywhere, rather than limiting them to a single store. One Wisconsin bank got in trouble with the Secret Service during the 1964 coin shortage by issuing wooden nickels to alleviate the problem. As long as they are not used as a form of general currency, they are acceptable.

Chapter 84

WORLD COINS

*For those tired of multi-billion mintages, the world offers unlimited possibilities.
It takes some persuading to convince collectors that despite the strange
languages, world coins are made just like they are here in the U.S.*

Q: Why is Philippines spelled Filipinas on recent coins?

Filipinas is the spelling in the native Tagalog language. When the Philippines gained
independence, they removed English from their coins and substituted Tagalog.

Q: How many different countries have issued coins?

In modern times, or since about 1700, the *Standard Catalog of World Coins* figure is
about 1,400. This includes a number of cities, states, provinces and other political
entities, as well as religious groups that have struck coins.

Q: Which countries are producing the most gold?

The top five in order of quantity are South Africa, Russia, Canada, China, and the U.S.

**Q: A fellow collector claims he can identify the country of origin of similar coins from
Norway and Sweden from the mid 1800s just by looking at the obverse. How does he do it?**

Look a little closer, and you will note that on the coins of Sweden, SVERIGE is
before NORR in the legend. On the Norwegian coins the order is reversed. This lasted
until 1871.

**Q: The statement is made that Hitler never appeared on a German coin. How about the
coins that were shipped into Austria before that country was taken over?**

The complete statement reads "an official German coin." The pieces you refer to were
clandestine pieces matching the Austrian denominations up to five shillings, which
were struck by the Austrian Nazi party as a fund-raising scheme. Possession was
illegal, and party members would blackmail unsuspecting businessmen who received
the pieces hidden in goods shipments from Germany. One variety carried the bust
of Hitler.

**Q: Did the early Greeks use a standard system of coinage where multiples of smaller
denominations matched the weights of the smaller units?**

My source indicates that they "fudged" a bit on the bigger coins. For example, although
the multiples of the obol, which was the smallest common coin, were exact, when it
came to the multiples of the drachm we begin to find differences. The standard weights
of the drachm were from 60 to 85 grains. The didrachm (2 drachm) weights were
double - 120 to 170 grains, but the tetradrachm weights (4 drachm), were only 220 to
280 grains instead of the 240 to 340 range, and the decadrachms (10 drachm) weighed
from 560 to 670 grains when they really should have weighed from 600 to 850 grains.

Q: I have a Mexican coin with a G.R. countermark. What does that stand for?

British Caribbean colonies used many Mexican coins. The G.R. indicates their use
during the reign of George III. G.R. is the abbreviation of the Latin, "Georgius Rex" or
"King George."

The Italian fantasy coins with Mussolini.

Q: I have an Italian 20 lira coin with Mussolini on it that I can't find in the catalog. What is it?

It's a privately struck fantasy coin. Street merchants did a thriving business with these, selling them to tourists back in the 1960s and 1970s. The 20 lire come in silver, silvered brass, brass and gold. There is also a 1943 gold 100 lire weighing 31.89 grams and 35 mm in diameter. This comes in two types of gold and in silvered brass. It was listed as a pattern/fantasy in a 1980 auction catalog. We list both denominations in the Krause Unusual World Coins catalog. There's also a 100 lire with King Vittorio Emanuel III, which is included in the same group. The pieces do have some collector value, but not as coins. There are no official native country coins bearing the bust of "Il Duche," a statement that is also true for Adolf Hitler and Joseph Stalin.

Q: Are there any examples of coins which use both Roman and Arabic numerals in the date?

I found a listing for two such coins, the groschens of Brandenburg, a province in Germany, which were dated 150II for 1502 and 150III for 1503. There is also an Austrian groschen of 1513 which has the date represented as MDX13. Readers may know of others.

Q: What was the first nickel-alloy coin to bear the head of a monarch?

Queen Victoria of England appeared in 1869 on the Jamaica copper-nickel half penny and penny, and a farthing of the same metal with her portrait was issued there in 1880. King Leopold I of Belgium beat her to the punch, however, appearing on the 1860 20 centimes, a less well-known denomination. The 5 and 10-centime coins of 1860 were also struck in copper-nickel but did not bear the bust of the King, instead showing a lion. The first pure nickel coin bearing a monarch was the Italian 1919 50 centisime with the bust of King Victor Emanuelle.

Q: Something was said about some coins that predicted the term of office of a country's ruler?

You're thinking of the coins of Paraguay. They showed the five-year terms of the country's dictator, General A. Stroessner. The most recent was the "8th Term" issued in 1988 and dated 1988-1993.

Q: Did anyone find any more of those Philippine 1969 1 sentimo overdates you reported in 1993?

Lots of them have been reported, but so far, of all the reports coming in, nobody has one of the Philippine coins without the overdate. The punching apparently was done on the master die. One reader has several rolls that he checked and all were the overdate variety. It looks like a normal date for the 1969 one sentimo would be a real rarity. Mintage was 12 million, so unless one without the overdate shows up we have to assume that the variety traces to the master die.

Q: Are there instances in other countries of coin denomination in two sizes for the same year?

In the U.S. the three-cent silver and three-cent nickel overlapped from 1865 through 1873. Portugal in 1969 had two size 20 centavos, measuring 20.5 and 16.0 mm. Finland's 1952 1 and 5 markka come in two sizes, as do the 1881 Colombia 2 1/2 centavos. Canada had large and small cents in 1920. Norway had two different designs and two different sizes for the 5 ore in two different years (1952 and 1973.) There are probably enough others to form an interesting collection.

Q: The word "Ducat" supposedly comes from the gold ducat d'oro of Venice, which bore the word "DVCAT." Is this correct?

The first Venetian gold ducat d'oro was struck in 1284, more than 30 years after Florence and Genoa struck similar gold coins, but none of the three is the real source of the term. Ducat actually traces back to silver coins struck by Roger II (1102-54) and William I (1154-66) of Sicily from 1140 onward, coming from dvcatus apuliae. The legend reads: "SIT TIBI CHRISTE, DATUS, QUEM TU REGIS, ISTE DUCATUS," which translates as: "May this royal ducat be dedicated to thee O Christ." The term "ducat" was first applied to the silver grossi of Venice in 1202, but this coin did not bear the inscription. The coin was initially referred to as a ducatus, later ducat. The silver coins were known as ducati argenti (silver) and the gold coins as ducati aurii (gold), with the emphasis gradually shifting to the gold. This was the same pattern as that followed by the florin, first a silver coin, later gold.

The ducat name is still used in Austria, Czechoslovakia and the Netherlands.

Q: Where can I cash in a quantity of world coins?

Sorry, but none of the U.S. banks will convert coins (only paper money), and even in Europe banks that handle foreign exchange won't touch coins. There are several possibilities, including starting a coin collection. You also might try to find someone visiting the country of origin and sell the coins that way. You can also donate them to a charity for a tax credit. For example, UNICEF would welcome those world coins. For future reference, in most international airports there are usually collection boxes for travelers to dispose of their coins, which are donated to various charities.

Q: Is the U.S. the only country to issue the same coin as two denominations - the half dime and the nickel?

Among others, Germany has the 50 pfennig and half mark, France has the 50 centime and half franc. Also there are the U.S. 50 cents and half dollar and disme, dime and 10 cents, although as noted in a previous question, "10 Cents" was not an official denomination.

Q: What was the "Wheaties International Coin Collection?"
As part of a company promotion, it contained 15 world coins, the latest dated 1954, and a world map showing where the coins came from. With the set was an offer for a "mystery set" of another "entirely different" group of 15 coins for 25 cents and a Wheaties box top. There have been several similar promotions. MacDonald's passed out foreign coins to their customers about 1993 or 1994. There was a similar promotion years ago by Kraft cheese. Kraft Foods in 1957 purchased some 12 million foreign coins that were used as an advertising promotion, with a packet of coins being sold as a premium. Westinghouse Electric Corporation in 1958 used some three million foreign coins in a similar promotion, except that they passed out bags of seven coins free to anybody who came in the store to look at appliances. Kellogg's also had a similar promotion. That's enough to start a promotion collection.

Q: What's the story on a reputed French 5 franc coin that is worth "a million francs?"
Napoleon reputedly had one of the new 5 franc pieces hollowed out and enclosed a check for one million francs. This was purely a publicity stunt to popularize the coins bearing Napoleon's bust. However, at last report, the French Treasury still has funds ready to pay the person who discovers the coin.

Q: What was the first use of aluminum for circulating coins?
The earliest use for a circulating coin was in the 1907 British West Africa 1/10 penny and East Africa one cent. The U.S. Mint made an aluminum pattern in 1851, which was probably among the first attempts to use the metal for coinage. At that time aluminum was expensive, on a par with silver. Once a cheap method of recovering it from ore was discovered, the price dropped very quickly.

Q: I know invasion coins, but "evasion" coins?
Evasion coins had their beginnings in the 1700s in England, where it was worth your life to counterfeit gold or silver, but because of a loophole in the law, faking copper coinage was only a misdemeanor. Counterfeiters "evaded" that part of the law by putting variations of BRITANNIA on their coins, such as BRITONS RULE, GEORGE RULES, BRITANNIAS ISLES or even BONNIE GIRL. Given the general illiteracy of the population, these pieces, which skirted or evaded the law, were usually readily accepted.

Q: What period of time is covered by the Roman coinage?
Rome was a Monarchy from 753-510 BCE, then a Republic from 509-27 BCE and finally an Empire from 27 BCE to 476 CE. The last (Western) Empire coins were those of Romulus Augustulus in 476 CE. The Christian Roman Empire lasted some 1,200 years, ending in 1204 CE. The Roman republic and imperial coinage covered a span of more than 700 years. The first Roman silver coins were struck about 269 BCE. The Rome Mint became an Ostrogothic Mint in the 5th century CE.

Q: There are conflicting mintage figures for the Yemen 1969 2 riyal Apollo 11 coins. Which are correct?
The *Standard Catalog of World Coins* now lists four varieties for the 1969 coin, in proof and uncirculated, with mintages of 200 proofs for two varieties, and 1,000 proofs (restrikes) for the other two. The first two varieties list 7,583 uncirculated coins. These figures conflict with a published contemporary report that the Valcambia Mint in Switzerland struck 52,700 "sets" of the coins. Perhaps our readers can help.

Q: Is it true that not all mermaids are female?

All the mermaids are in fact female, but there is at least one "merman." A Greek silver didrachm of Itanus shows a male. It dates to the 4th century BCE. I don't know whether this spoils the story or not, but the merman is actually Triton, the god of rivers.

Syria 1 Lira 1974.

Q: I have a "Banque de Syrie" 1/2-piastre coin which is dated 1921 on one side with what looks like 1971 on the other, except that the "7" is reversed. Is this a mint error, and what country is it from?

You have a 1921 coin from Syria. The date on what is actually the obverse is in Arabic numerals. The symbol for "2" does indeed look similar to a reversed "7," but both dates read 1921.

Q: There are lots of bi-metal coins like our current clad coins, but are there any tri-metal pieces?

One suggested is the emergency money issued in Ghent, Belgium during the German occupation of World War II. It was reportedly struck on an iron core, brass plated on one side and copper plated on the other. I'm not aware of any national currency that would fit the title.

Q: Is it a fact that at one time when silver prices were very low there was a ban on importing silver coins of other countries into the United States?

In 1935 the Treasury Department banned the import of any silver coins that contained silver worth more than the face value of the coin. Among those noted as falling under the provisions of this regulation were coins of at least 10 countries - Bolivia, Chile, China, Costa Rica, Colombia, Hong Kong, Mexico, Peru, Salvador and Uruguay. At the time, the silver content of the American silver dollar was worth 55 cents.

Q: Which actual coins were called doubloons?

The name and term was applied to the 2-escudo coins of Spain, and those were struck at several of the North and South American mints. Doubloon stems from dobla, and means big double, or in this case, a double escudo.

Q: I have a "thing" for butterflies. Are there any coins with butterflies on them?

There are several. A few of the listings include the Papua, New Guinea gold 100 kina in 1978 with a bird wing butterfly, a 1990 gold and a 1992 platinum 100-kina with a Queen Alexandra butterfly, a 1993 50-kina in gold and a 1992 five-kina in silver. Panama struck a 1983 500 balboas in gold with an owl butterfly. The Cook Islands struck a 1992 silver and a 1994 gold $50 with a poplar admiral butterfly. Among older coins with butterflies is the 1733 silver death thaler of King Augustus II of Poland.

A Hungary 1943 5 pengo that looks like President Johnson.

Q: Isn't there a Hungarian coin with a Lyndon Johnson bust?

The 1943 5-pengo design does look like LBJ, but actually is Admiral Horthy. Some of the Turkish coins with Ataturk's bust also resemble Johnson.

Q: Are there any other coins than the Spanish eight reales (Pieces of eight) that were cut into parts?

There are plenty of them around to start a collection. Many of the Caribbean countries cut coins or punched out the centers. Some modern Mexican coins have been cut in half. Many other coins were cut earlier.

Chapter 85

RESOURCES

Krause Publications
700 E. State St.
Iola, WI 54990
(715) 445-2214
Numismatic News
Coins Magazine
World Coin News
Bank Note Reporter
Coin Prices Magazine
Numismatic Catalogs
Club Guide
Show Guide

American Numismatic Association
818 N. Cascade Ave.
Colorado Springs, CO 80903-3279

American Numismatic Society
Broadway at 155th
New York, NY 10032
(212) 234-3130

Bureau of Engraving and Printing
14th & C Streets, SW
Washington, DC 20228
(202) 874-3019

U.S. Mint Headquarters
801 9th Street NW
Washington, DC 20220

If you have a question, please include a loose 1st class stamp and write to me at the address for Krause Publications above. Please do not send any coins until they are requested.